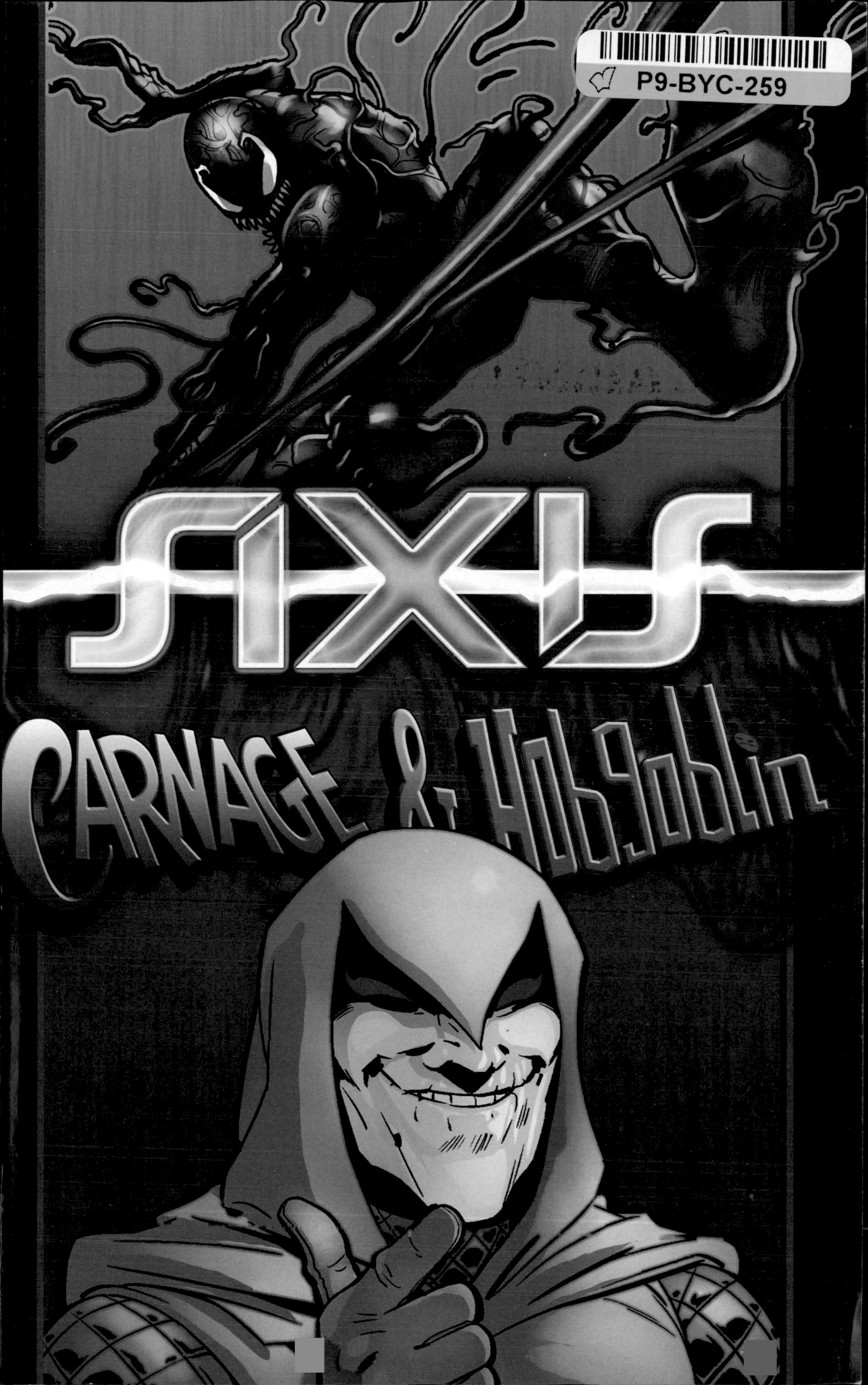
AXIS
CARNAGE & HOBGOBLIN

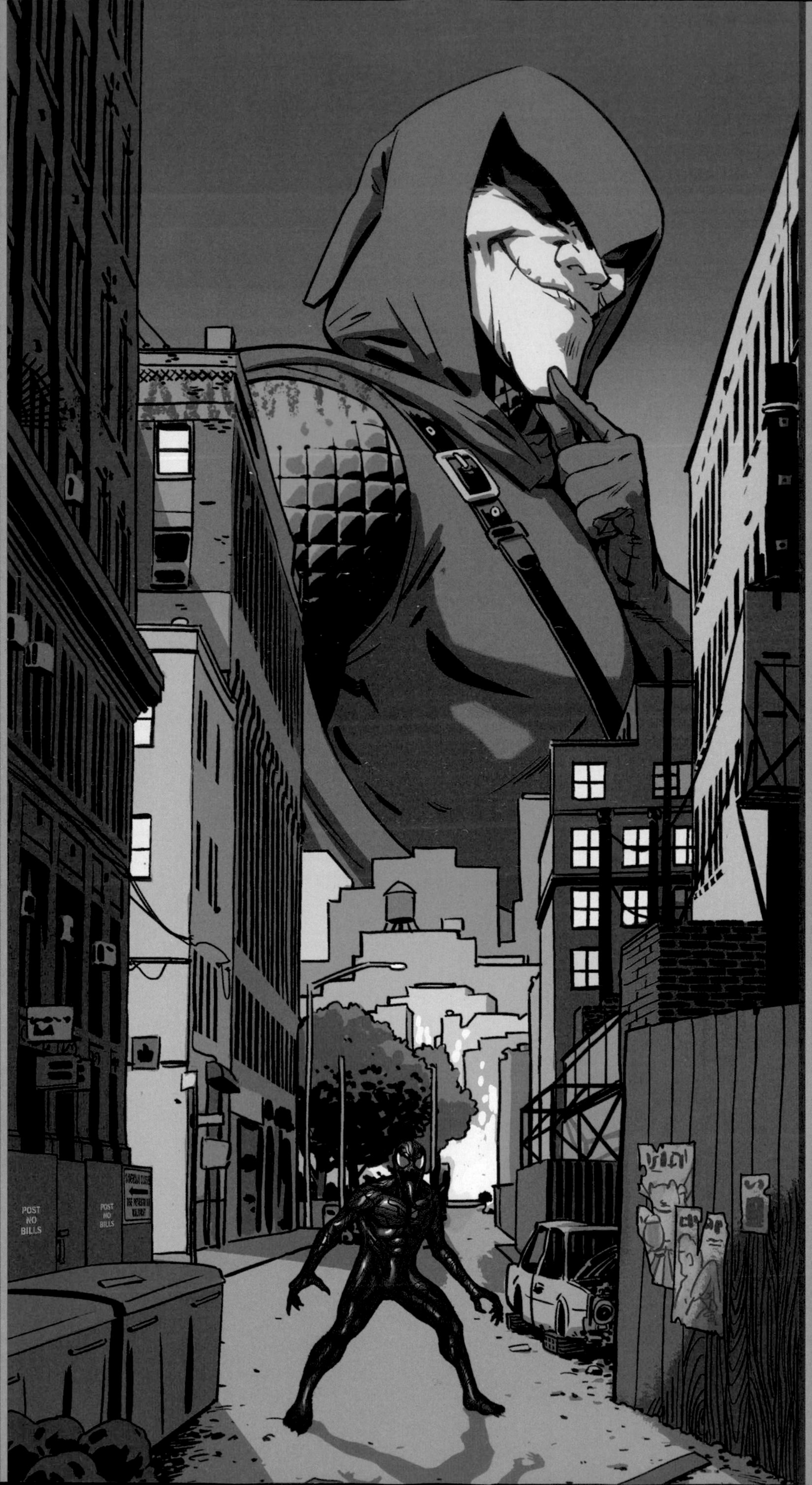
POST
NO
BILLS
POST
NO
BILLS

CARNAGE & HOBGOBLIN

CARNAGE

WRITER: **RICK SPEARS**

ARTIST: **GERMÁN PERALTA**

COLORIST: **RAIN BEREDO**

LETTERER: **VC'S JOE SABINO**

COVER ART: **ALEXANDER LOZANO**

ASSISTANT EDITOR: **CHARLES BEACHAM**

EDITOR: **NICK LOWE**

HOBGOBLIN

WRITER: **KEVIN SHINICK**

PENCILER/COLORIST: **JAVIER RODRIGUEZ**

INKER: **ALVARO LOPEZ**

ART, #2, PP. 8 &17: **WILL SLINEY**

COLORISTS, #2: **MUNTSA VICENTE** WITH **VERONICA GANDINI** (PP. 8 & 17)

LETTERER: **VC'S CLAYTON COWLES**

COVER ART: **JAVIER RODRIGUEZ**

EDITOR: **ELLIE PYLE**

SENIOR EDITOR: **NICK LOWE**

COLLECTION EDITOR: **SARAH BRUNSTAD**

ASSOCIATE MANAGING EDITOR: **ALEX STARBUCK**

EDITORS, SPECIAL PROJECTS: **JENNIFER GRÜNWALD & MARK D. BEAZLEY**

SENIOR EDITOR, SPECIAL PROJECTS: **JEFF YOUNGQUIST** SVP PRINT, SALES & MARKETING: **DAVID GABRIEL**

BOOK DESIGNER: **NELSON RIBEIRO**

EDITOR IN CHIEF: **AXEL ALONSO** CHIEF CREATIVE OFFICER: **JOE QUESADA**

PUBLISHER: **DAN BUCKLEY** EXECUTIVE PRODUCER: **ALAN FINE**

AXIS: CARNAGE & HOBGOBLIN. Contains material originally published in magazine form as AXIS: HOBGOBLIN #1-3 and AXIS: CARNAGE #1-3. First printing 2015. ISBN# 978-0-7851-9311-1. Published by MARVEL WORLDWIDE, INC., a subsidiary of MARVEL ENTERTAINMENT, LLC. OFFICE OF PUBLICATION: 135 West 50th Street, New York, NY 10020. Copyright © 2014 and 2015 Marvel Characters, Inc. All rights reserved. All characters featured in this issue and the distinctive names and likenesses thereof, and all related indicia are trademarks of Marvel Characters, Inc. No similarity between any of the names, characters, persons, and/or institutions in this magazine with those of any living or dead person or institution is intended, and any such similarity which may exist is purely coincidental. **Printed in Canada.** ALAN FINE, EVP - Office of the President, Marvel Worldwide, Inc. and EVP & CMO Marvel Characters B.V.; DAN BUCKLEY, Publisher & President - Print, Animation & Digital Divisions; JOE QUESADA, Chief Creative Officer; TOM BREVOORT, SVP of Publishing; DAVID BOGART, SVP of Operations & Procurement, Publishing; C.B. CEBULSKI, SVP of Creator & Content Development; DAVID GABRIEL, SVP Print, Sales & Marketing; JIM O'KEEFE, VP of Operations & Logistics; DAN CARR, Executive Director of Publishing Technology; SUSAN CRESPI, Editorial Operations Manager; ALEX MORALES, Publishing Operations Manager; STAN LEE, Chairman Emeritus. For information regarding advertising in Marvel Comics or on Marvel.com, please contact Niza Disla, Director of Marvel Partnerships, at ndisla@marvel.com. For Marvel subscription inquiries, please call 800-217-9158. **Manufactured between 12/26/2014 and 2/2/2015 by SOLISCO PRINTERS, SCOTT, QC, CANADA.**

10 9 8 7 6 5 4 3 2 1

AXIS

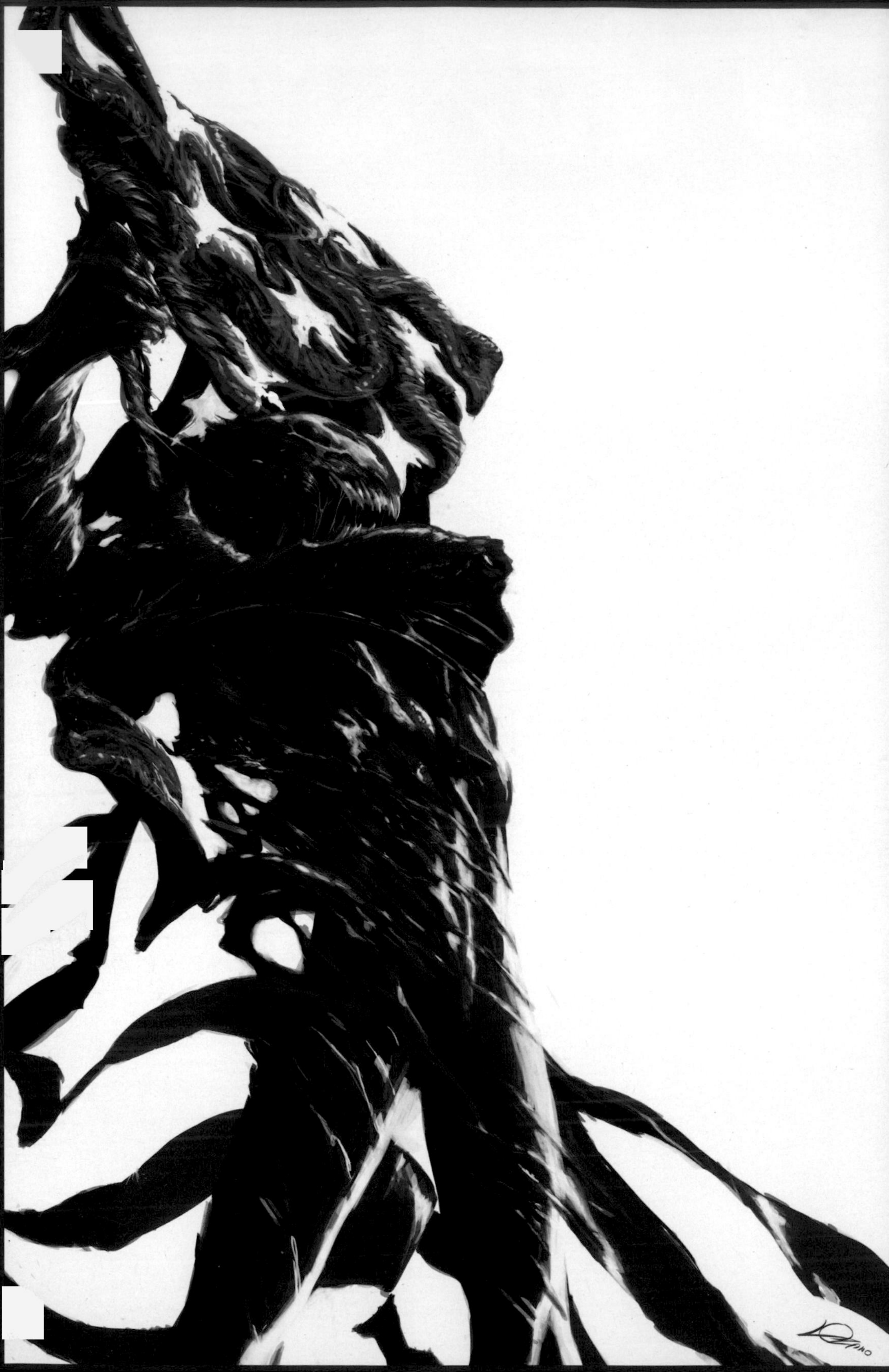

CARNAGE #1

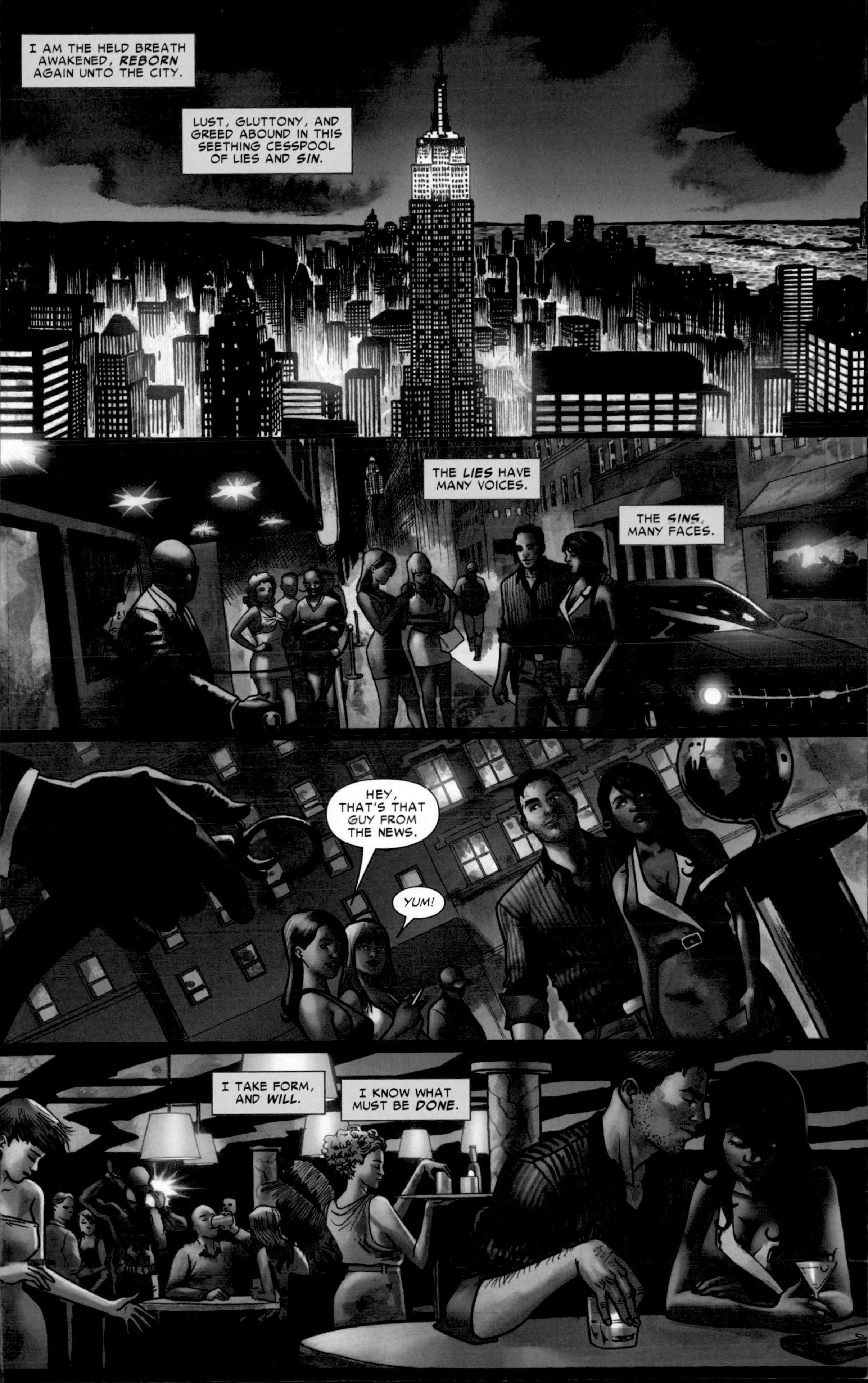
I AM THE HELD BREATH AWAKENED, REBORN AGAIN UNTO THE CITY.
LUST, GLUTTONY, AND GREED ABOUND IN THIS SEETHING CESSPOOL OF LIES AND SIN.
THE LIES HAVE MANY VOICES.
THE SINS, MANY FACES.
HEY, THAT'S THAT GUY FROM THE NEWS.
YUM!
I TAKE FORM, AND WILL.
I KNOW WHAT MUST BE DONE.

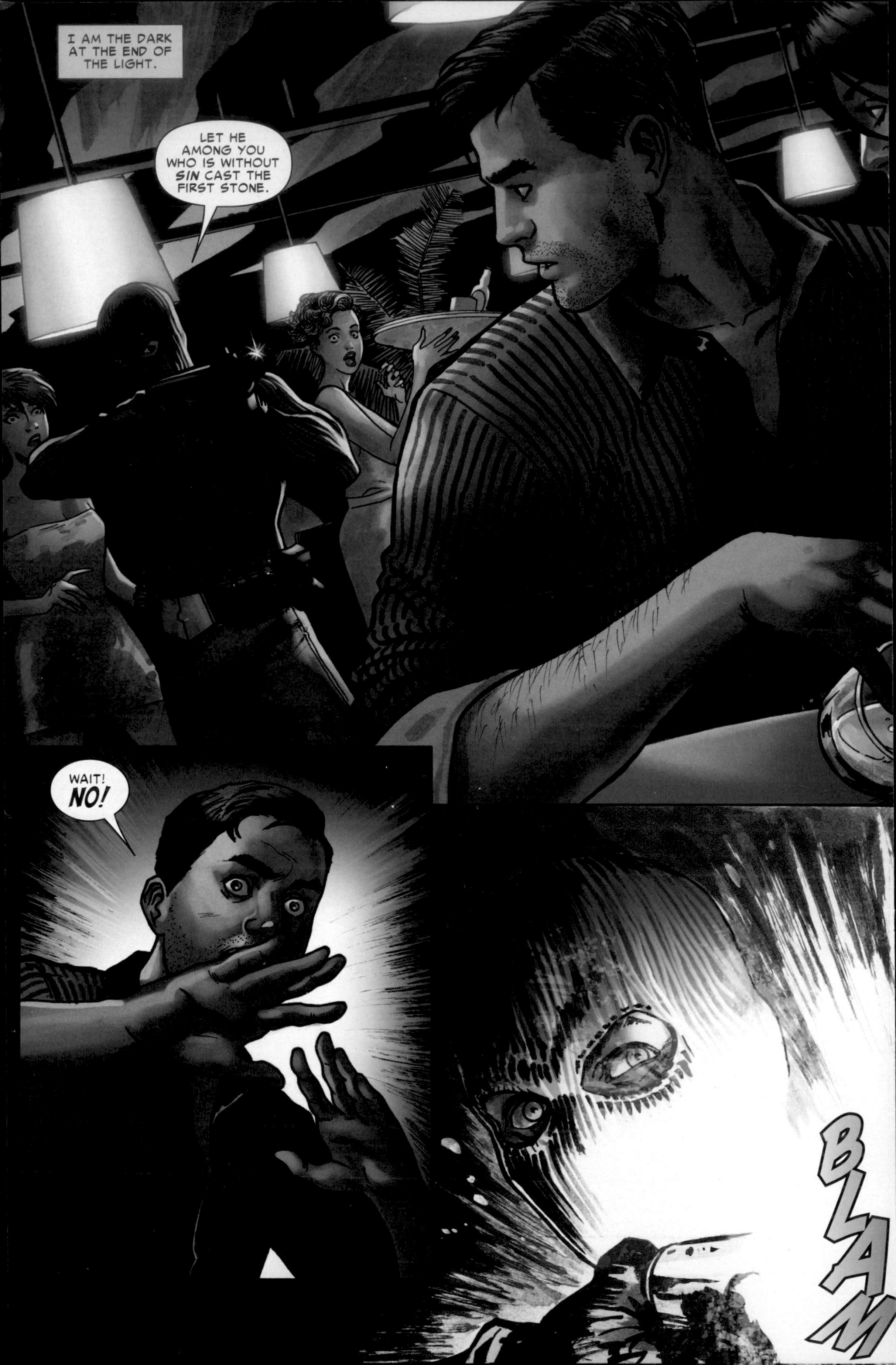
I AM THE DARK AT THE END OF THE LIGHT.
LET HE AMONG YOU WHO IS WITHOUT SIN CAST THE FIRST STONE.
WAIT! NO!
BLAM

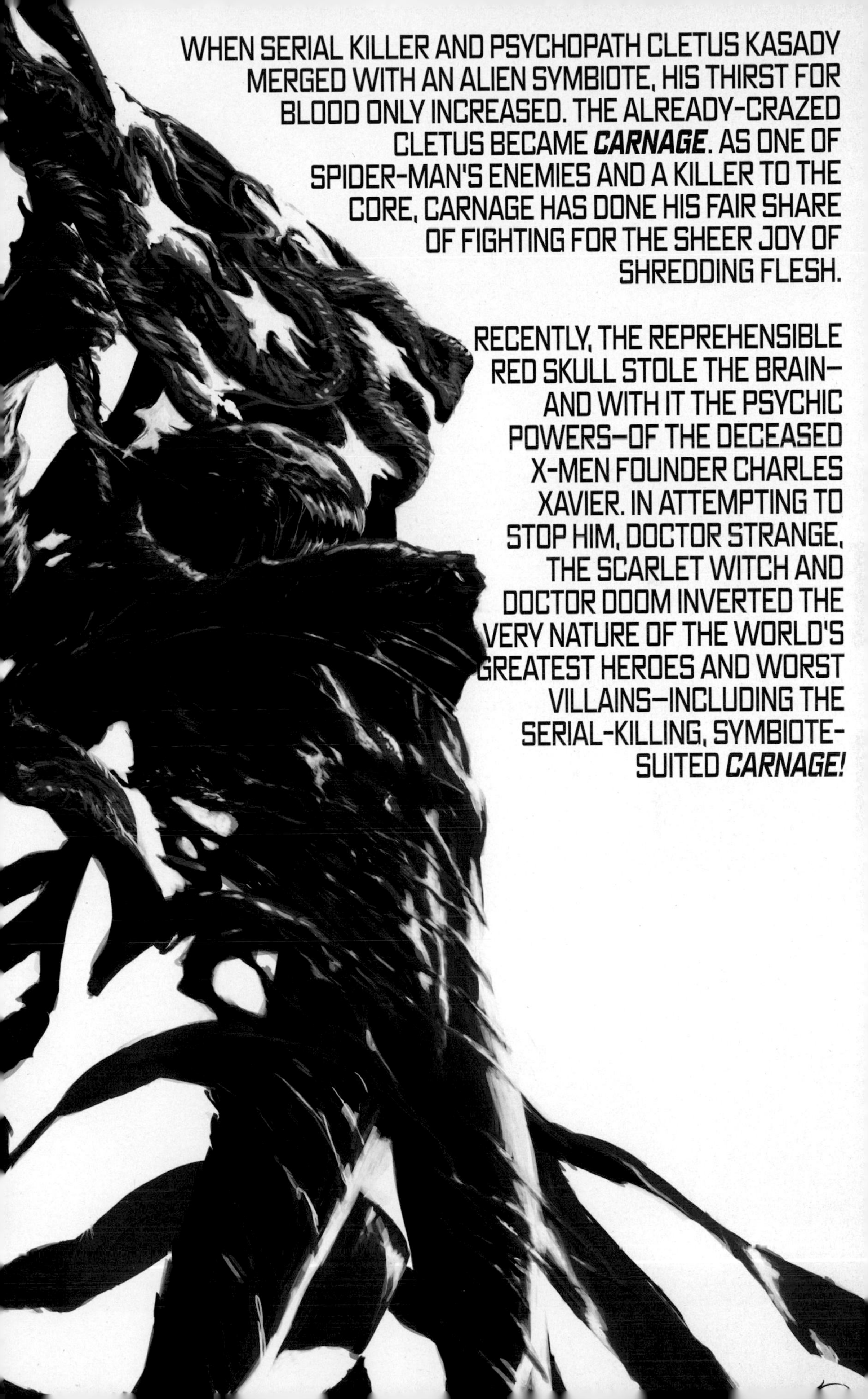

WHEN SERIAL KILLER AND PSYCHOPATH CLETUS KASADY MERGED WITH AN ALIEN SYMBIOTE, HIS THIRST FOR BLOOD ONLY INCREASED. THE ALREADY-CRAZED CLETUS BECAME ***CARNAGE***. AS ONE OF SPIDER-MAN'S ENEMIES AND A KILLER TO THE CORE, CARNAGE HAS DONE HIS FAIR SHARE OF FIGHTING FOR THE SHEER JOY OF SHREDDING FLESH.

RECENTLY, THE REPREHENSIBLE RED SKULL STOLE THE BRAIN—AND WITH IT THE PSYCHIC POWERS—OF THE DECEASED X-MEN FOUNDER CHARLES XAVIER. IN ATTEMPTING TO STOP HIM, DOCTOR STRANGE, THE SCARLET WITCH AND DOCTOR DOOM INVERTED THE VERY NATURE OF THE WORLD'S GREATEST HEROES AND WORST VILLAINS—INCLUDING THE SERIAL-KILLING, SYMBIOTE-SUITED ***CARNAGE!***

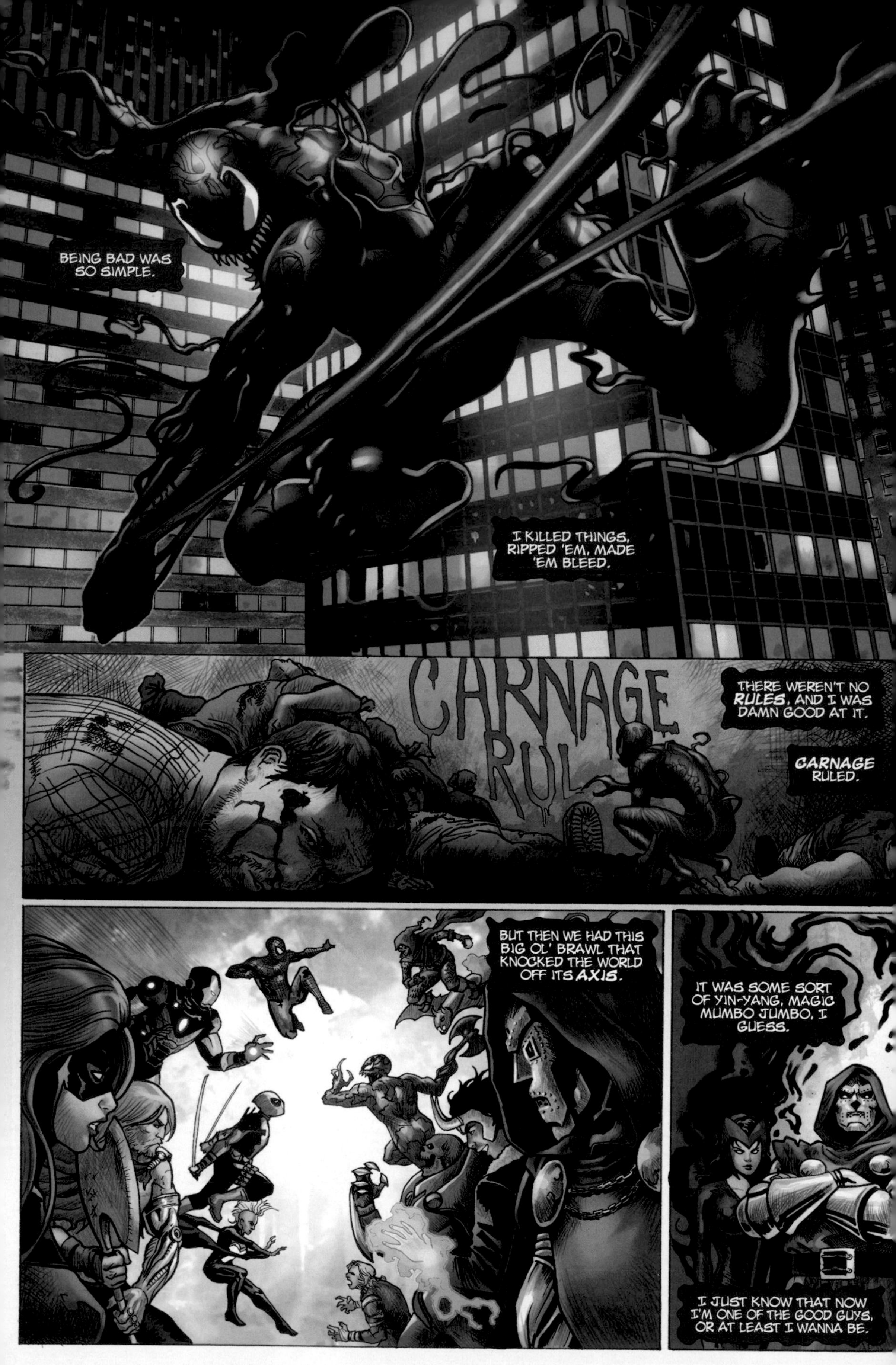
BEING BAD WAS SO SIMPLE.
I KILLED THINGS, RIPPED 'EM, MADE 'EM BLEED.
CARNAGE RUL
THERE WEREN'T NO RULES, AND I WAS DAMN GOOD AT IT.
CARNAGE RULED.
BUT THEN WE HAD THIS BIG OL' BRAWL THAT KNOCKED THE WORLD OFF ITS AXIS.
IT WAS SOME SORT OF YIN-YANG, MAGIC MUMBO JUMBO, I GUESS.
I JUST KNOW THAT NOW I'M ONE OF THE GOOD GUYS, OR AT LEAST I WANNA BE.

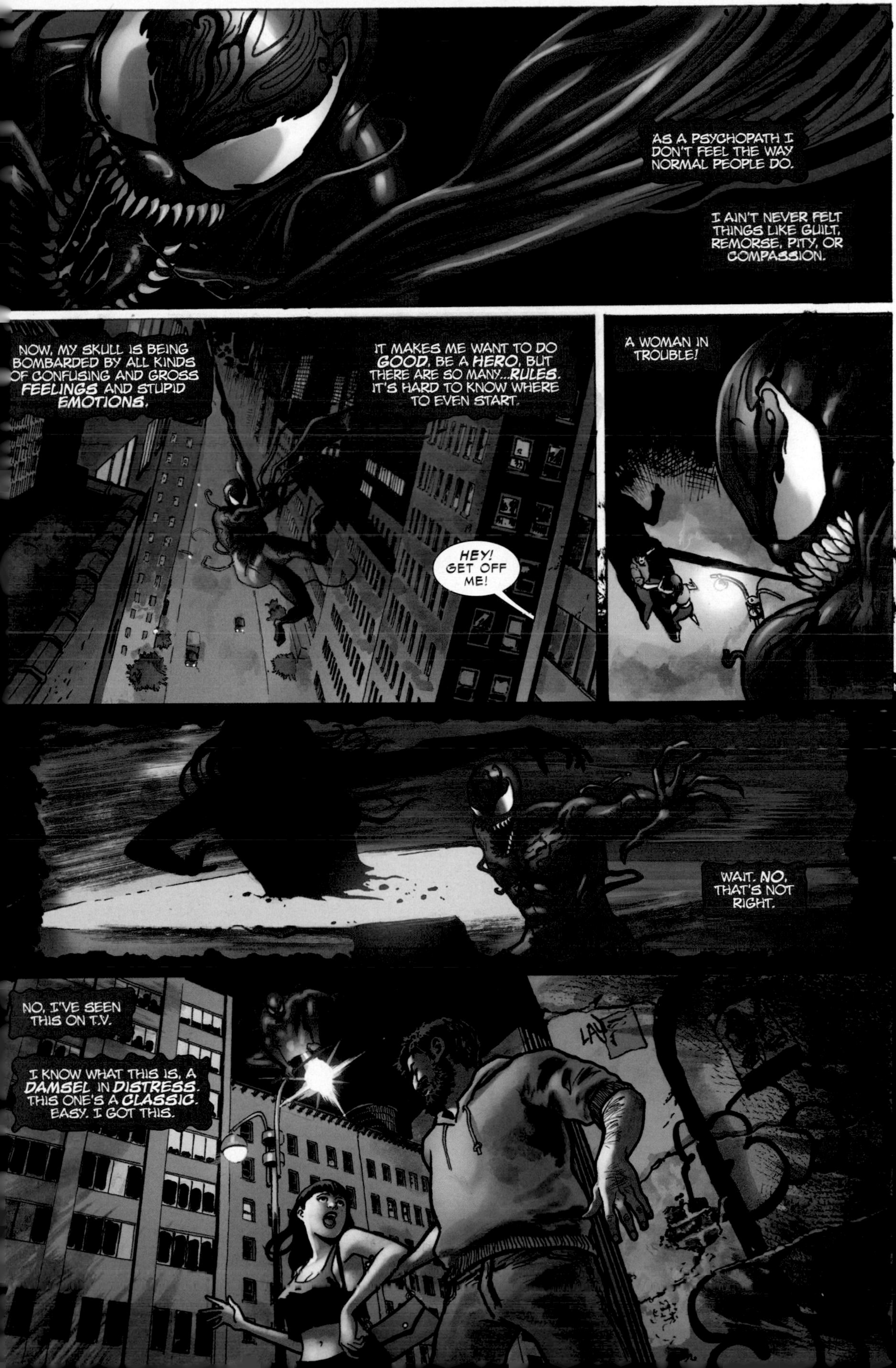
AS A PSYCHOPATH I DON'T FEEL THE WAY NORMAL PEOPLE DO.
I AIN'T NEVER FELT THINGS LIKE GUILT, REMORSE, PITY, OR COMPASSION.
NOW, MY SKULL IS BEING BOMBARDED BY ALL KINDS OF CONFUSING AND GROSS FEELINGS AND STUPID EMOTIONS.
IT MAKES ME WANT TO DO GOOD, BE A HERO, BUT THERE ARE SO MANY...RULES. IT'S HARD TO KNOW WHERE TO EVEN START.
HEY! GET OFF ME!
A WOMAN IN TROUBLE!
WAIT. NO, THAT'S NOT RIGHT.
NO, I'VE SEEN THIS ON T.V.
I KNOW WHAT THIS IS, A DAMSEL IN DISTRESS. THIS ONE'S A CLASSIC. EASY. I GOT THIS.

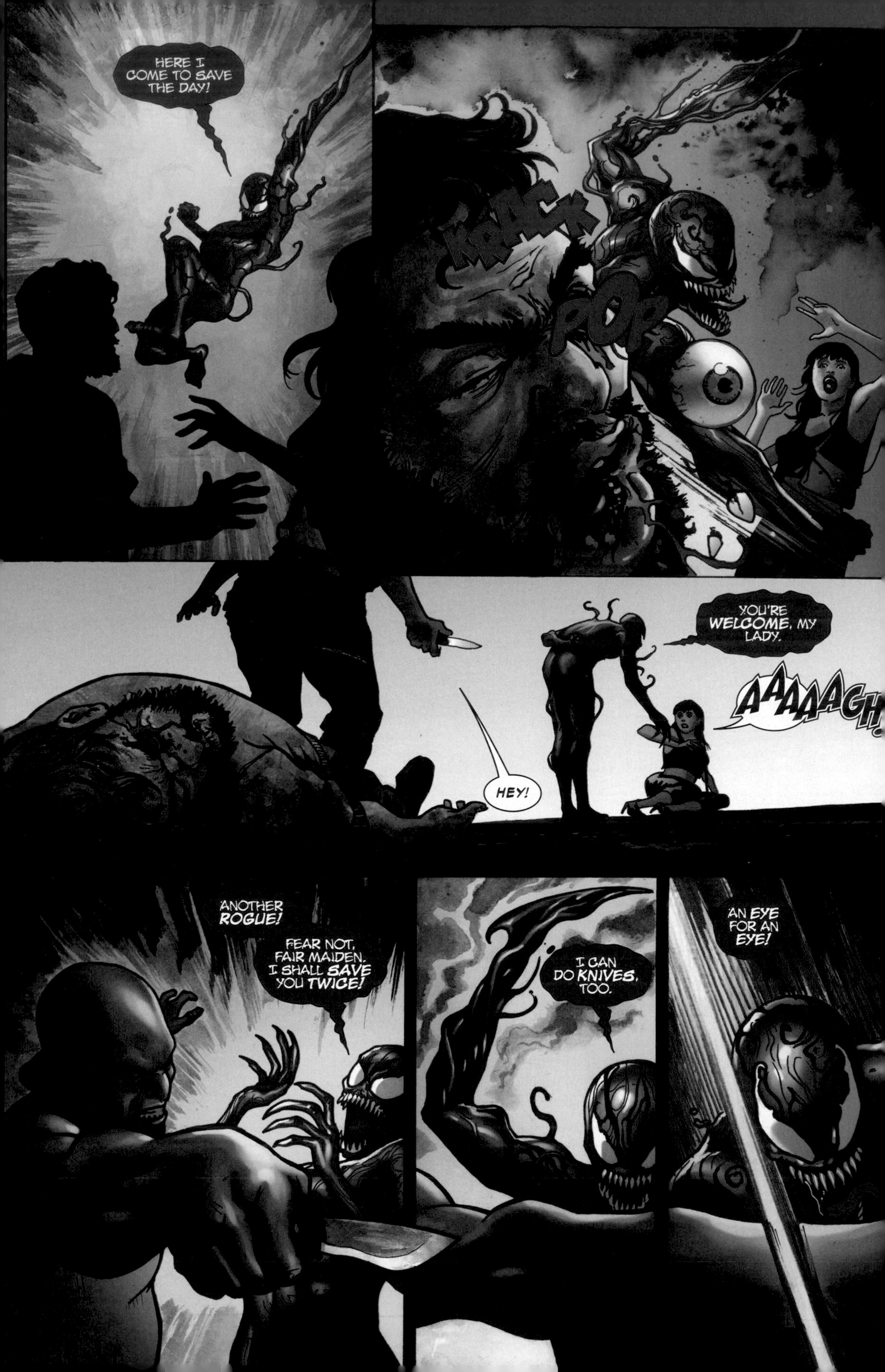
HERE I COME TO SAVE THE DAY!
KRACK
POP
YOU'RE WELCOME, MY LADY.
AAAAAGH!
HEY!
ANOTHER ROGUE!
FEAR NOT, FAIR MAIDEN. I SHALL SAVE YOU TWICE!
I CAN DO KNIVES, TOO.
AN EYE FOR AN EYE!

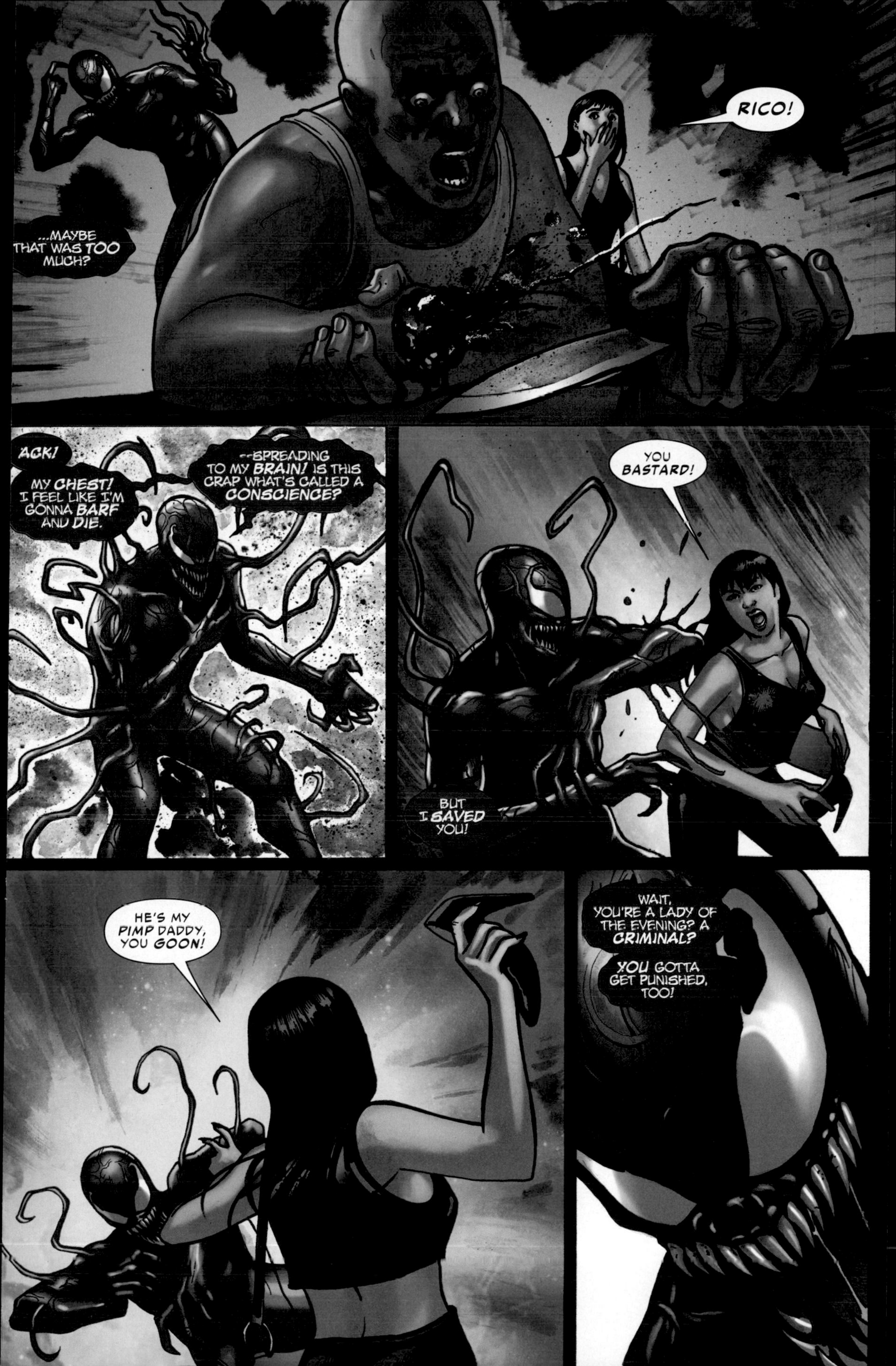
RICO!
...MAYBE THAT WAS TOO MUCH?
ACK!
MY CHEST! I FEEL LIKE I'M GONNA BARF AND DIE.
--SPREADING TO MY BRAIN! IS THIS CRAP WHAT'S CALLED A CONSCIENCE?
YOU BASTARD!
BUT I SAVED YOU!
HE'S MY PIMP DADDY, YOU GOON!
WAIT, YOU'RE A LADY OF THE EVENING? A CRIMINAL?
YOU GOTTA GET PUNISHED, TOO!

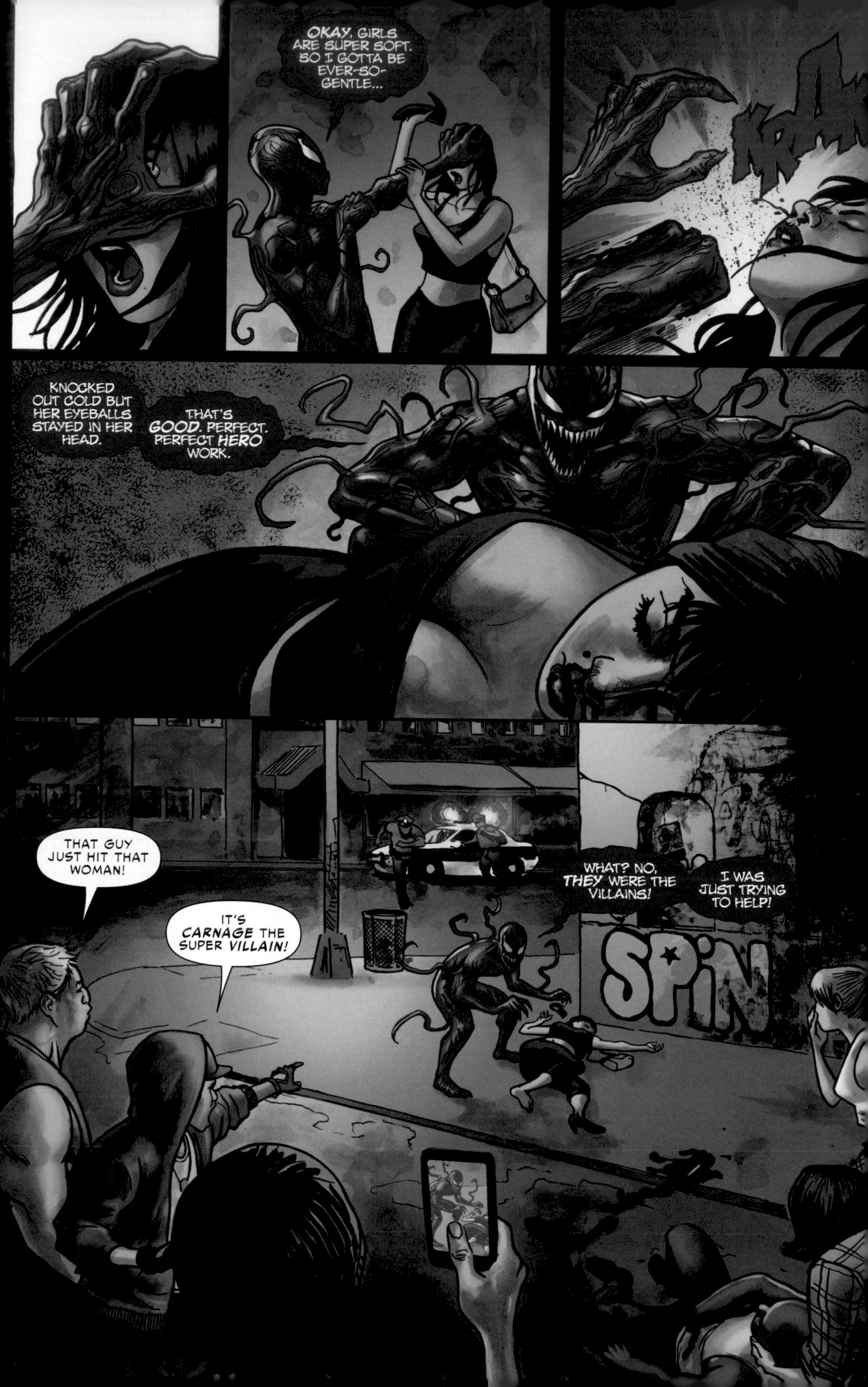
OKAY, GIRLS ARE SUPER SOFT. SO I GOTTA BE EVER-SO-GENTLE...
KNOCKED OUT COLD BUT HER EYEBALLS STAYED IN HER HEAD.
THAT'S GOOD. PERFECT. PERFECT HERO WORK.
THAT GUY JUST HIT THAT WOMAN!
IT'S CARNAGE THE SUPER VILLAIN!
WHAT? NO, THEY WERE THE VILLAINS!
I WAS JUST TRYING TO HELP!
SPIN

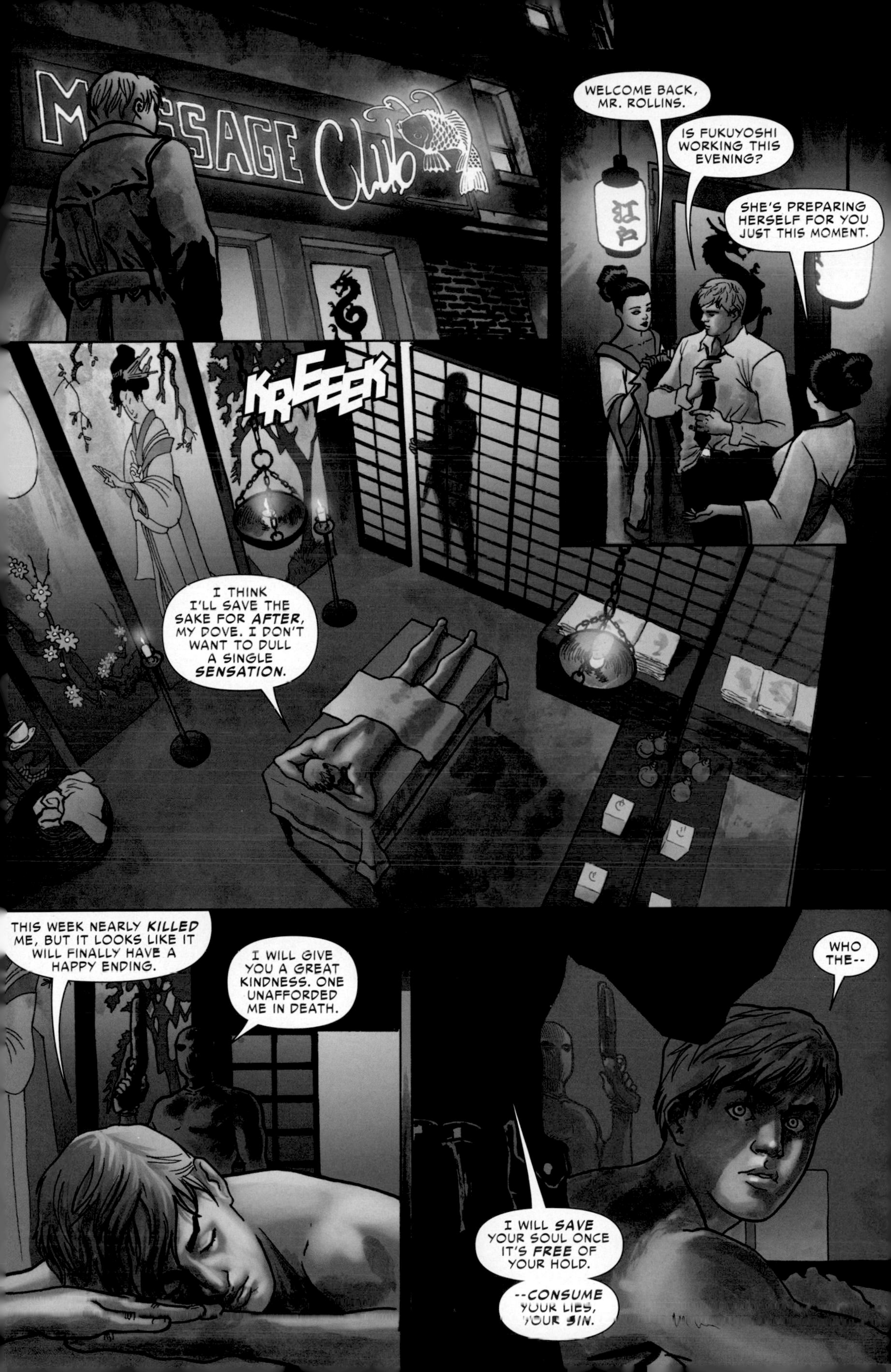
MASSAGE Club
WELCOME BACK, MR. ROLLINS.
IS FUKUYOSHI WORKING THIS EVENING?
SHE'S PREPARING HERSELF FOR YOU JUST THIS MOMENT.
KREEEK
I THINK I'LL SAVE THE SAKE FOR AFTER, MY DOVE. I DON'T WANT TO DULL A SINGLE SENSATION.
THIS WEEK NEARLY KILLED ME, BUT IT LOOKS LIKE IT WILL FINALLY HAVE A HAPPY ENDING.
I WILL GIVE YOU A GREAT KINDNESS. ONE UNAFFORDED ME IN DEATH.
WHO THE--
I WILL SAVE YOUR SOUL ONCE IT'S FREE OF YOUR HOLD.
--CONSUME YOUR LIES, YOUR SIN.

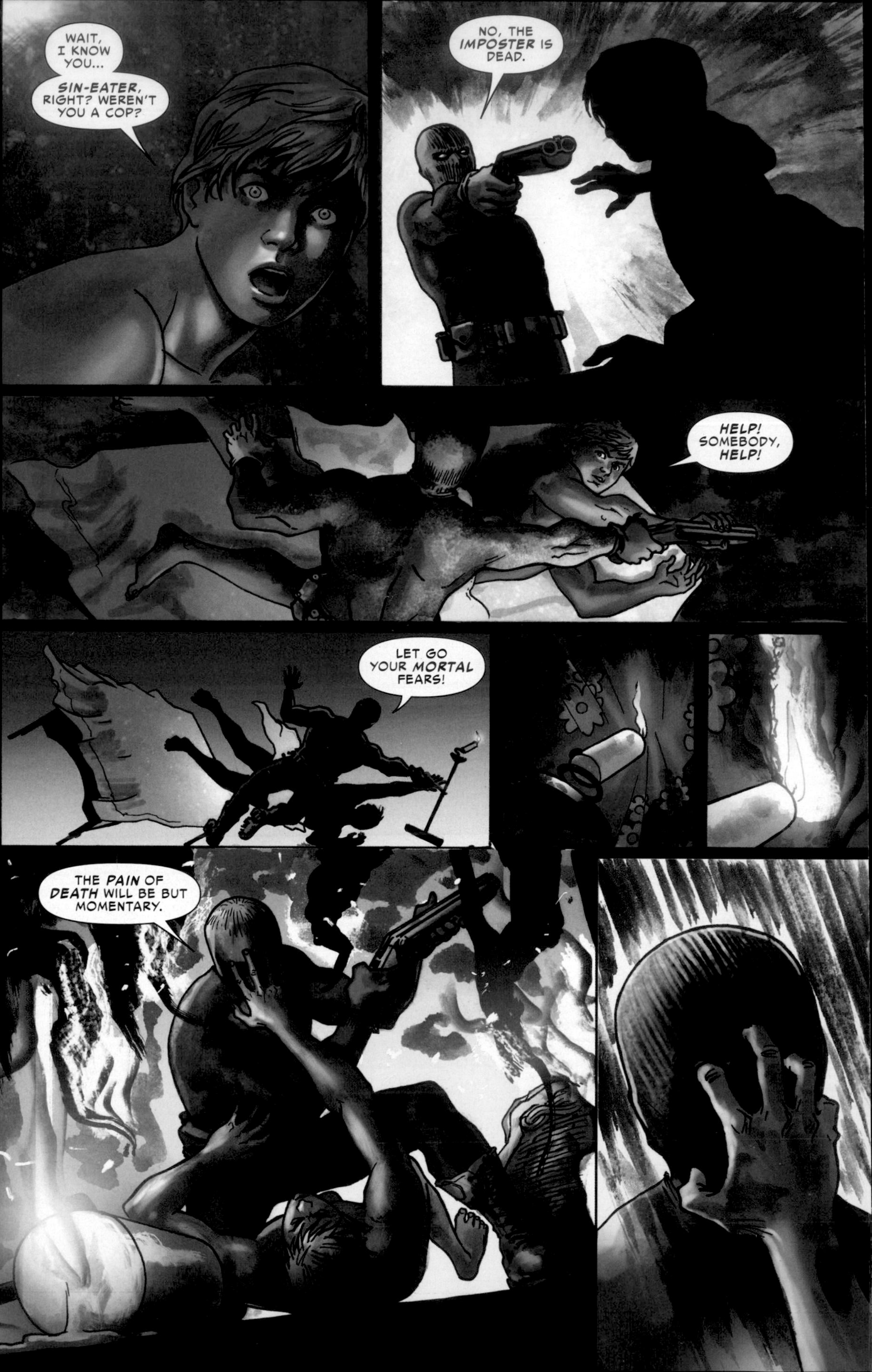
WAIT, I KNOW YOU...
SIN-EATER, RIGHT? WEREN'T YOU A COP?
NO, THE IMPOSTER IS DEAD.
HELP! SOMEBODY, HELP!
LET GO YOUR MORTAL FEARS!
THE PAIN OF DEATH WILL BE BUT MOMENTARY.

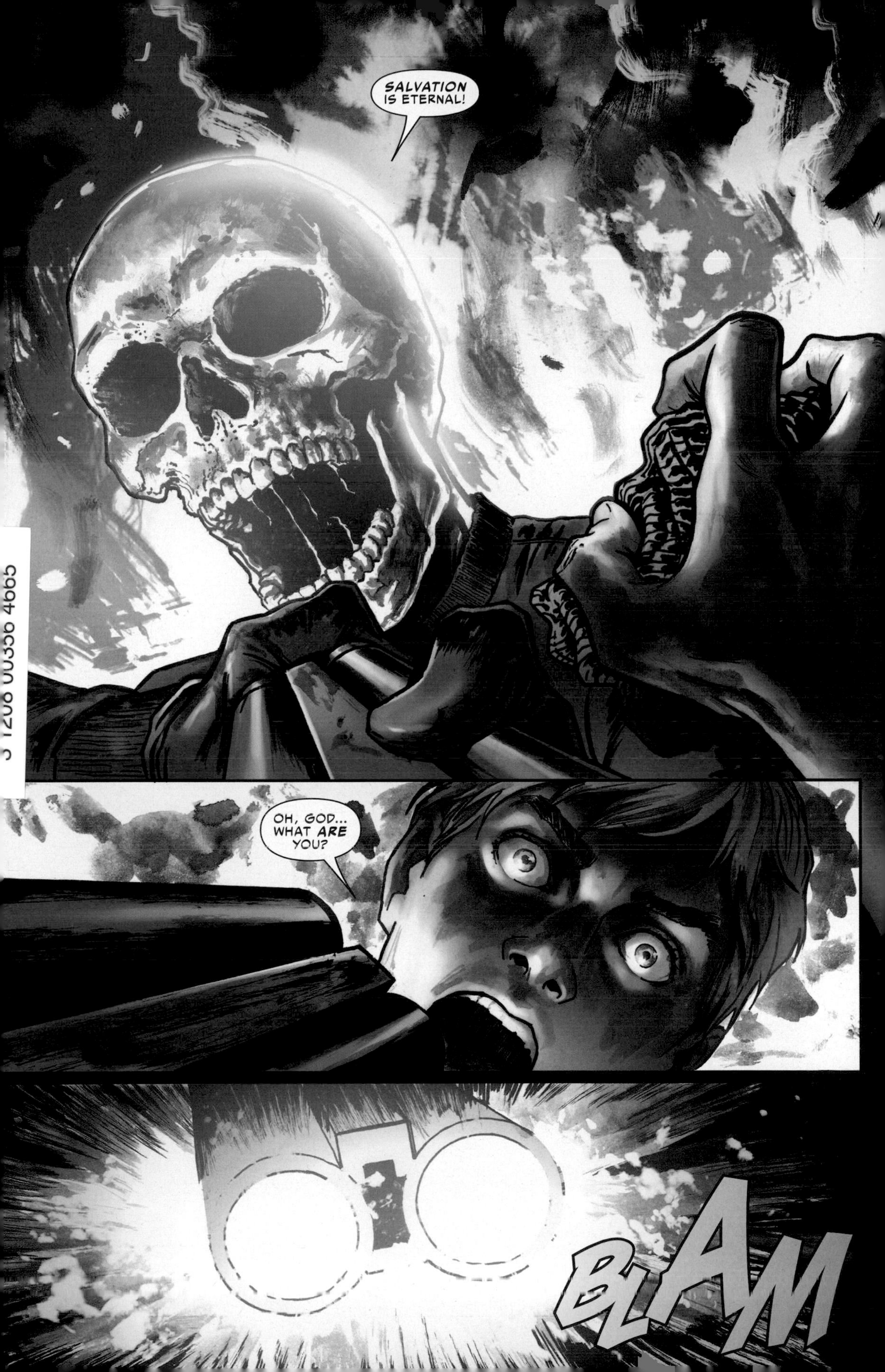
SALVATION IS ETERNAL!
OH, GOD... WHAT *ARE* YOU?
BLAM

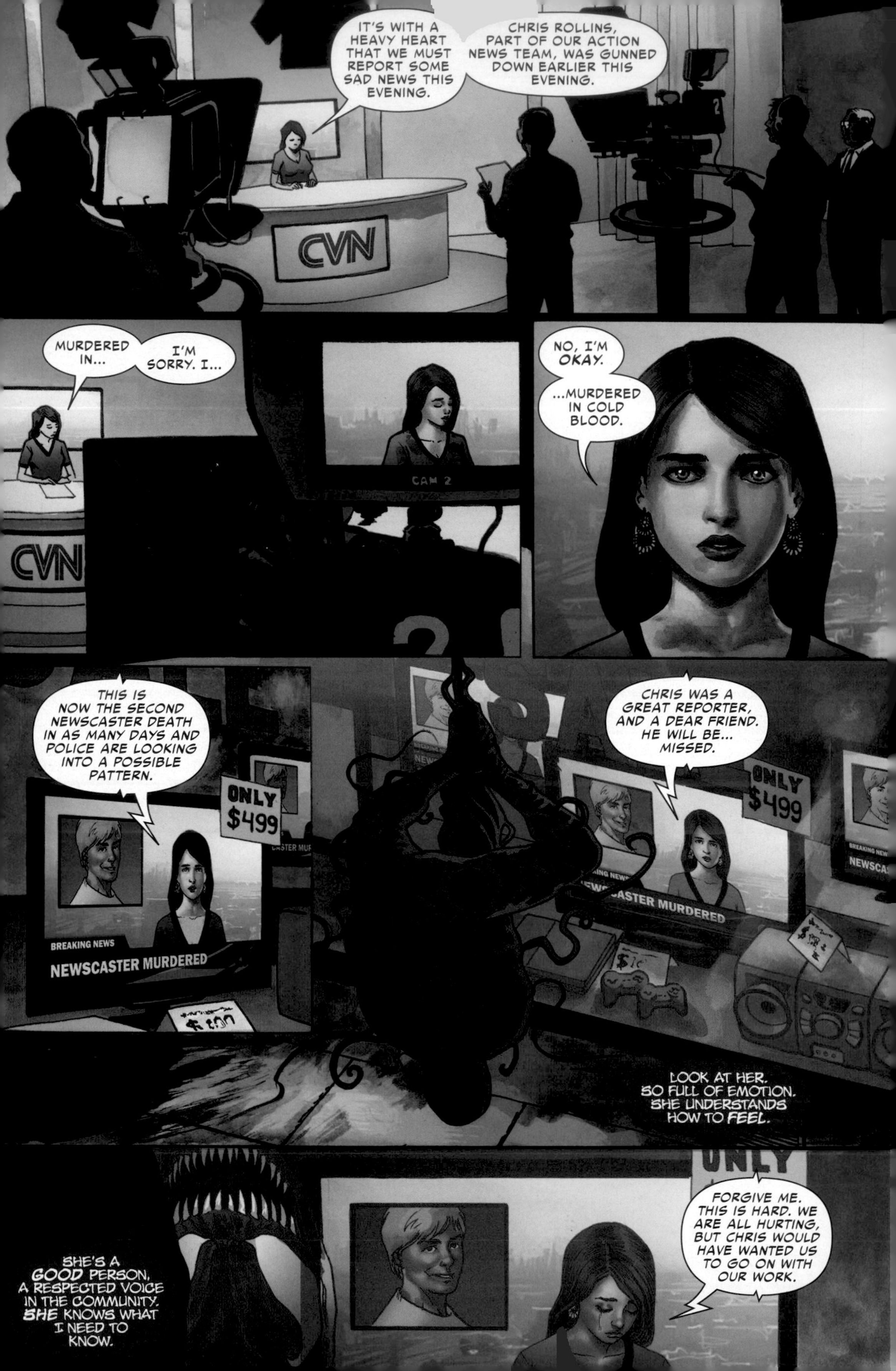
IT'S WITH A HEAVY HEART THAT WE MUST REPORT SOME SAD NEWS THIS EVENING.
CHRIS ROLLINS, PART OF OUR ACTION NEWS TEAM, WAS GUNNED DOWN EARLIER THIS EVENING.
CVN
MURDERED IN...
I'M SORRY. I...
CVN
CAM 2
NO, I'M OKAY.
...MURDERED IN COLD BLOOD.
THIS IS NOW THE SECOND NEWSCASTER DEATH IN AS MANY DAYS AND POLICE ARE LOOKING INTO A POSSIBLE PATTERN.
ONLY $499
BREAKING NEWS
NEWSCASTER MURDERED
CHRIS WAS A GREAT REPORTER, AND A DEAR FRIEND. HE WILL BE... MISSED.
ONLY $499
NEWSCASTER MURDERED
LOOK AT HER. SO FULL OF EMOTION. SHE UNDERSTANDS HOW TO FEEL.
ONLY
FORGIVE ME. THIS IS HARD. WE ARE ALL HURTING, BUT CHRIS WOULD HAVE WANTED US TO GO ON WITH OUR WORK.
SHE'S A GOOD PERSON, A RESPECTED VOICE IN THE COMMUNITY. SHE KNOWS WHAT I NEED TO KNOW.

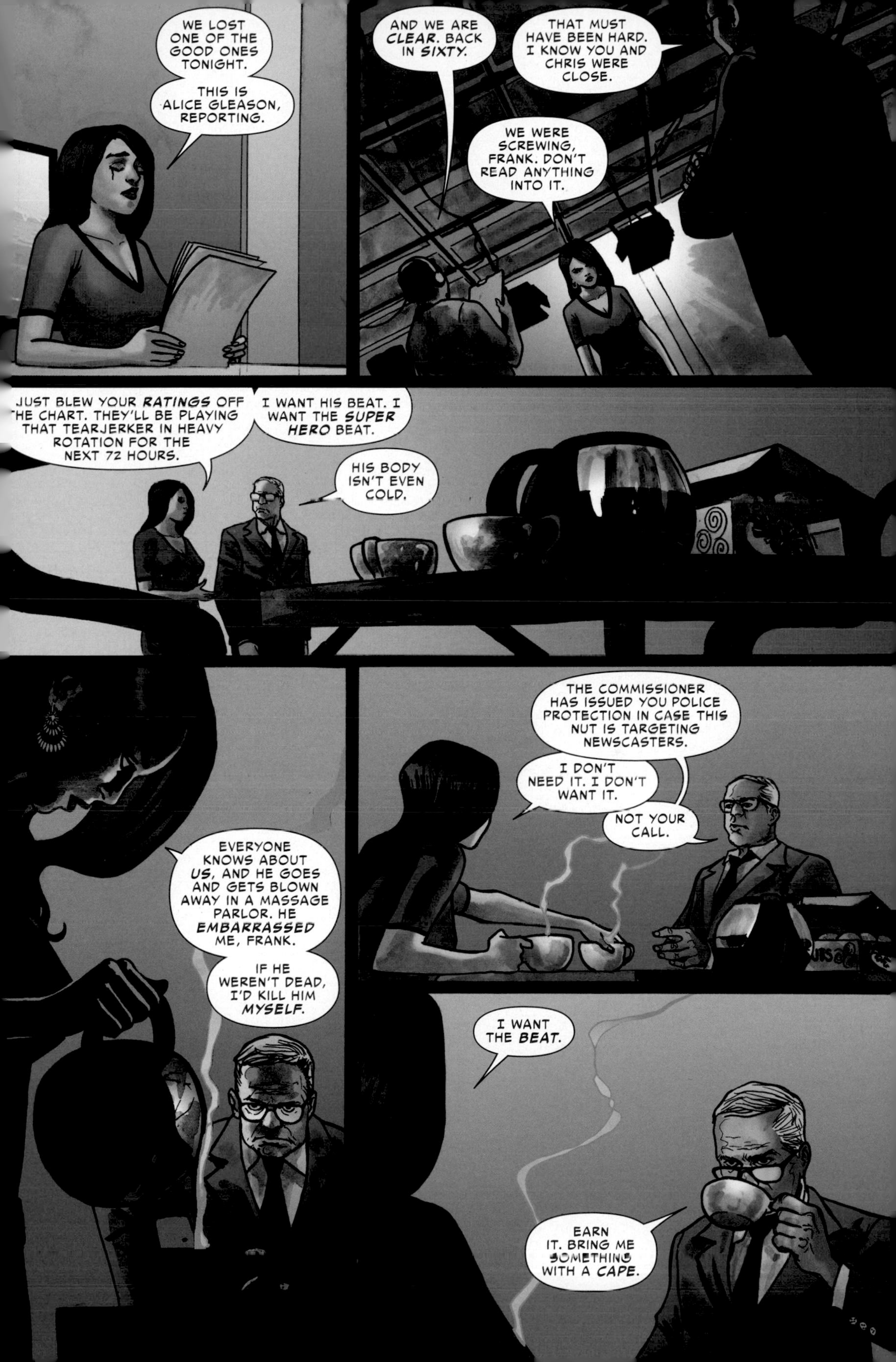
WE LOST ONE OF THE GOOD ONES TONIGHT.
THIS IS ALICE GLEASON, REPORTING.
AND WE ARE *CLEAR*. BACK IN *SIXTY*.
THAT MUST HAVE BEEN HARD. I KNOW YOU AND CHRIS WERE CLOSE.
WE WERE SCREWING, FRANK. DON'T READ ANYTHING INTO IT.
JUST BLEW YOUR *RATINGS* OFF THE CHART. THEY'LL BE PLAYING THAT TEARJERKER IN HEAVY ROTATION FOR THE NEXT 72 HOURS.
I WANT HIS BEAT. I WANT THE *SUPER HERO* BEAT.
HIS BODY ISN'T EVEN COLD.
EVERYONE KNOWS ABOUT *US*, AND HE GOES AND GETS BLOWN AWAY IN A MASSAGE PARLOR. HE *EMBARRASSED* ME, FRANK.
IF HE WEREN'T DEAD, I'D KILL HIM *MYSELF*.
THE COMMISSIONER HAS ISSUED YOU POLICE PROTECTION IN CASE THIS NUT IS TARGETING NEWSCASTERS.
I DON'T NEED IT. I DON'T WANT IT.
NOT YOUR CALL.
I WANT THE *BEAT*.
EARN IT. BRING ME SOMETHING WITH A *CAPE*.

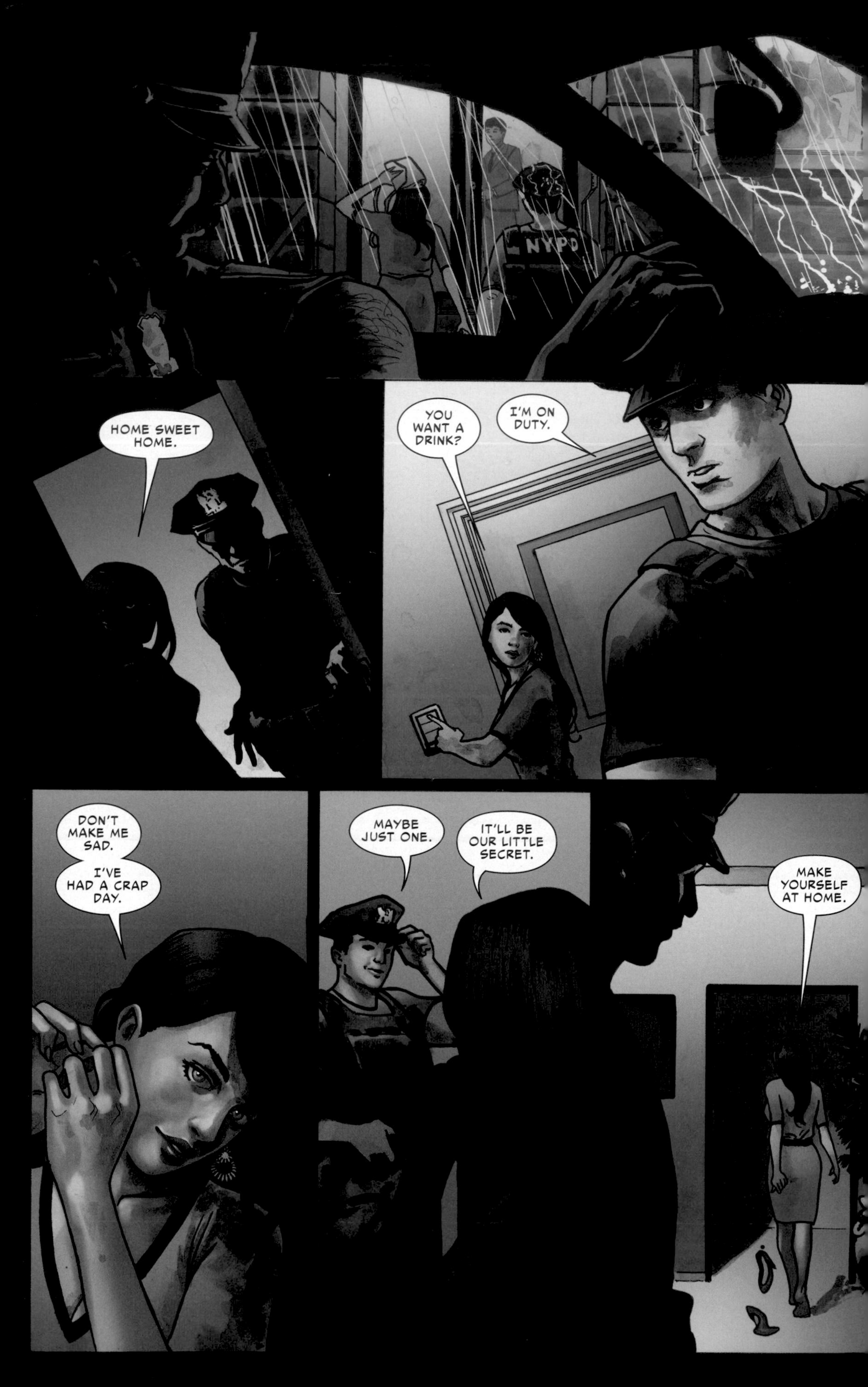
NYPD
HOME SWEET HOME.
YOU WANT A DRINK?
I'M ON DUTY.
DON'T MAKE ME SAD.
I'VE HAD A CRAP DAY.
MAYBE JUST ONE.
IT'LL BE OUR LITTLE SECRET.
MAKE YOURSELF AT HOME.

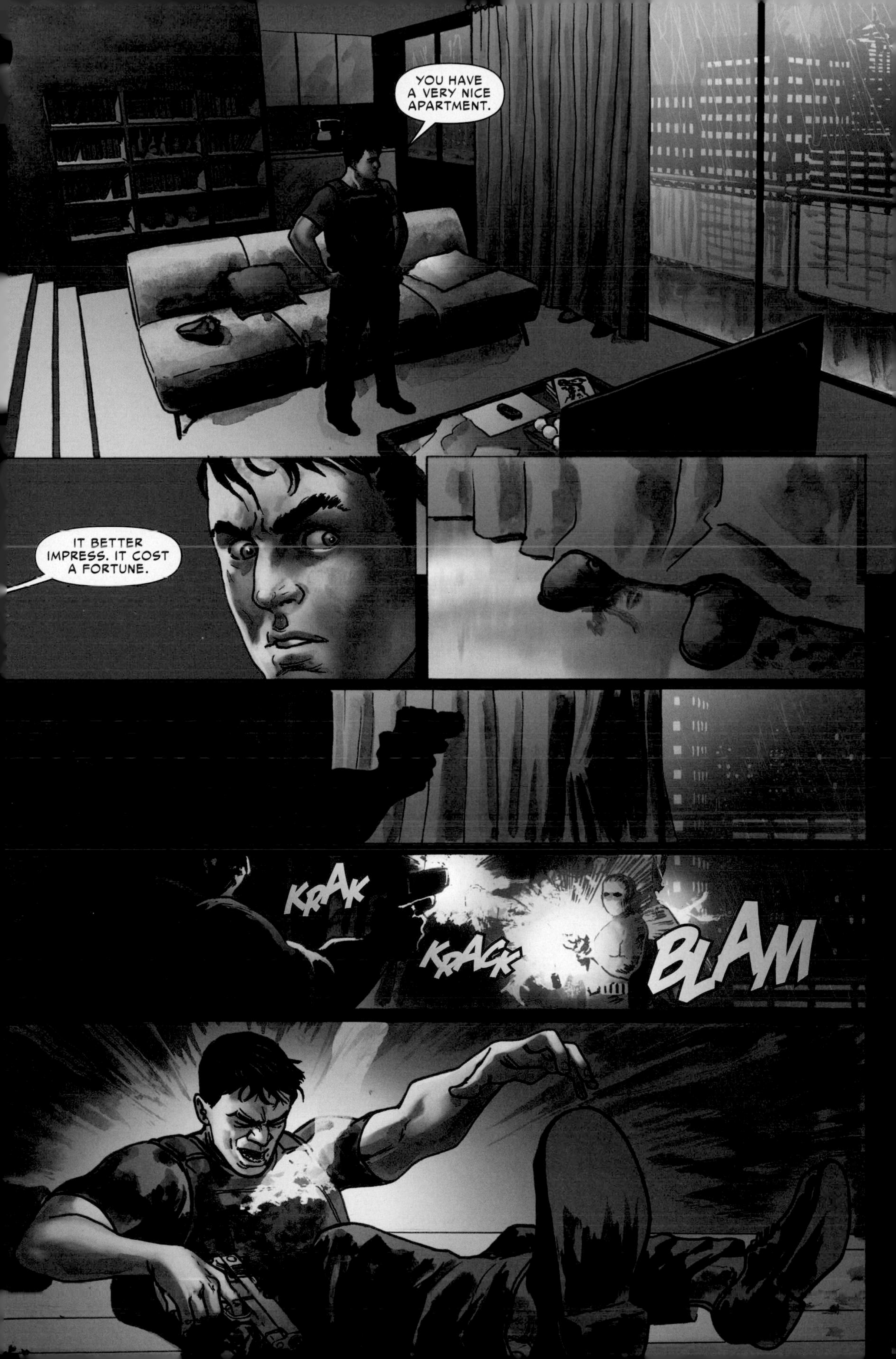
YOU HAVE A VERY NICE APARTMENT.
IT BETTER IMPRESS. IT COST A FORTUNE.
KRAK
KRACK
BLAM

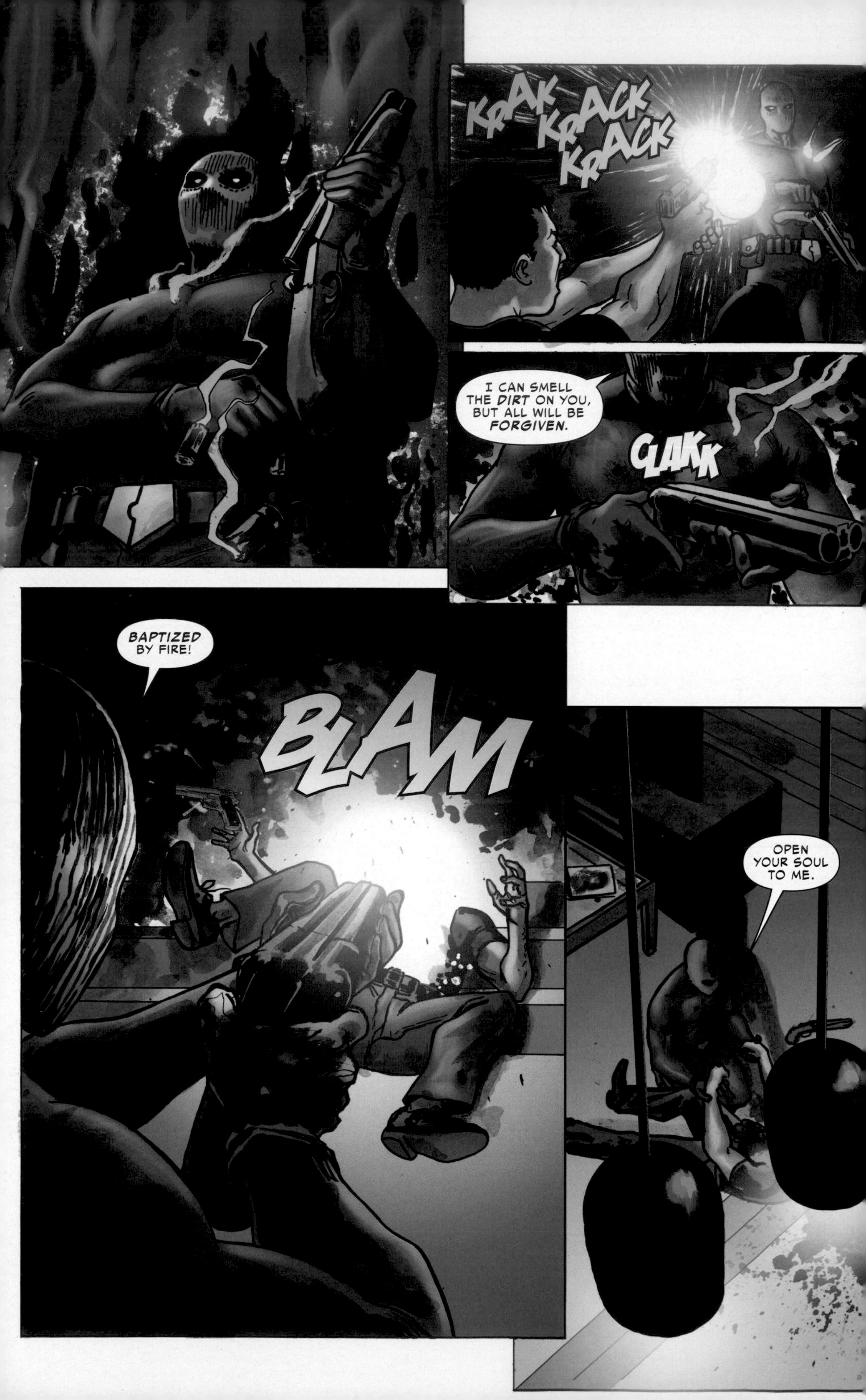
KRAK KRACK KRACK
I CAN SMELL THE DIRT ON YOU, BUT ALL WILL BE FORGIVEN.
CLAKK
BAPTIZED BY FIRE!
BLAM
OPEN YOUR SOUL TO ME.

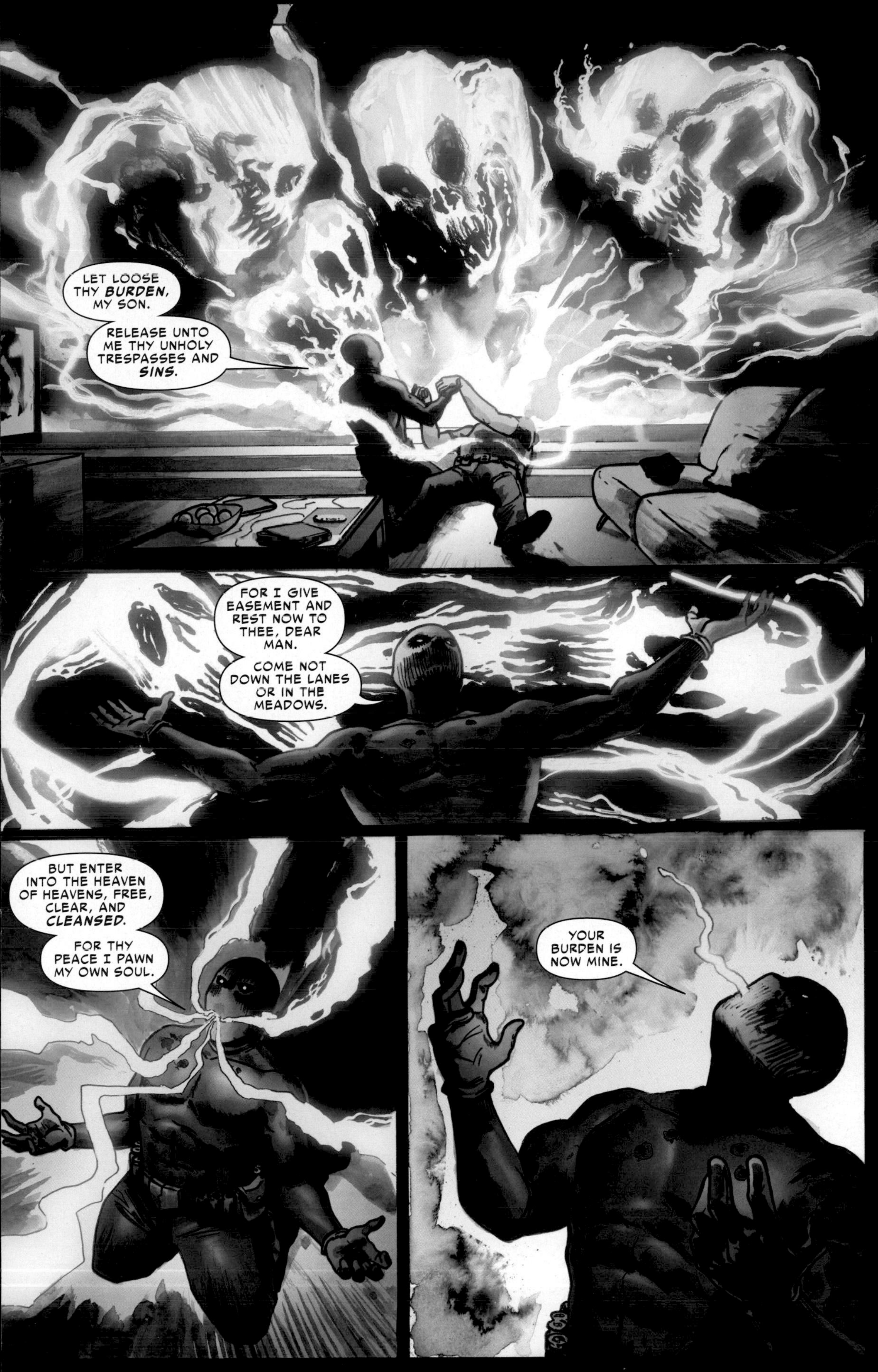
LET LOOSE THY BURDEN, MY SON.
RELEASE UNTO ME THY UNHOLY TRESPASSES AND SINS.
FOR I GIVE EASEMENT AND REST NOW TO THEE, DEAR MAN.
COME NOT DOWN THE LANES OR IN THE MEADOWS.
BUT ENTER INTO THE HEAVEN OF HEAVENS, FREE, CLEAR, AND CLEANSED.
FOR THY PEACE I PAWN MY OWN SOUL.
YOUR BURDEN IS NOW MINE.

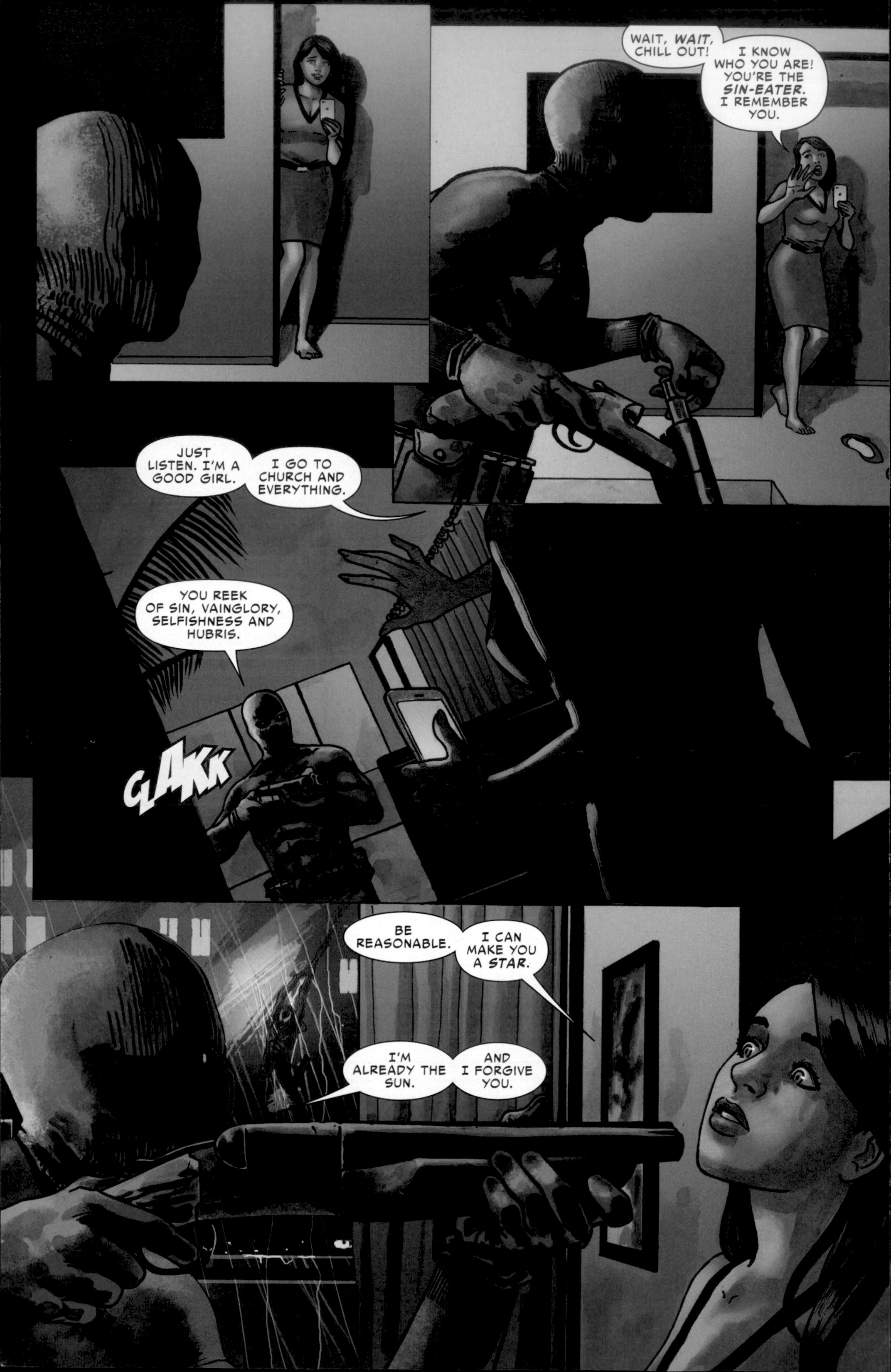
WAIT, WAIT, CHILL OUT!
I KNOW WHO YOU ARE! YOU'RE THE SIN-EATER. I REMEMBER YOU.
JUST LISTEN. I'M A GOOD GIRL.
I GO TO CHURCH AND EVERYTHING.
YOU REEK OF SIN, VAINGLORY, SELFISHNESS AND HUBRIS.
CLAKK
BE REASONABLE.
I CAN MAKE YOU A STAR.
I'M ALREADY THE SUN.
AND I FORGIVE YOU.

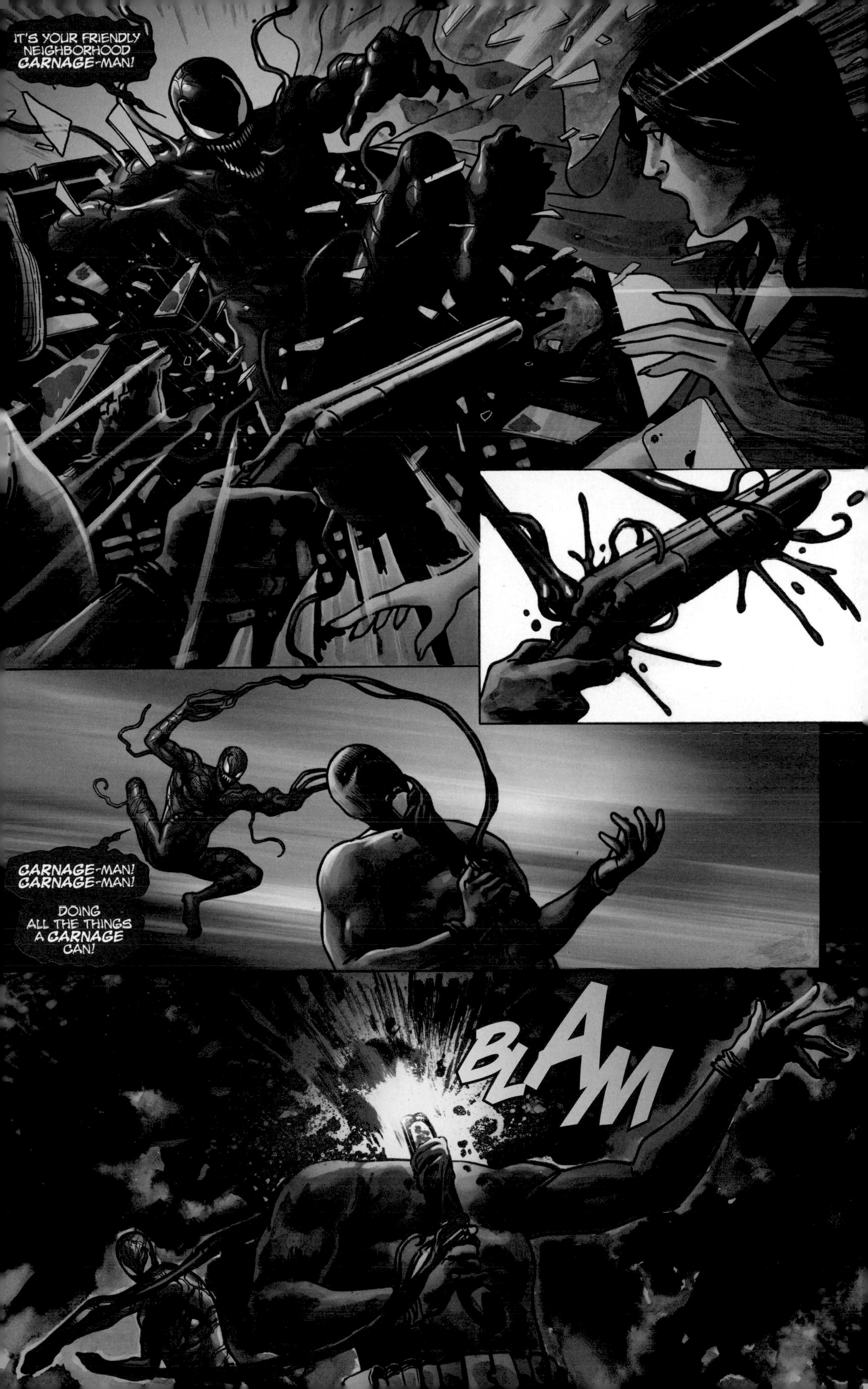
IT'S YOUR FRIENDLY NEIGHBORHOOD CARNAGE-MAN!
CARNAGE-MAN! CARNAGE-MAN!
DOING ALL THE THINGS A CARNAGE CAN!
BLAM

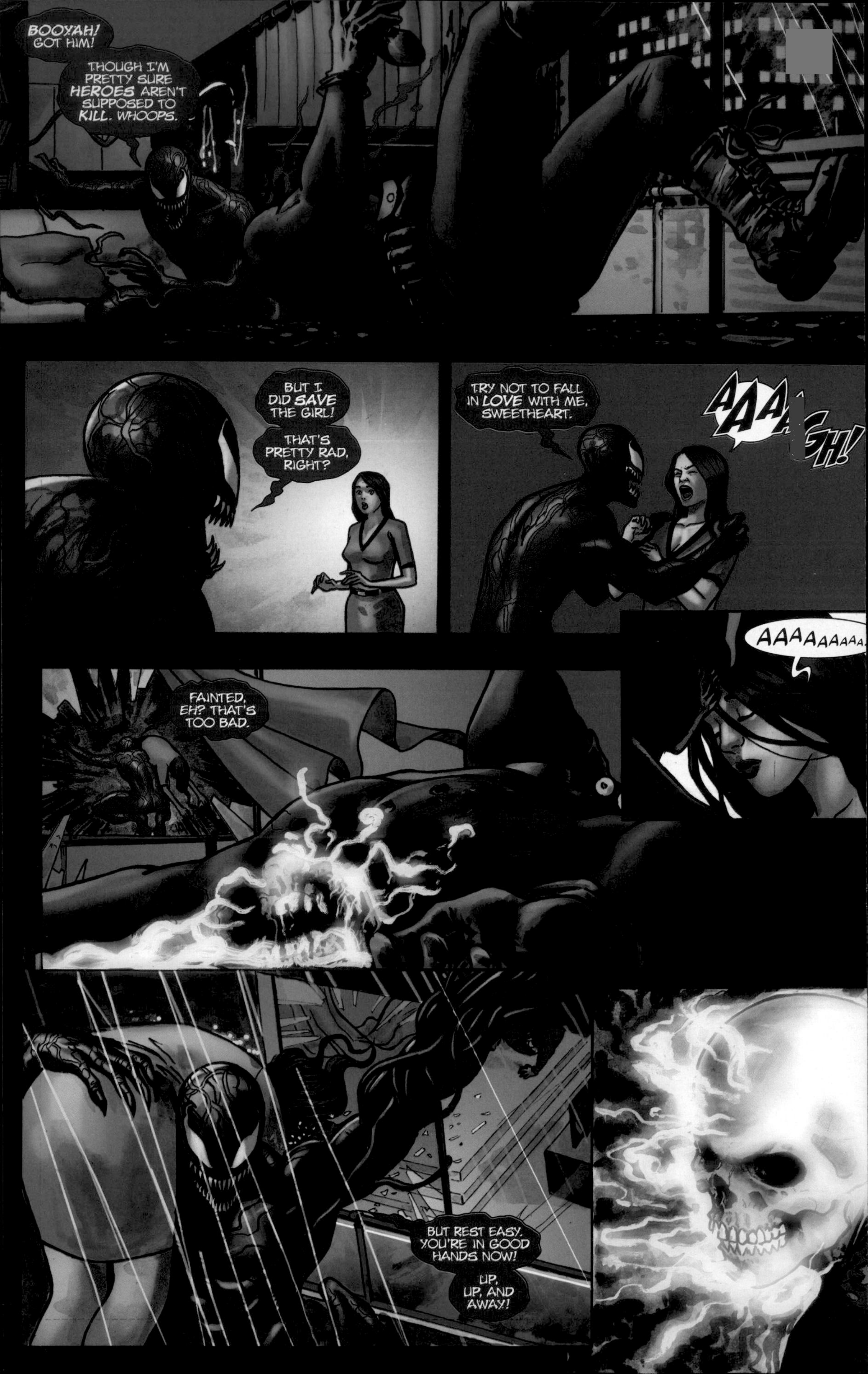
BOOYAH! GOT HIM!
THOUGH I'M PRETTY SURE HEROES AREN'T SUPPOSED TO KILL. WHOOPS.
BUT I DID SAVE THE GIRL!
THAT'S PRETTY RAD, RIGHT?
TRY NOT TO FALL IN LOVE WITH ME, SWEETHEART.
AAAAAAAAA
FAINTED, EH? THAT'S TOO BAD.
BUT REST EASY. YOU'RE IN GOOD HANDS NOW!
UP, UP, AND AWAY!

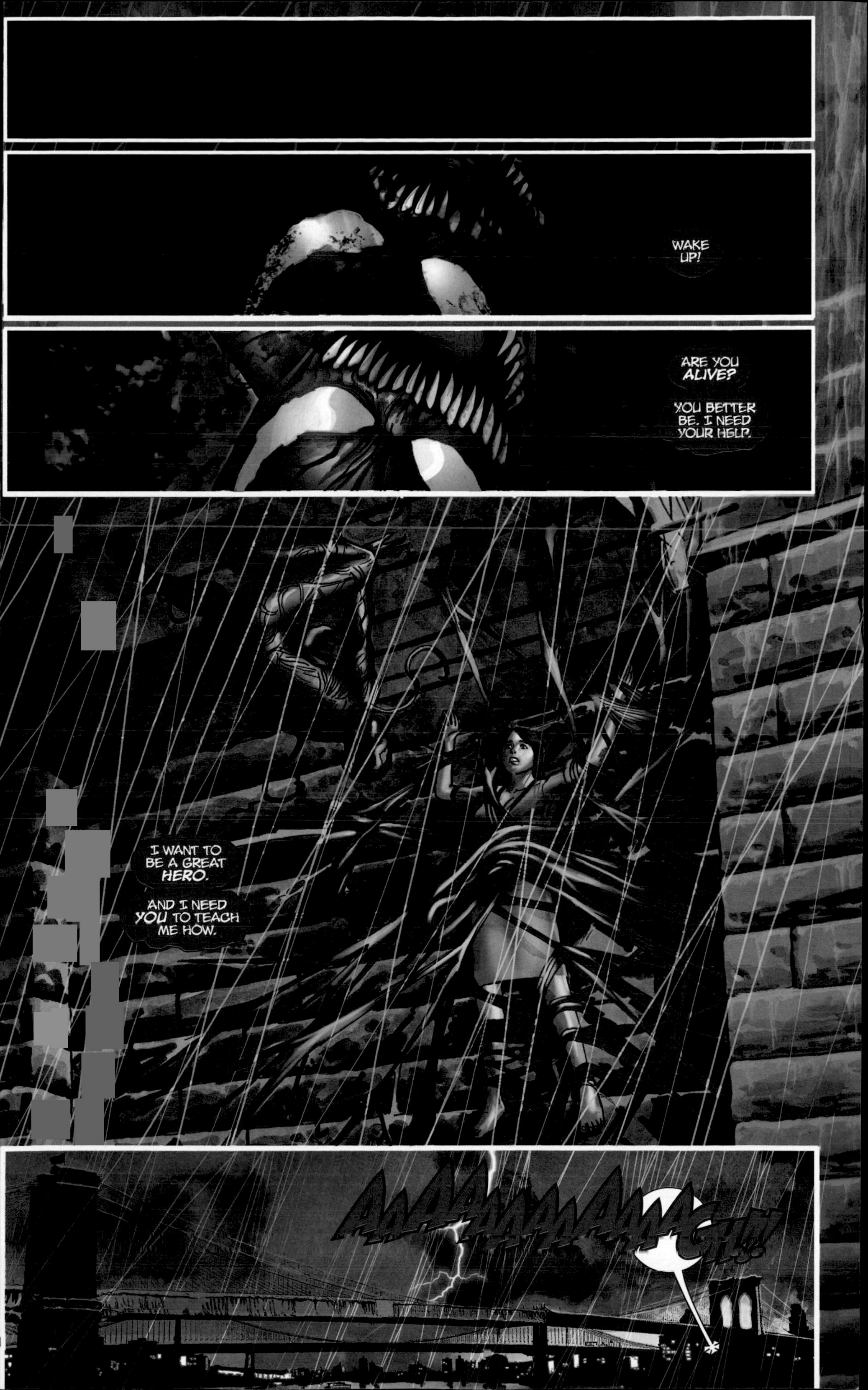
WAKE UP!
ARE YOU ALIVE?
YOU BETTER BE. I NEED YOUR HELP.
I WANT TO BE A GREAT HERO.
AND I NEED YOU TO TEACH ME HOW.
AAAAAAAAAAAGH!!

AXIS

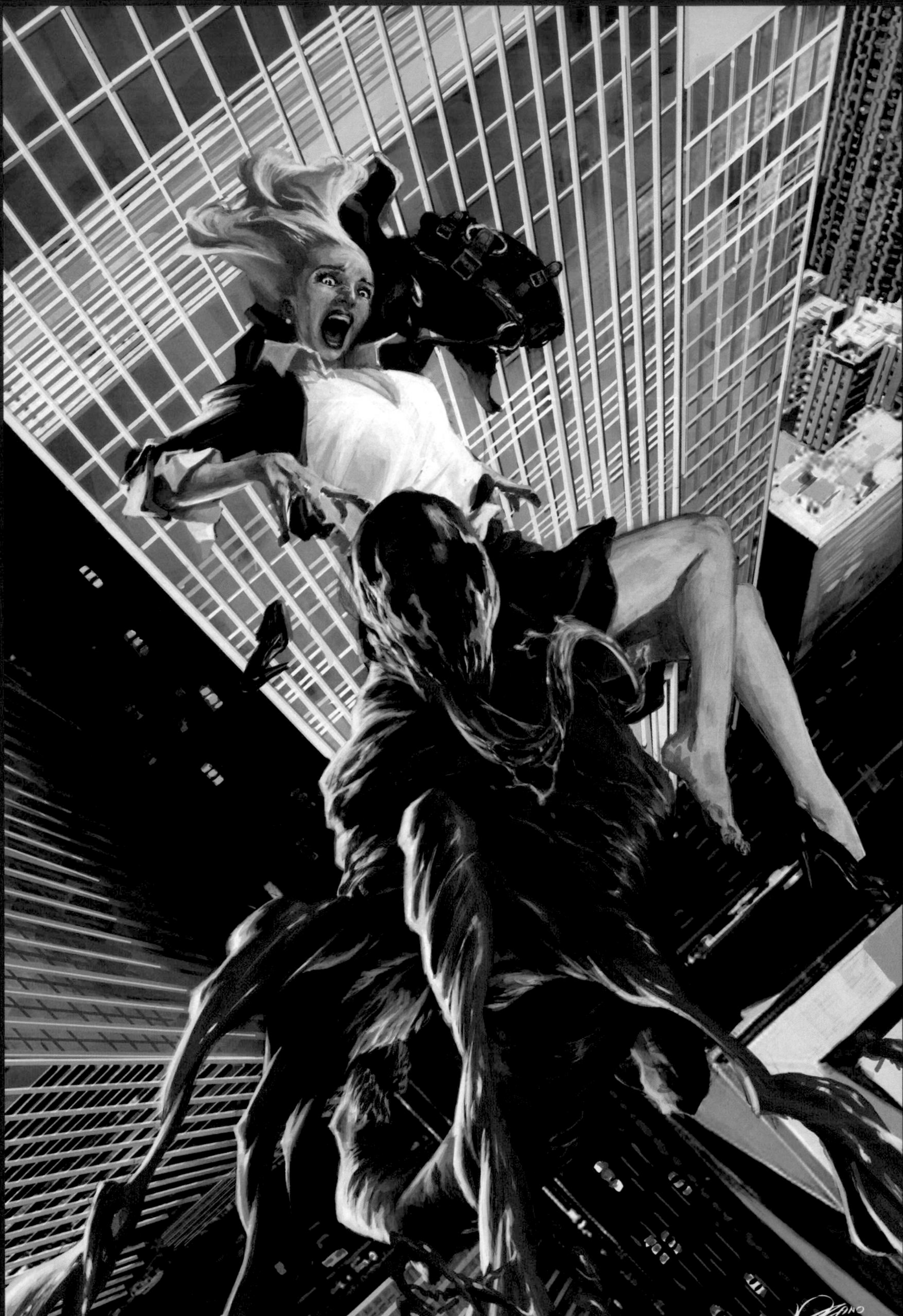

CARNAGE #2

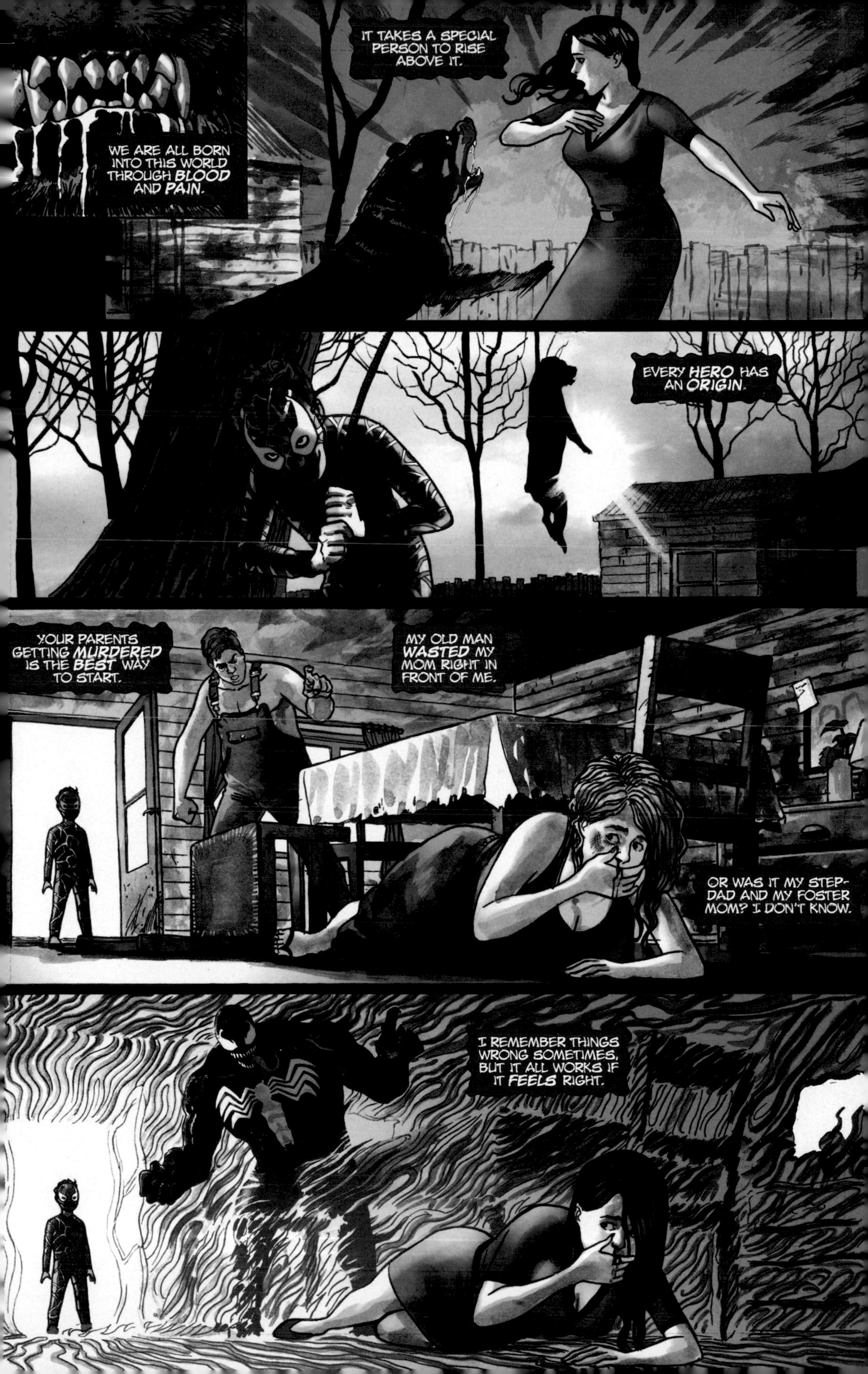
WE ARE ALL BORN INTO THIS WORLD THROUGH BLOOD AND PAIN.
IT TAKES A SPECIAL PERSON TO RISE ABOVE IT.
EVERY HERO HAS AN ORIGIN.
YOUR PARENTS GETTING MURDERED IS THE BEST WAY TO START.
MY OLD MAN WASTED MY MOM RIGHT IN FRONT OF ME.
OR WAS IT MY STEP-DAD AND MY FOSTER MOM? I DON'T KNOW.
I REMEMBER THINGS WRONG SOMETIMES, BUT IT ALL WORKS IF IT FEELS RIGHT.

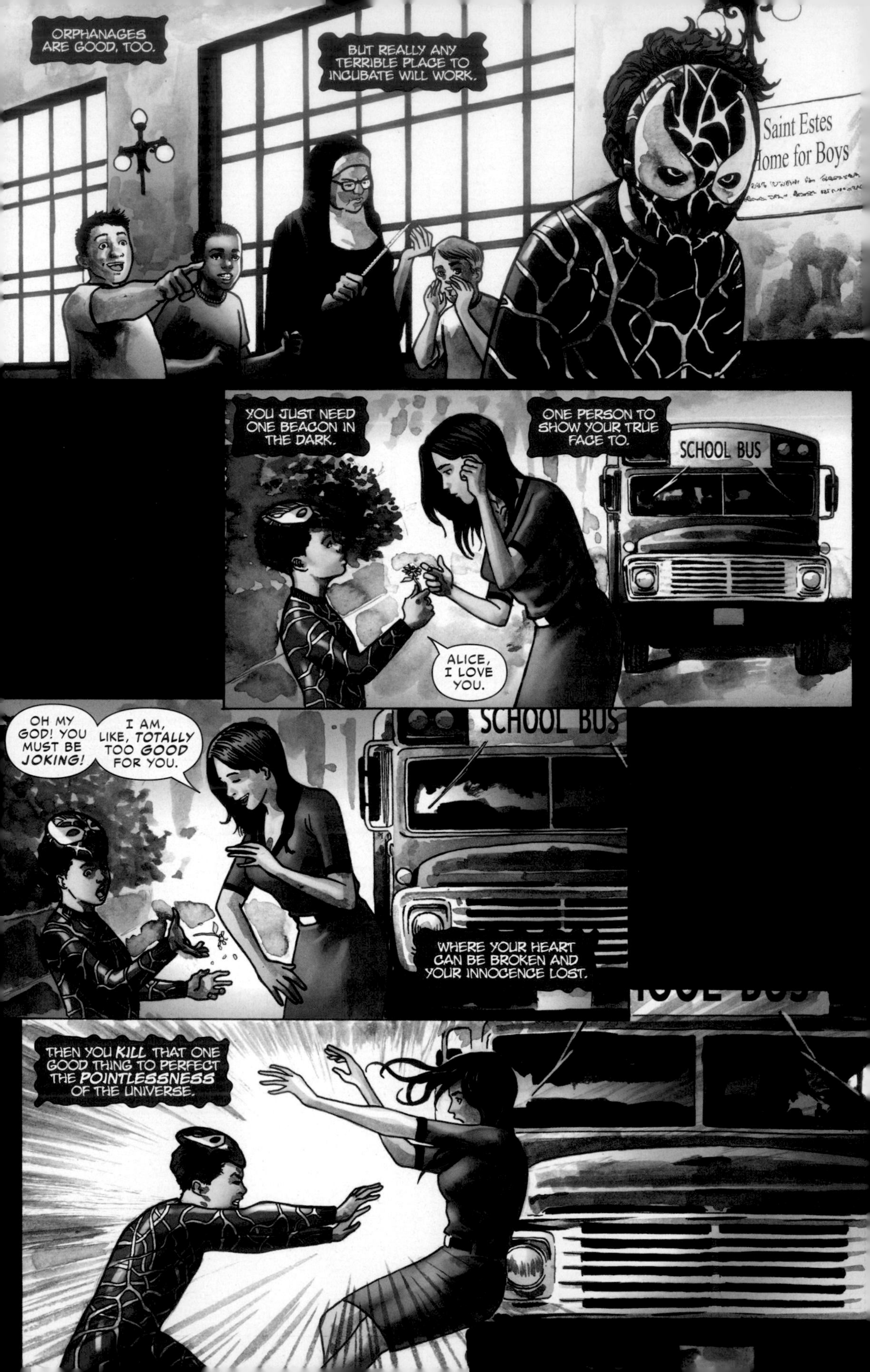

ORPHANAGES ARE GOOD, TOO.
BUT REALLY ANY TERRIBLE PLACE TO INCUBATE WILL WORK.
Saint Estes Home for Boys
YOU JUST NEED ONE BEACON IN THE DARK.
ONE PERSON TO SHOW YOUR TRUE FACE TO.
SCHOOL BUS
ALICE, I LOVE YOU.
OH MY GOD! YOU MUST BE JOKING!
I AM, LIKE, TOTALLY TOO GOOD FOR YOU.
SCHOOL BUS
WHERE YOUR HEART CAN BE BROKEN AND YOUR INNOCENCE LOST.
THEN YOU KILL THAT ONE GOOD THING TO PERFECT THE POINTLESSNESS OF THE UNIVERSE.

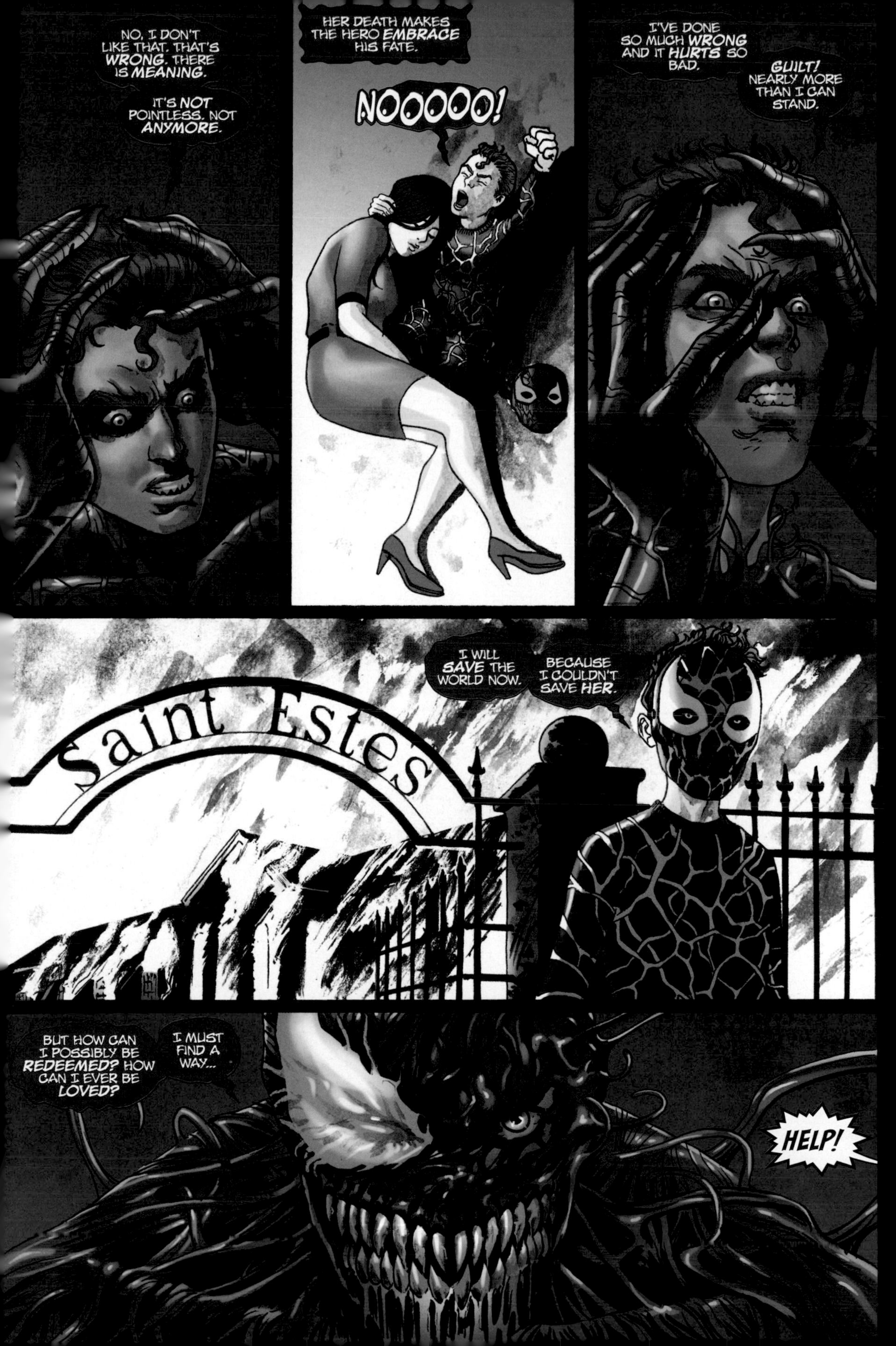
NO, I DON'T LIKE THAT. THAT'S WRONG. THERE IS MEANING.
IT'S NOT POINTLESS. NOT ANYMORE.
HER DEATH MAKES THE HERO EMBRACE HIS FATE.
NOOOOO!
I'VE DONE SO MUCH WRONG AND IT HURTS SO BAD.
GUILT! NEARLY MORE THAN I CAN STAND.
Saint Estes
I WILL SAVE THE WORLD NOW.
BECAUSE I COULDN'T SAVE HER.
BUT HOW CAN I POSSIBLY BE REDEEMED? HOW CAN I EVER BE LOVED?
I MUST FIND A WAY...
HELP!

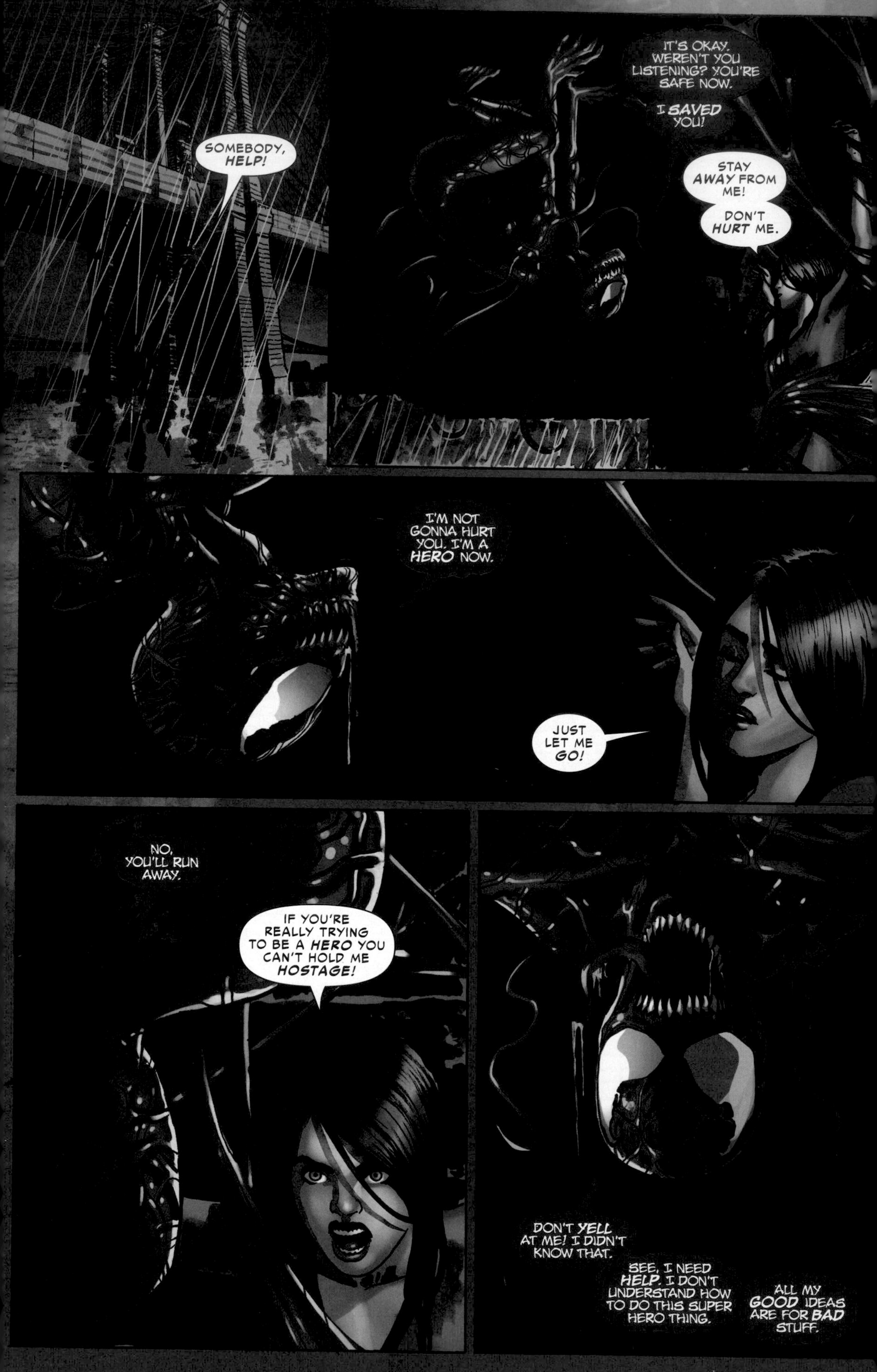
SOMEBODY, HELP!
IT'S OKAY. WEREN'T YOU LISTENING? YOU'RE SAFE NOW.
I SAVED YOU!
STAY AWAY FROM ME!
DON'T HURT ME.
I'M NOT GONNA HURT YOU. I'M A HERO NOW.
JUST LET ME GO!
NO, YOU'LL RUN AWAY.
IF YOU'RE REALLY TRYING TO BE A HERO YOU CAN'T HOLD ME HOSTAGE!
DON'T YELL AT ME! I DIDN'T KNOW THAT.
SEE, I NEED HELP. I DON'T UNDERSTAND HOW TO DO THIS SUPER HERO THING.
ALL MY GOOD IDEAS ARE FOR BAD STUFF.

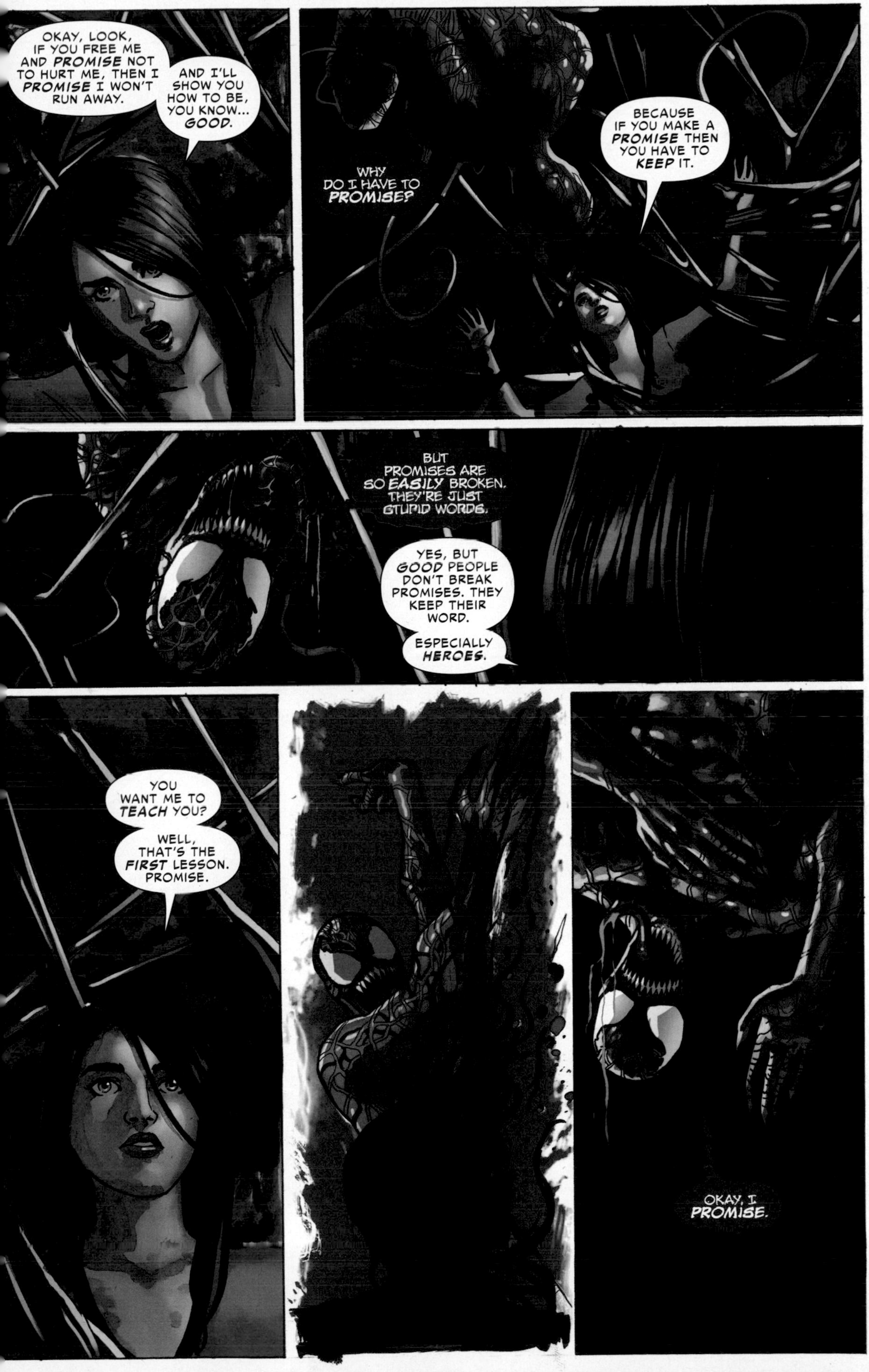
OKAY, LOOK, IF YOU FREE ME AND PROMISE NOT TO HURT ME, THEN I PROMISE I WON'T RUN AWAY.
AND I'LL SHOW YOU HOW TO BE, YOU KNOW... GOOD.
WHY DO I HAVE TO PROMISE?
BECAUSE IF YOU MAKE A PROMISE THEN YOU HAVE TO KEEP IT.
BUT PROMISES ARE SO EASILY BROKEN. THEY'RE JUST STUPID WORDS.
YES, BUT GOOD PEOPLE DON'T BREAK PROMISES. THEY KEEP THEIR WORD.
ESPECIALLY HEROES.
YOU WANT ME TO TEACH YOU?
WELL, THAT'S THE FIRST LESSON. PROMISE.
OKAY, I PROMISE.

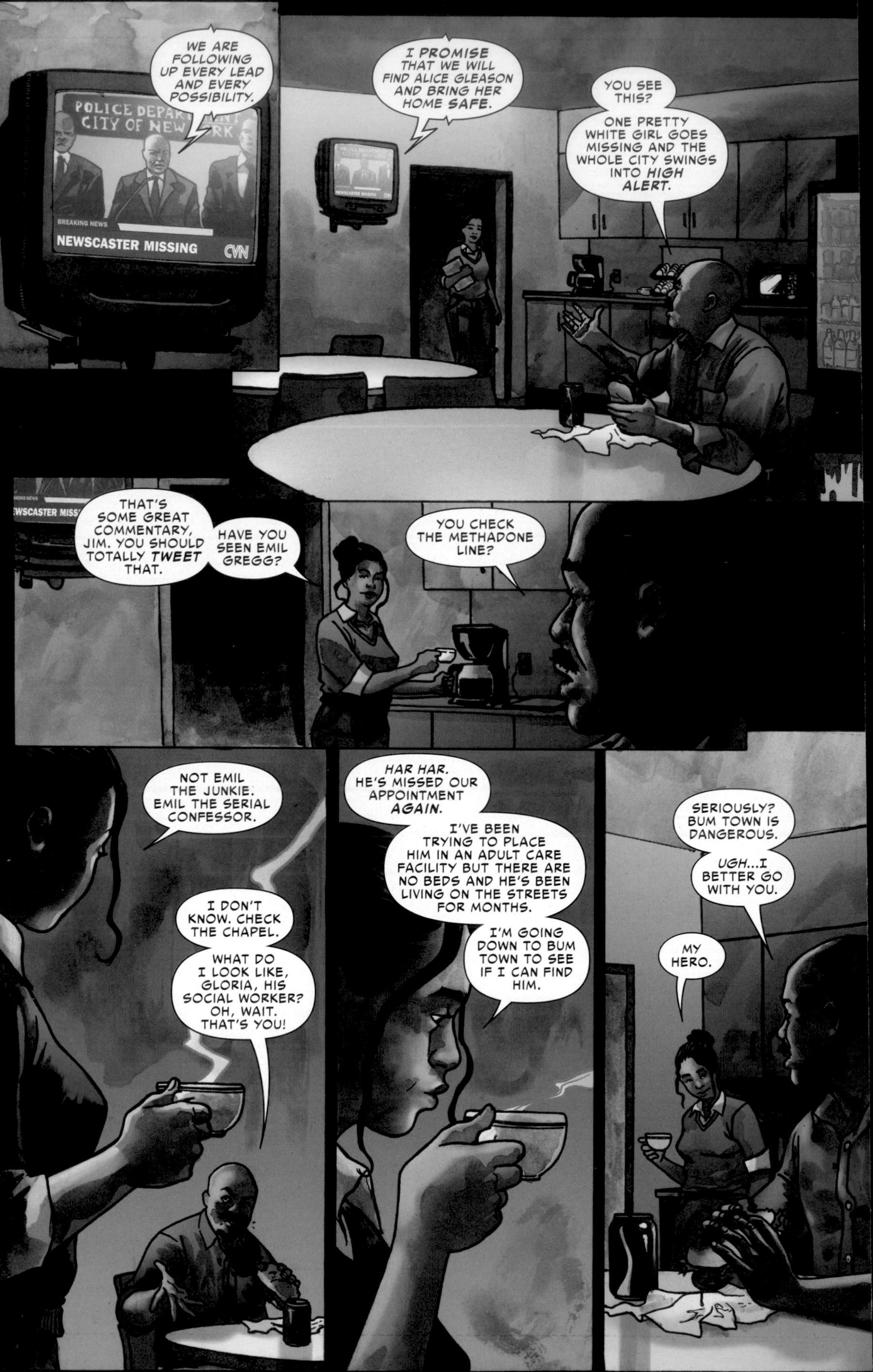
POLICE DEPAR... CITY OF NEW ...RK
BREAKING NEWS
NEWSCASTER MISSING
CVN
WE ARE FOLLOWING UP EVERY LEAD AND EVERY POSSIBILITY.
I PROMISE THAT WE WILL FIND ALICE GLEASON AND BRING HER HOME SAFE.
YOU SEE THIS?
ONE PRETTY WHITE GIRL GOES MISSING AND THE WHOLE CITY SWINGS INTO HIGH ALERT.
THAT'S SOME GREAT COMMENTARY, JIM. YOU SHOULD TOTALLY TWEET THAT.
HAVE YOU SEEN EMIL GREGG?
YOU CHECK THE METHADONE LINE?
NOT EMIL THE JUNKIE. EMIL THE SERIAL CONFESSOR.
I DON'T KNOW. CHECK THE CHAPEL.
WHAT DO I LOOK LIKE, GLORIA, HIS SOCIAL WORKER? OH, WAIT. THAT'S YOU!
HAR HAR. HE'S MISSED OUR APPOINTMENT AGAIN.
I'VE BEEN TRYING TO PLACE HIM IN AN ADULT CARE FACILITY BUT THERE ARE NO BEDS AND HE'S BEEN LIVING ON THE STREETS FOR MONTHS.
I'M GOING DOWN TO BUM TOWN TO SEE IF I CAN FIND HIM.
SERIOUSLY? BUM TOWN IS DANGEROUS.
UGH...I BETTER GO WITH YOU.
MY HERO.

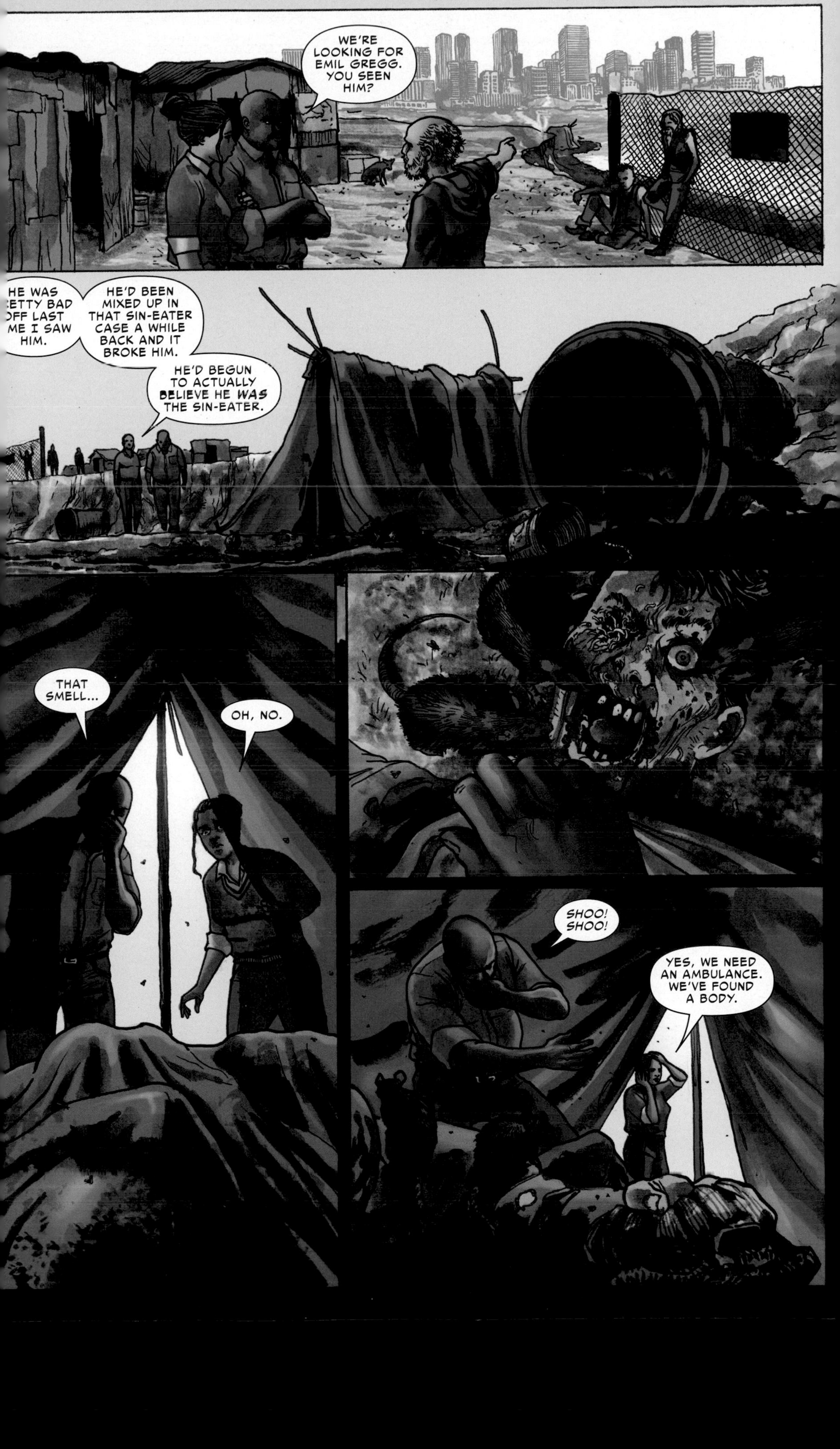
WE'RE LOOKING FOR EMIL GREGG. YOU SEEN HIM?
HE WAS ETTY BAD OFF LAST ME I SAW HIM.
HE'D BEEN MIXED UP IN THAT SIN-EATER CASE A WHILE BACK AND IT BROKE HIM.
HE'D BEGUN TO ACTUALLY BELIEVE HE WAS THE SIN-EATER.
THAT SMELL...
OH, NO.
SHOO! SHOO!
YES, WE NEED AN AMBULANCE. WE'VE FOUND A BODY.

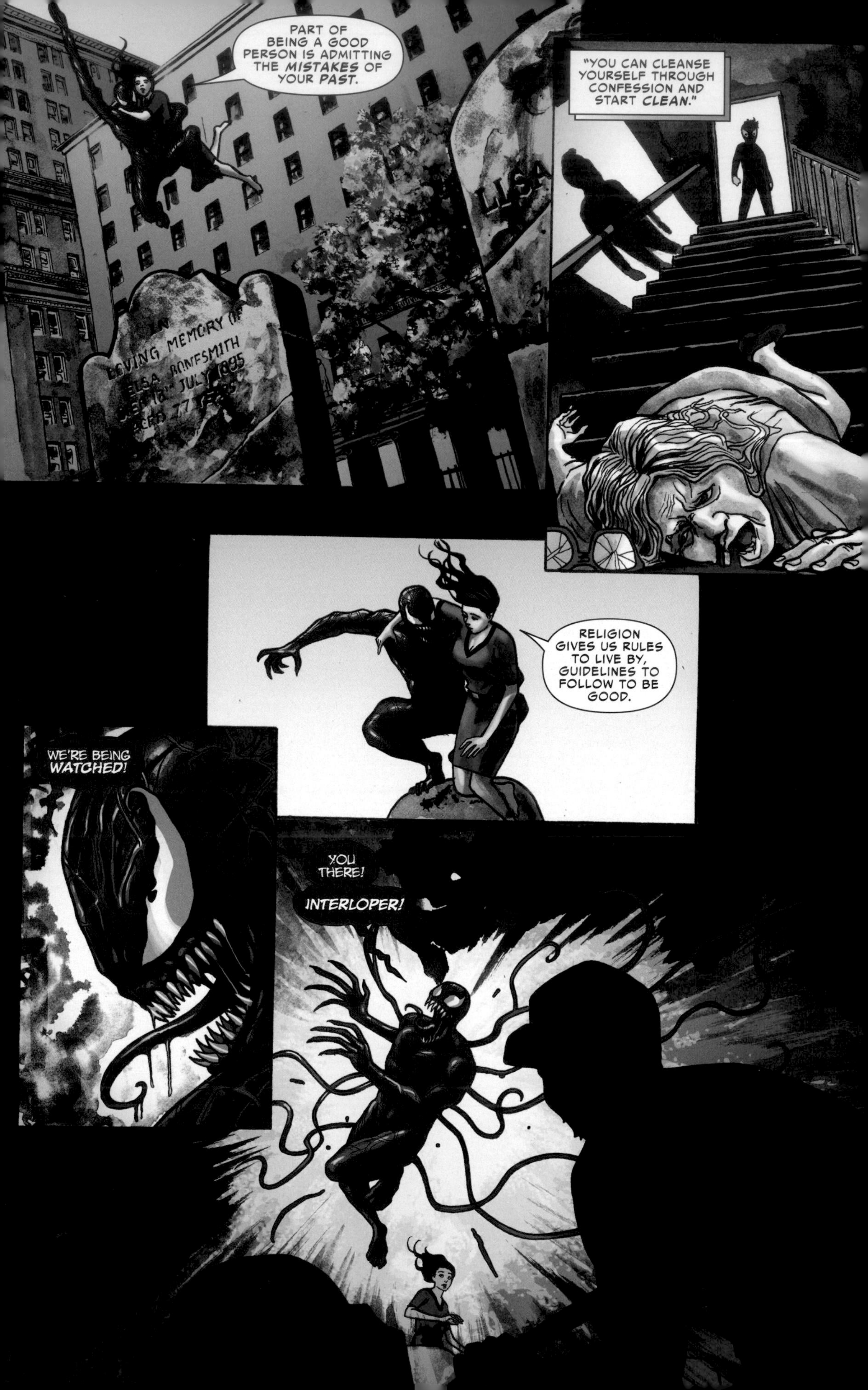
PART OF BEING A GOOD PERSON IS ADMITTING THE MISTAKES OF YOUR PAST.
IN LOVING MEMORY OF ELSA BONESMITH
"YOU CAN CLEANSE YOURSELF THROUGH CONFESSION AND START CLEAN."
RELIGION GIVES US RULES TO LIVE BY, GUIDELINES TO FOLLOW TO BE GOOD.
WE'RE BEING WATCHED!
YOU THERE!
INTERLOPER!

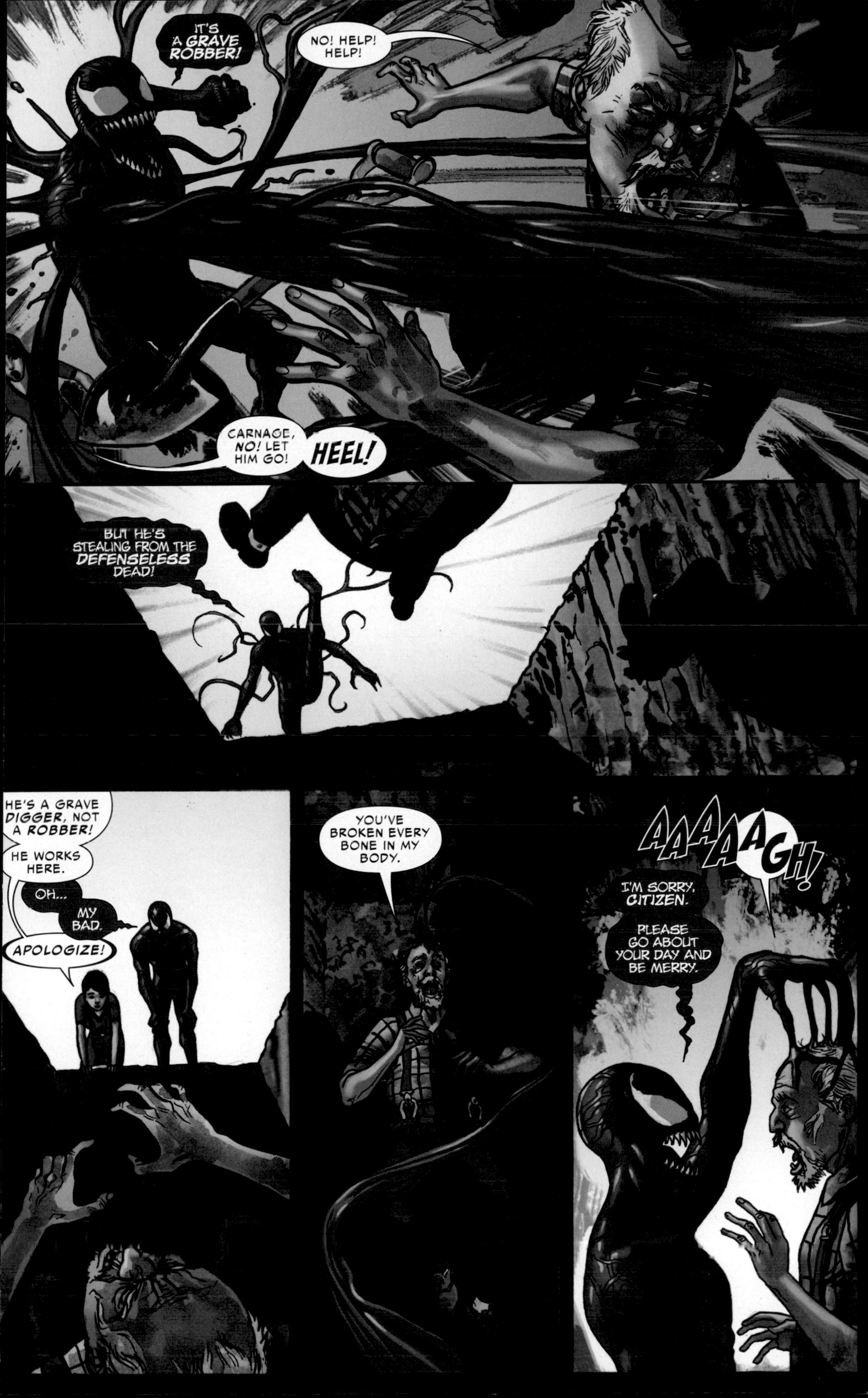
IT'S A GRAVE ROBBER!
NO! HELP! HELP!
CARNAGE, NO! LET HIM GO!
HEEL!
BUT HE'S STEALING FROM THE DEFENSELESS DEAD!
HE'S A GRAVE DIGGER, NOT A ROBBER!
HE WORKS HERE.
OH...
MY BAD.
APOLOGIZE!
YOU'VE BROKEN EVERY BONE IN MY BODY.
AAAAAGH!
I'M SORRY, CITIZEN.
PLEASE GO ABOUT YOUR DAY AND BE MERRY.

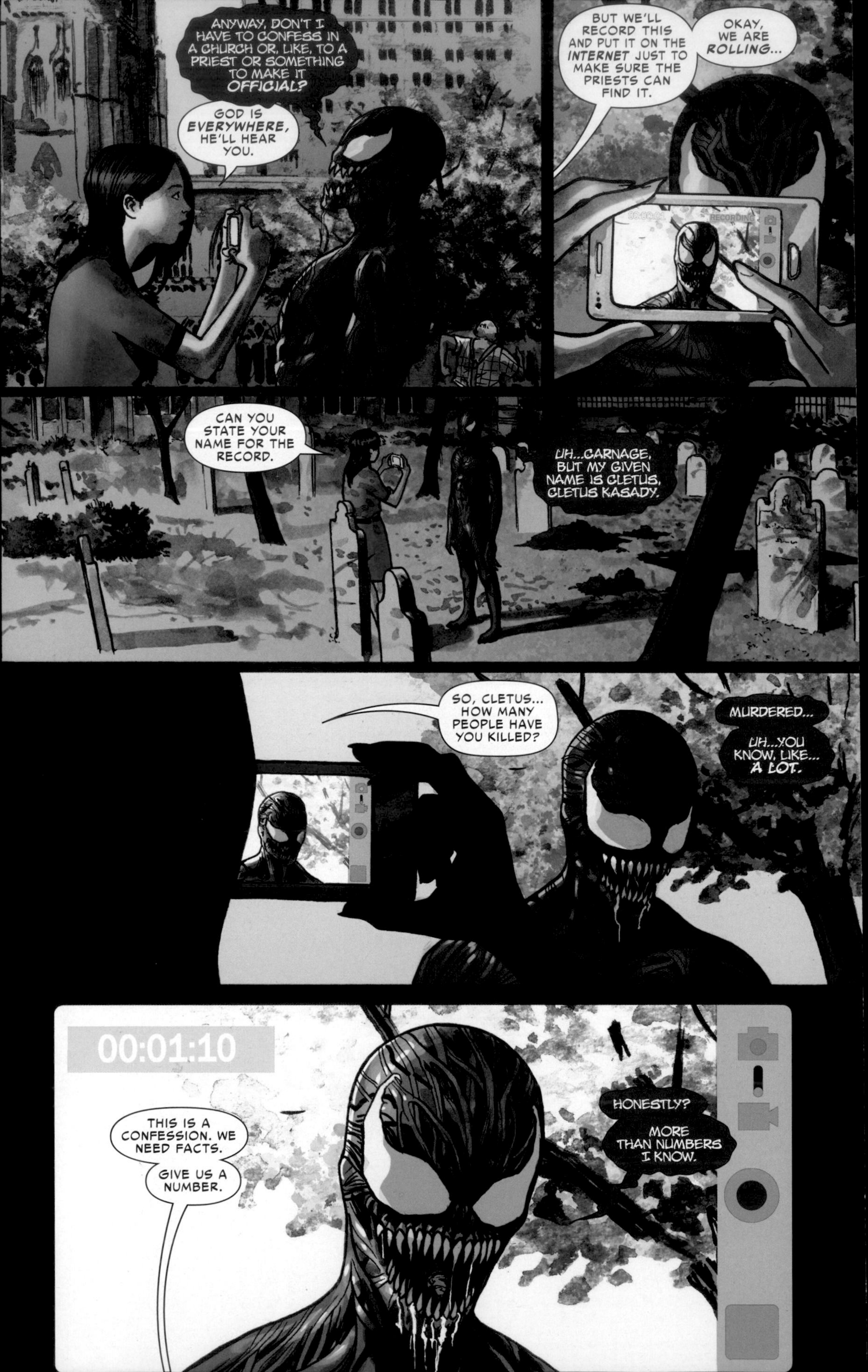
ANYWAY, DON'T I HAVE TO CONFESS IN A CHURCH OR, LIKE, TO A PRIEST OR SOMETHING TO MAKE IT OFFICIAL?
GOD IS EVERYWHERE, HE'LL HEAR YOU.
BUT WE'LL RECORD THIS AND PUT IT ON THE INTERNET JUST TO MAKE SURE THE PRIESTS CAN FIND IT.
OKAY, WE ARE ROLLING...
RECORDING
CAN YOU STATE YOUR NAME FOR THE RECORD.
UH...CARNAGE, BUT MY GIVEN NAME IS CLETUS, CLETUS KASADY.
SO, CLETUS... HOW MANY PEOPLE HAVE YOU KILLED?
MURDERED...
UH...YOU KNOW, LIKE... A LOT.
00:01:10
THIS IS A CONFESSION. WE NEED FACTS.
GIVE US A NUMBER.
HONESTLY?
MORE THAN NUMBERS I KNOW.

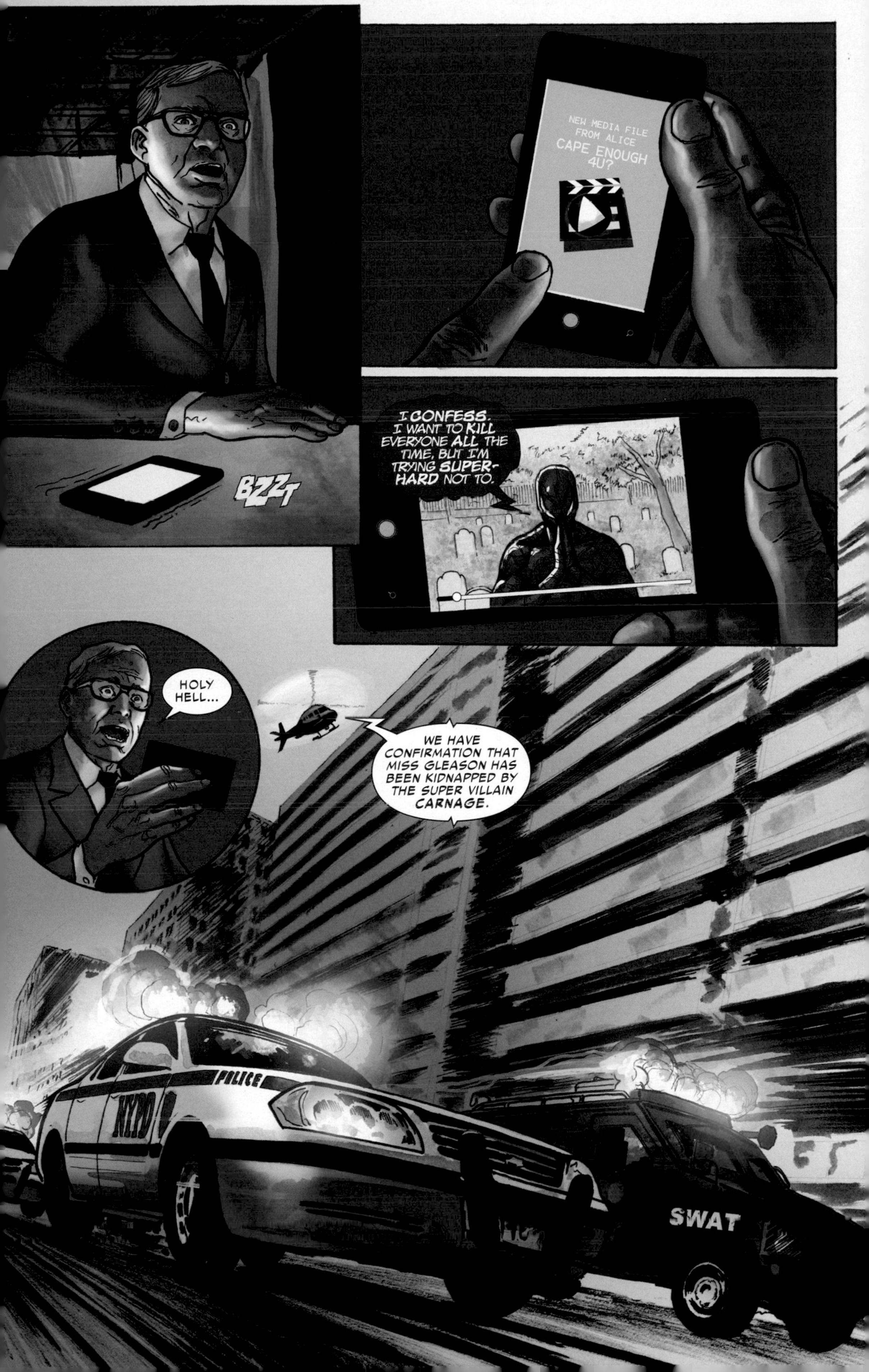
NEW MEDIA FILE FROM ALICE
CAPE ENOUGH 4U?
BZZT
I CONFESS. I WANT TO KILL EVERYONE ALL THE TIME, BUT I'M TRYING SUPER-HARD NOT TO.
HOLY HELL...
WE HAVE CONFIRMATION THAT MISS GLEASON HAS BEEN KIDNAPPED BY THE SUPER VILLAIN CARNAGE.
POLICE
NYPD
SWAT

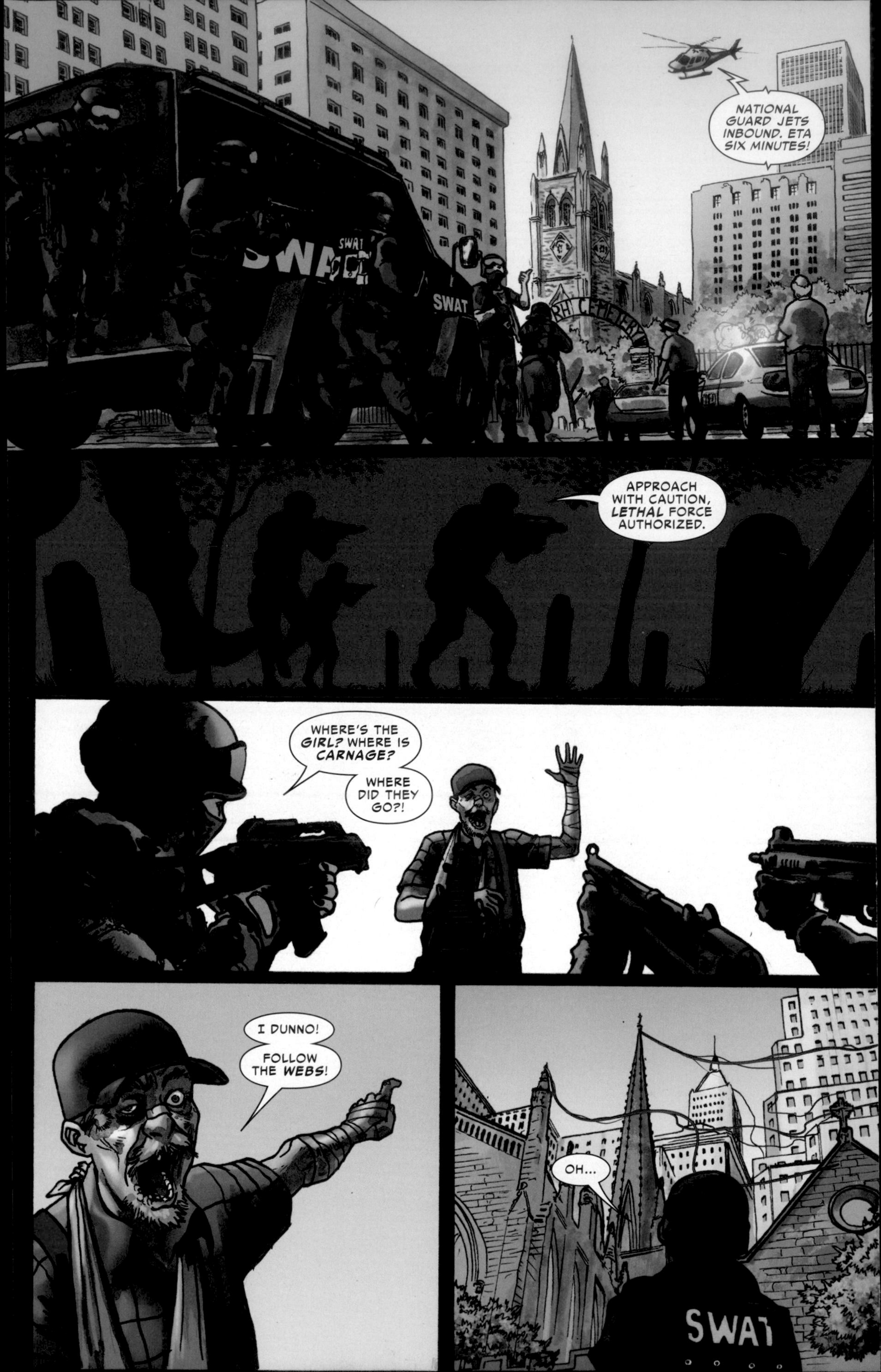
NATIONAL GUARD JETS INBOUND. ETA SIX MINUTES!
APPROACH WITH CAUTION, LETHAL FORCE AUTHORIZED.
WHERE'S THE GIRL? WHERE IS CARNAGE?
WHERE DID THEY GO?!
I DUNNO!
FOLLOW THE WEBS!
OH...
SWAT

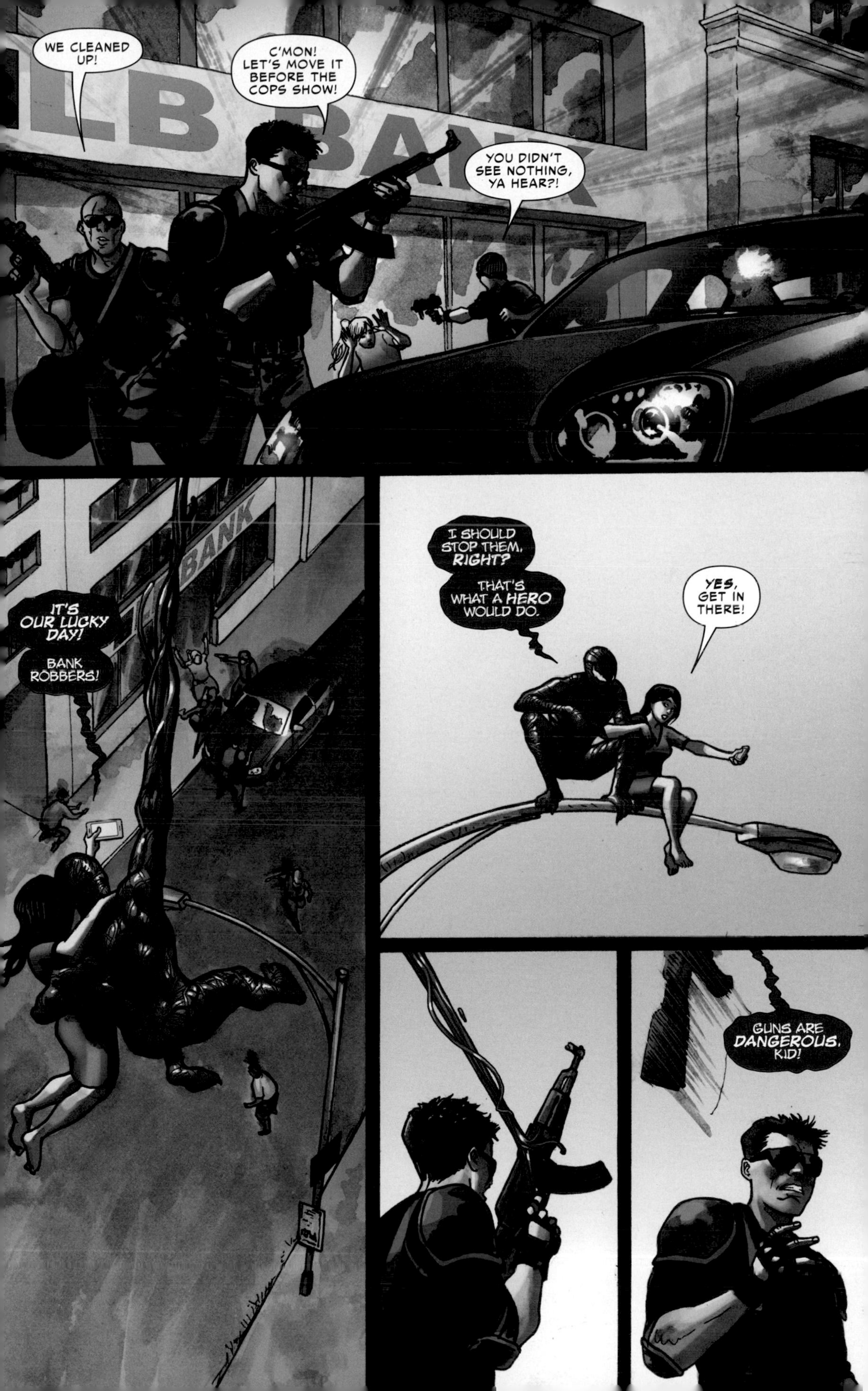
WE CLEANED UP!
C'MON! LET'S MOVE IT BEFORE THE COPS SHOW!
YOU DIDN'T SEE NOTHING, YA HEAR?!
LB BANK
BANK
IT'S OUR LUCKY DAY!
BANK ROBBERS!
I SHOULD STOP THEM, RIGHT?
THAT'S WHAT A HERO WOULD DO.
YES, GET IN THERE!
GUNS ARE DANGEROUS, KID!

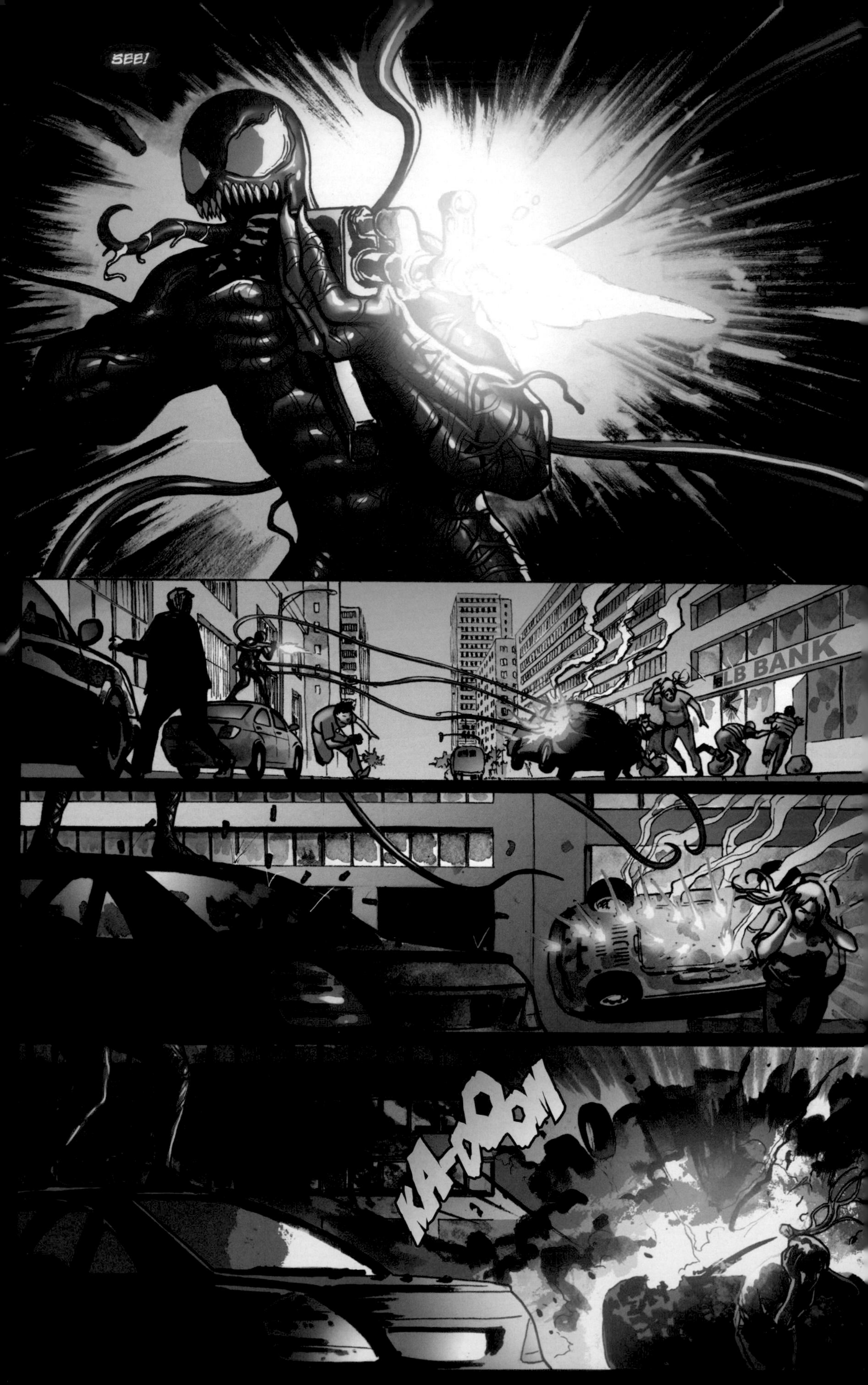
SBB!
LB BANK
KA-DOOM

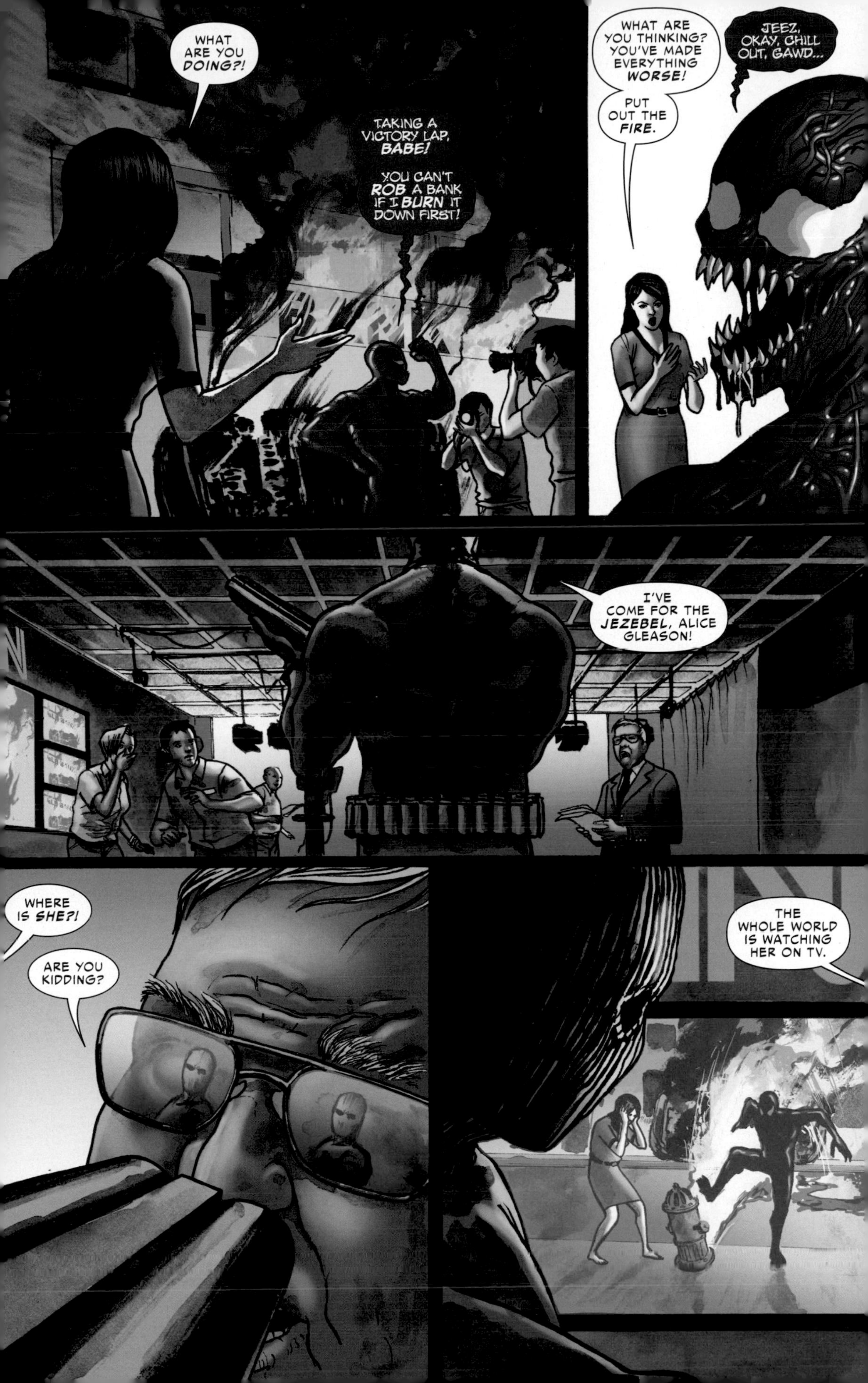
WHAT ARE YOU DOING?!
TAKING A VICTORY LAP, BABE!
YOU CAN'T ROB A BANK IF I BURN IT DOWN FIRST!
WHAT ARE YOU THINKING? YOU'VE MADE EVERYTHING WORSE!
PUT OUT THE FIRE.
JEEZ, OKAY, CHILL OUT, GAWD...
I'VE COME FOR THE JEZEBEL, ALICE GLEASON!
WHERE IS SHE?!
ARE YOU KIDDING?
THE WHOLE WORLD IS WATCHING HER ON TV.

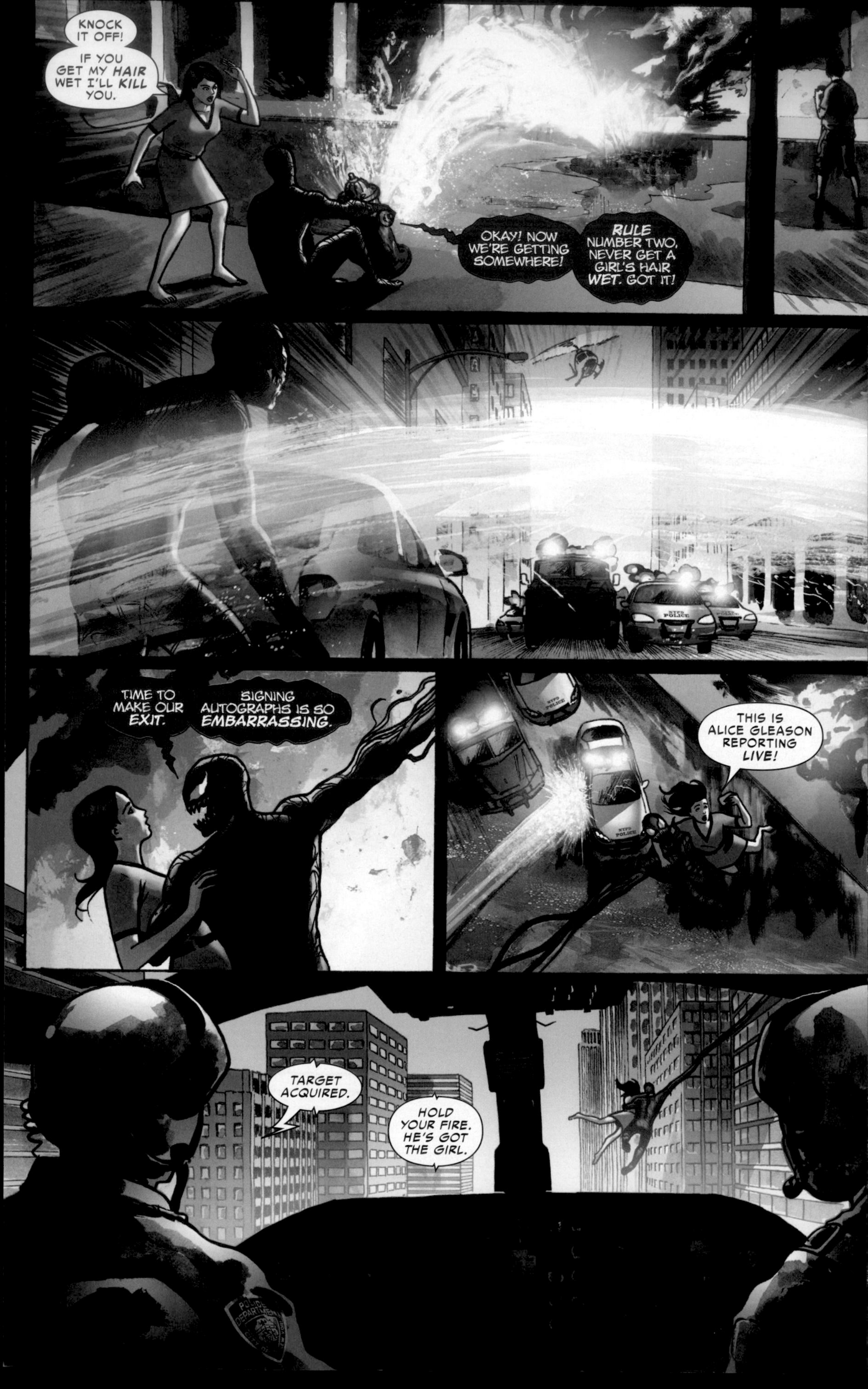
KNOCK IT OFF!
IF YOU GET MY HAIR WET I'LL KILL YOU.
OKAY! NOW WE'RE GETTING SOMEWHERE!
RULE NUMBER TWO, NEVER GET A GIRL'S HAIR WET. GOT IT!
TIME TO MAKE OUR EXIT.
SIGNING AUTOGRAPHS IS SO EMBARRASSING.
THIS IS ALICE GLEASON REPORTING LIVE!
TARGET ACQUIRED.
HOLD YOUR FIRE. HE'S GOT THE GIRL.

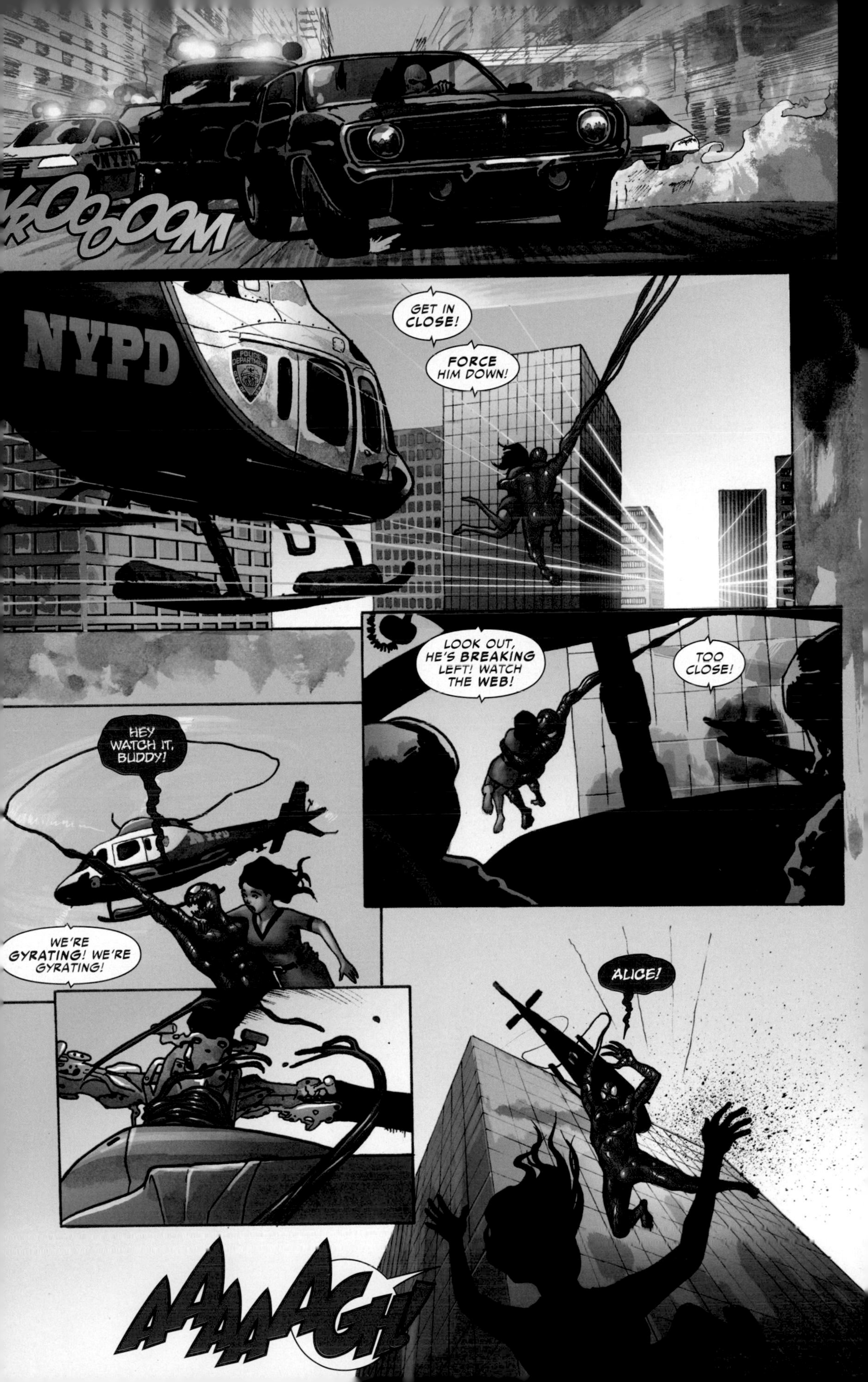
KROOOOOM
GET IN CLOSE!
FORCE HIM DOWN!
LOOK OUT, HE'S BREAKING LEFT! WATCH THE WEB!
TOO CLOSE!
HEY WATCH IT, BUDDY!
WE'RE GYRATING! WE'RE GYRATING!
ALICE!
AAAAAGH!

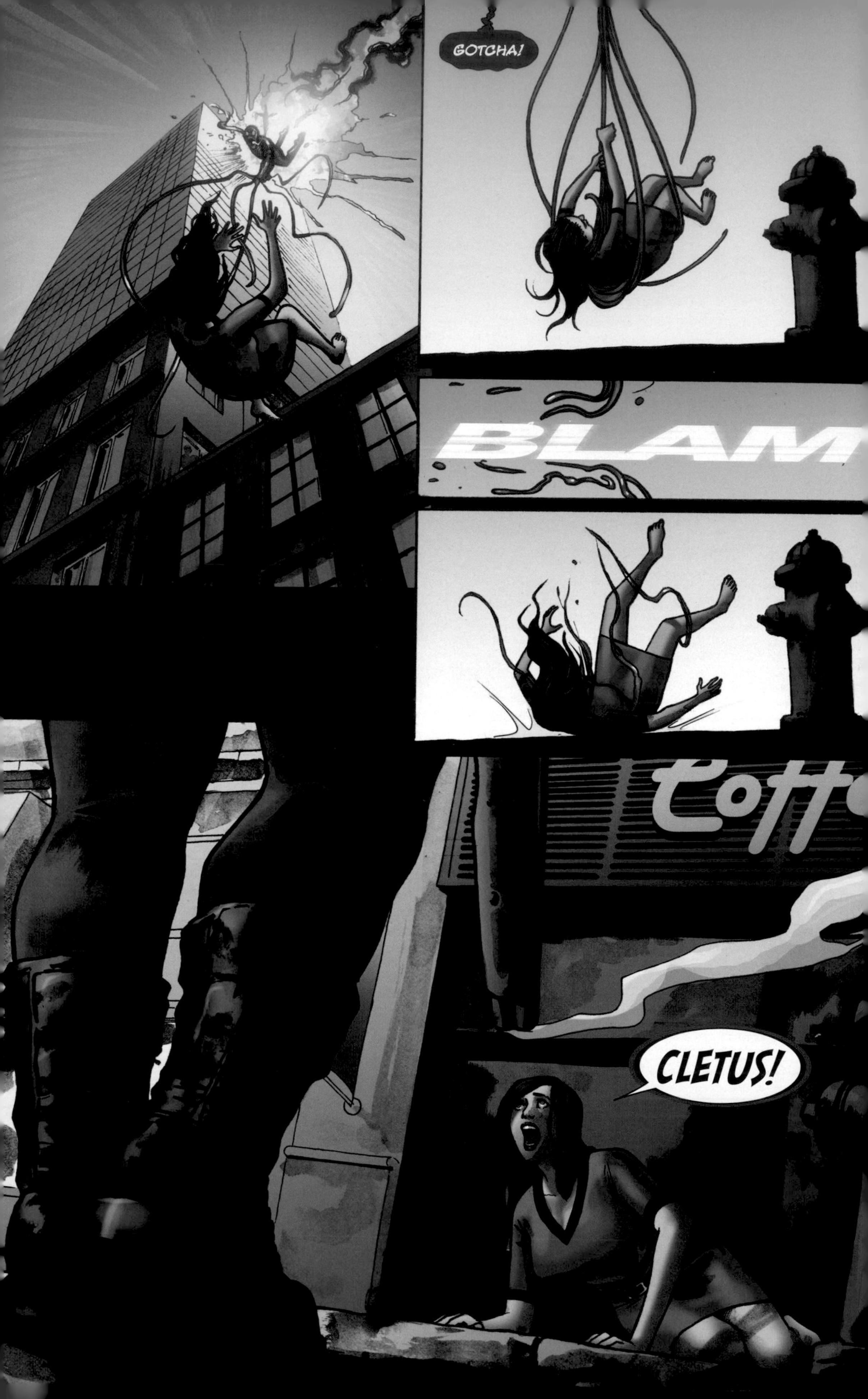
GOTCHA!
BLAM
COFF
CLETUS!

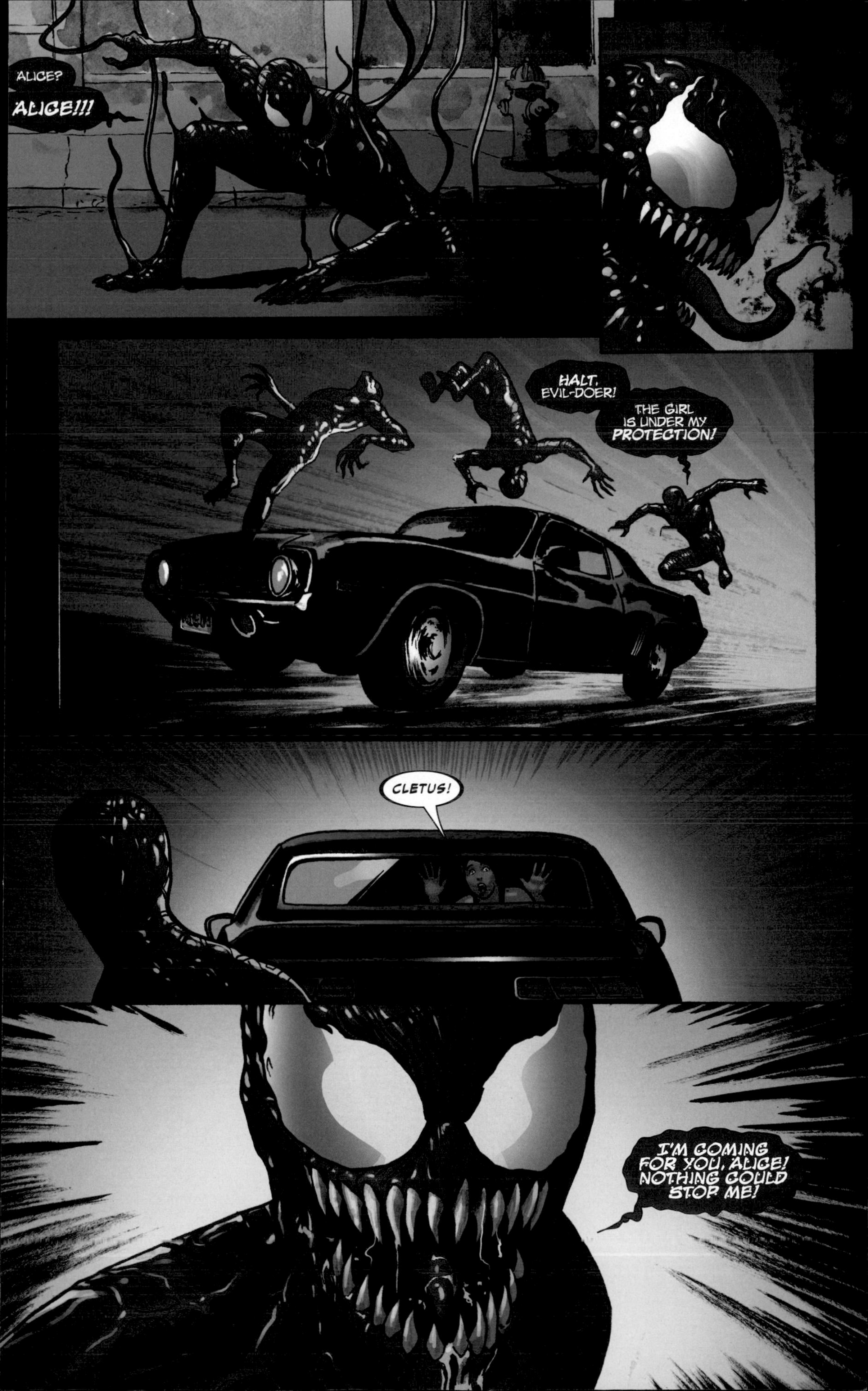
ALICE?
ALICE!!!
HALT, EVIL-DOER!
THE GIRL IS UNDER MY PROTECTION!
CLETUS!
I'M COMING FOR YOU, ALICE! NOTHING COULD STOP ME!

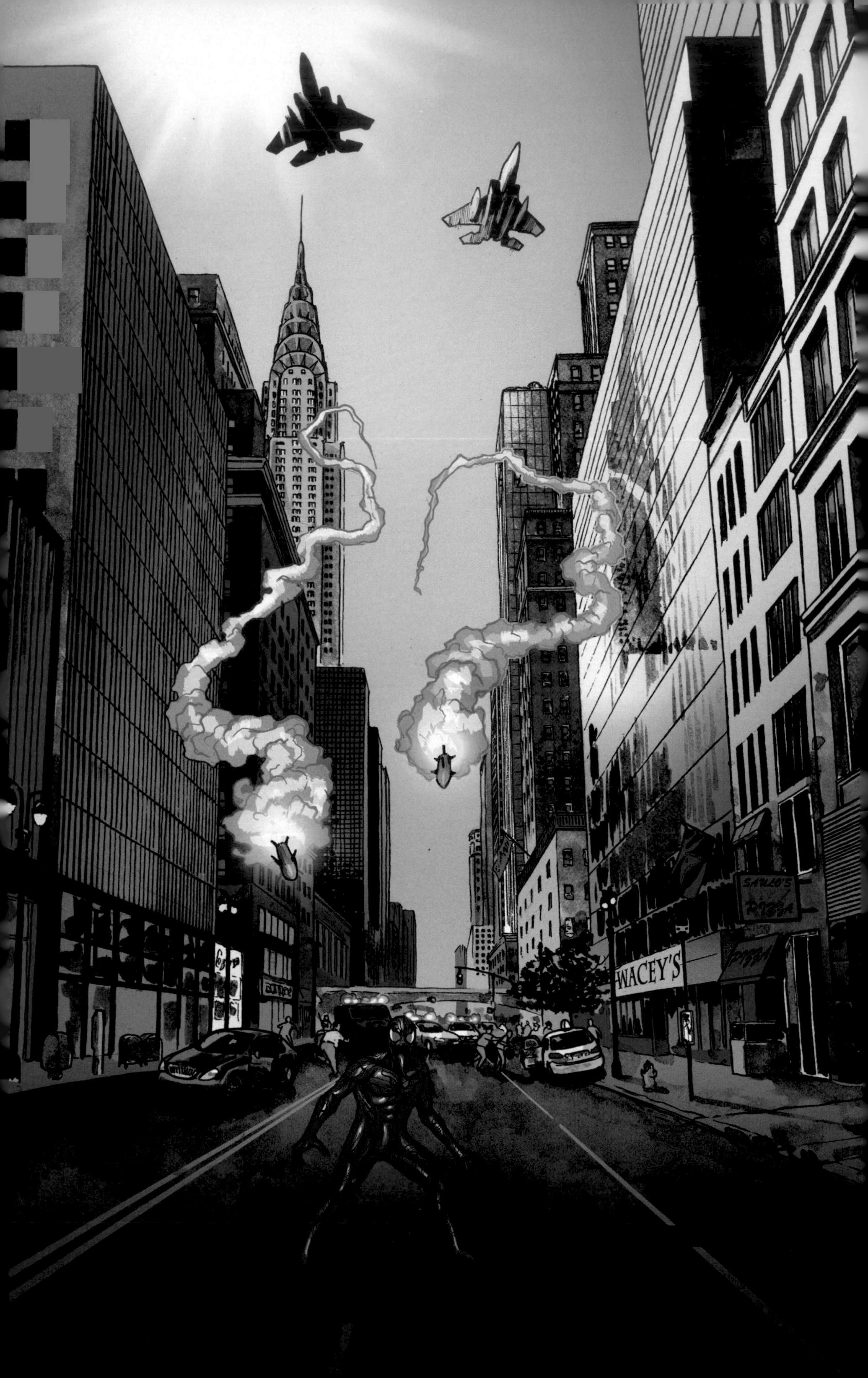
SAULO'S
PIZZA
WACEY'S
PIZZA

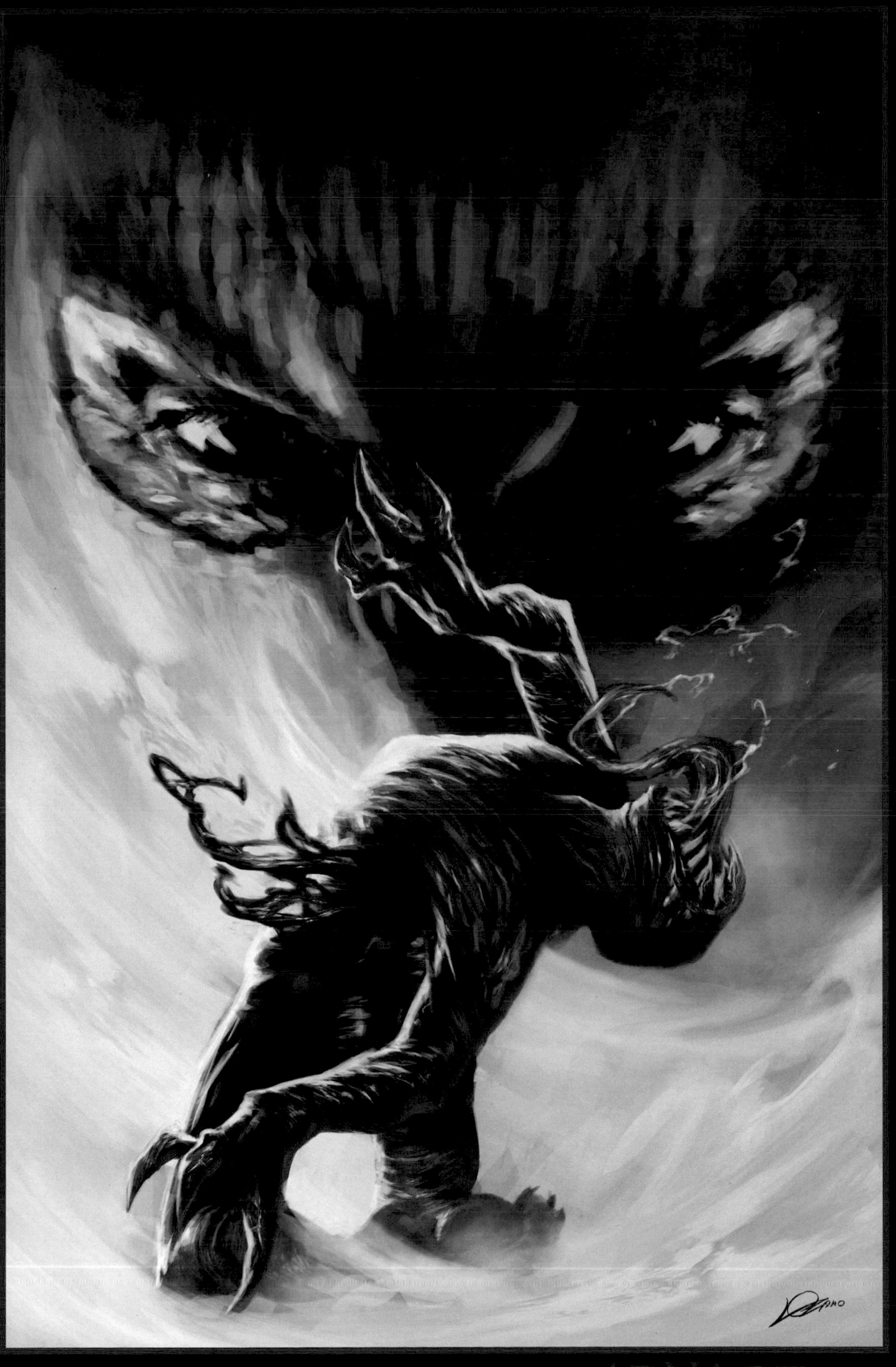
AXIS

CARNAGE #3

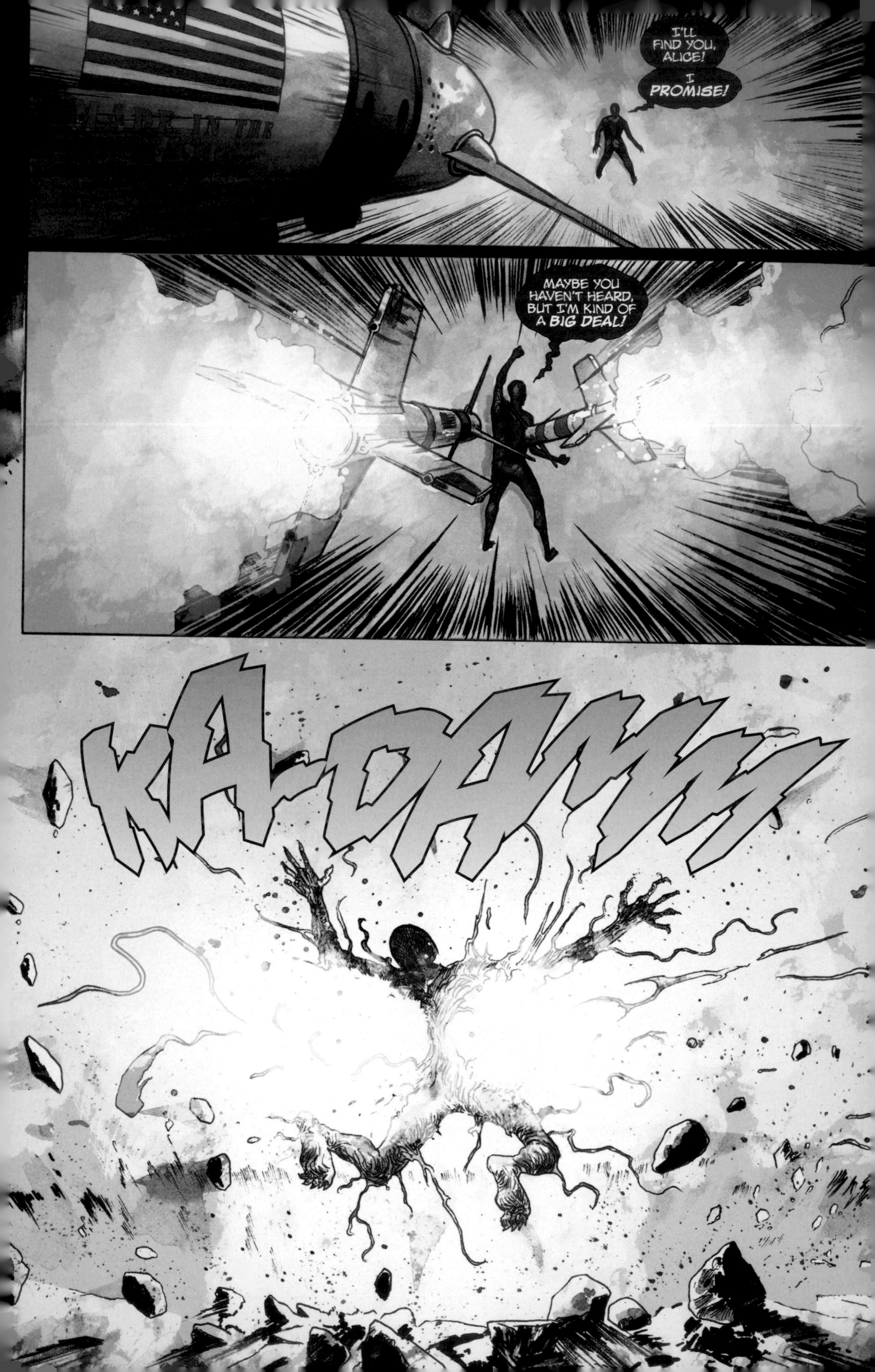
I'LL FIND YOU, ALICE!
I PROMISE!
MAYBE YOU HAVEN'T HEARD, BUT I'M KIND OF A BIG DEAL!
KA-DAMM

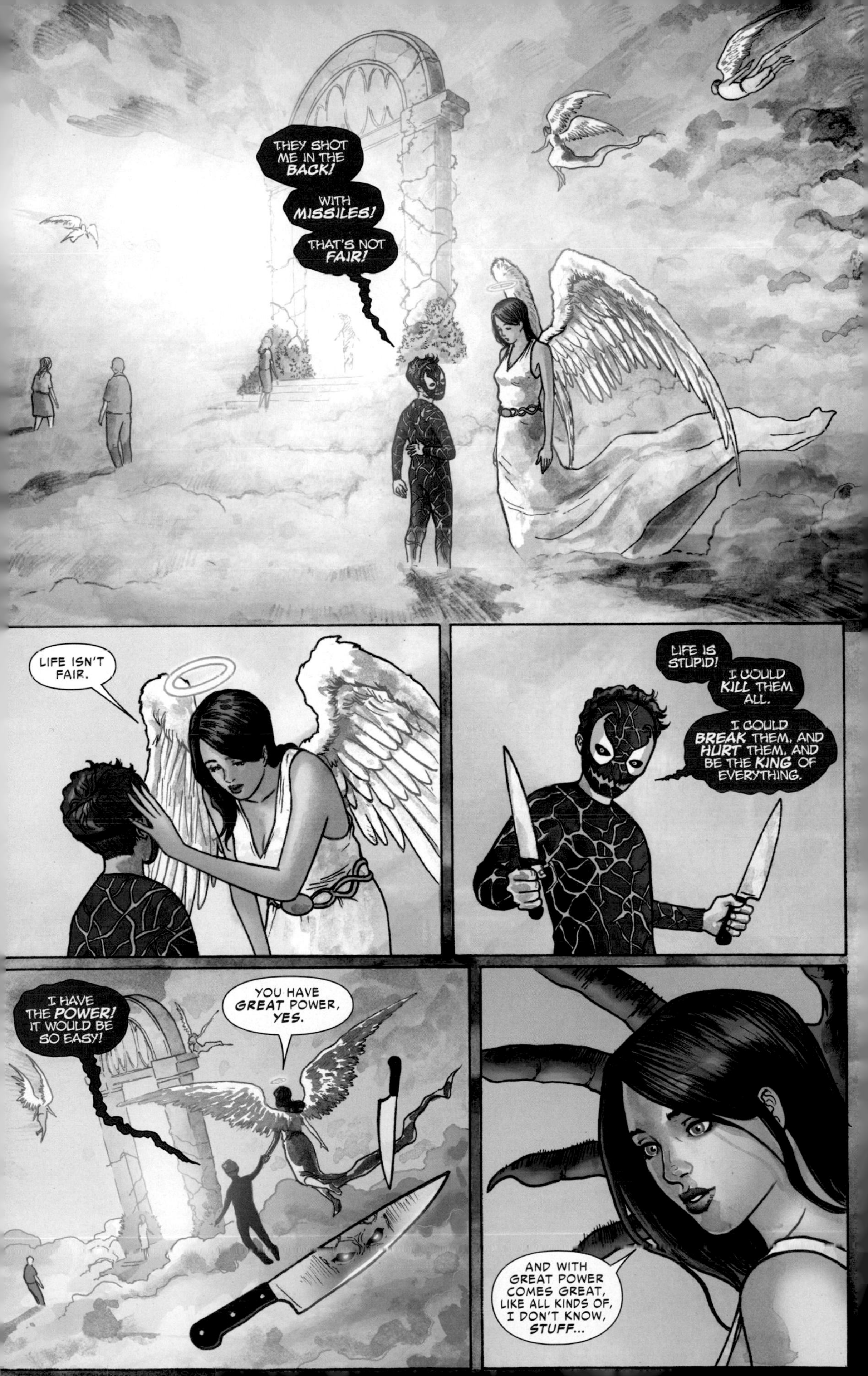
THEY SHOT ME IN THE BACK!
WITH MISSILES!
THAT'S NOT FAIR!
LIFE ISN'T FAIR.
LIFE IS STUPID!
I COULD KILL THEM ALL.
I COULD BREAK THEM, AND HURT THEM, AND BE THE KING OF EVERYTHING.
I HAVE THE POWER! IT WOULD BE SO EASY!
YOU HAVE GREAT POWER, YES.
AND WITH GREAT POWER COMES GREAT, LIKE ALL KINDS OF, I DON'T KNOW, STUFF...

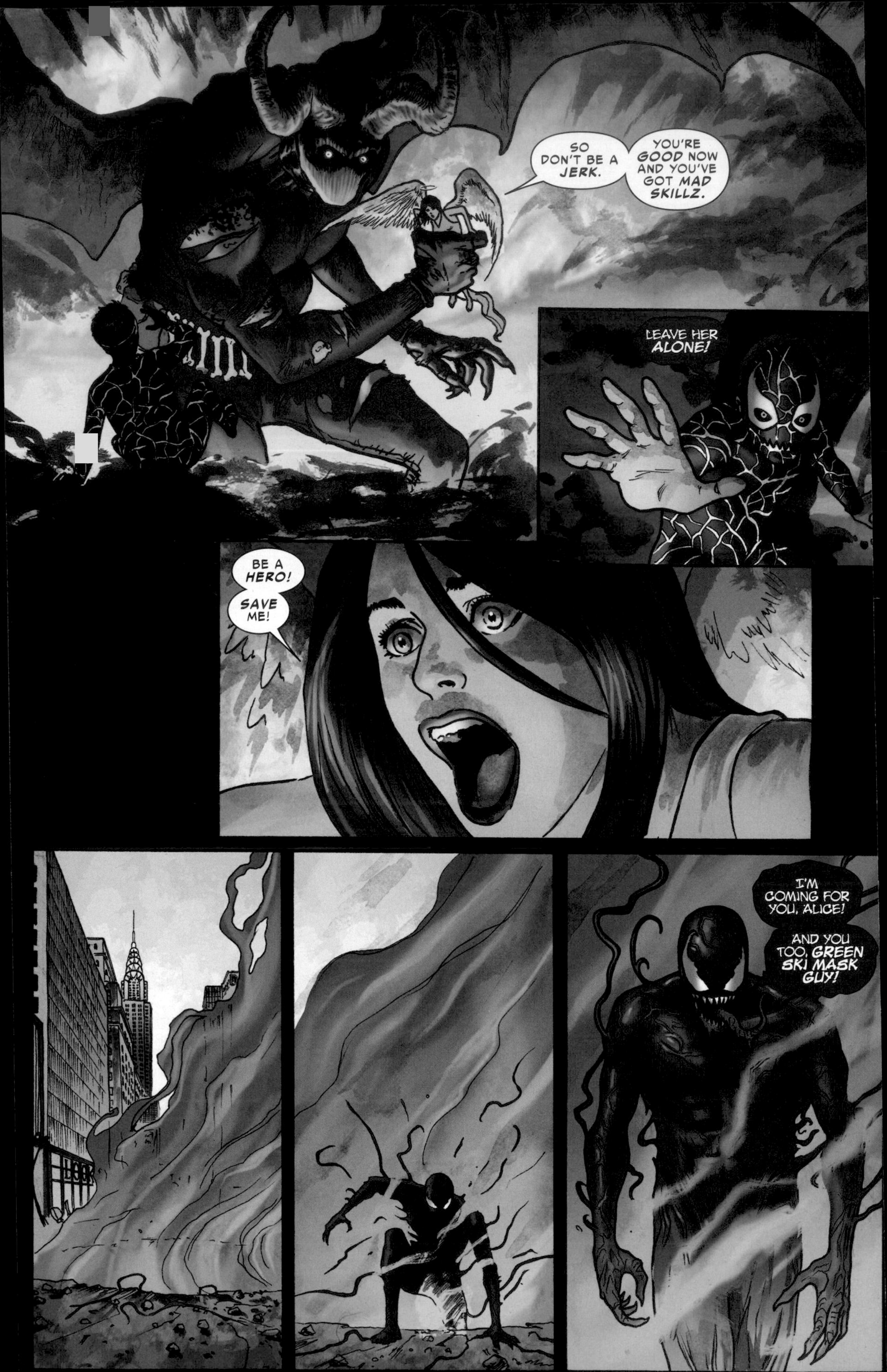
SO DON'T BE A JERK.
YOU'RE GOOD NOW AND YOU'VE GOT MAD SKILLZ.
LEAVE HER ALONE!
BE A HERO!
SAVE ME!
I'M COMING FOR YOU, ALICE!
AND YOU TOO, GREEN SKI MASK GUY!

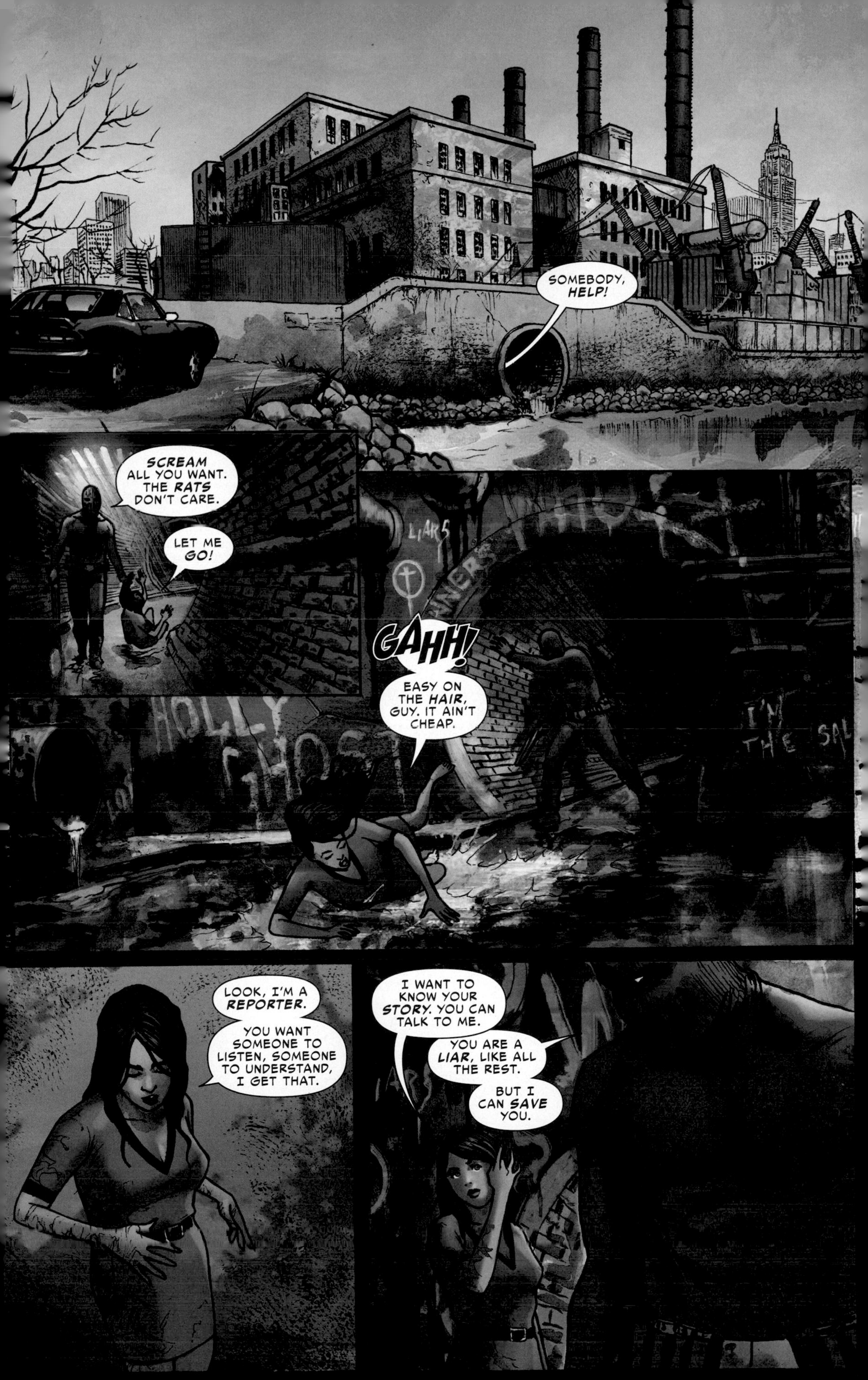
SOMEBODY, HELP!
SCREAM ALL YOU WANT. THE RATS DON'T CARE.
LET ME GO!
LIARS
GAHH!
EASY ON THE HAIR, GUY. IT AIN'T CHEAP.
LOOK, I'M A REPORTER.
YOU WANT SOMEONE TO LISTEN, SOMEONE TO UNDERSTAND, I GET THAT.
I WANT TO KNOW YOUR STORY. YOU CAN TALK TO ME.
YOU ARE A LIAR, LIKE ALL THE REST.
BUT I CAN SAVE YOU.

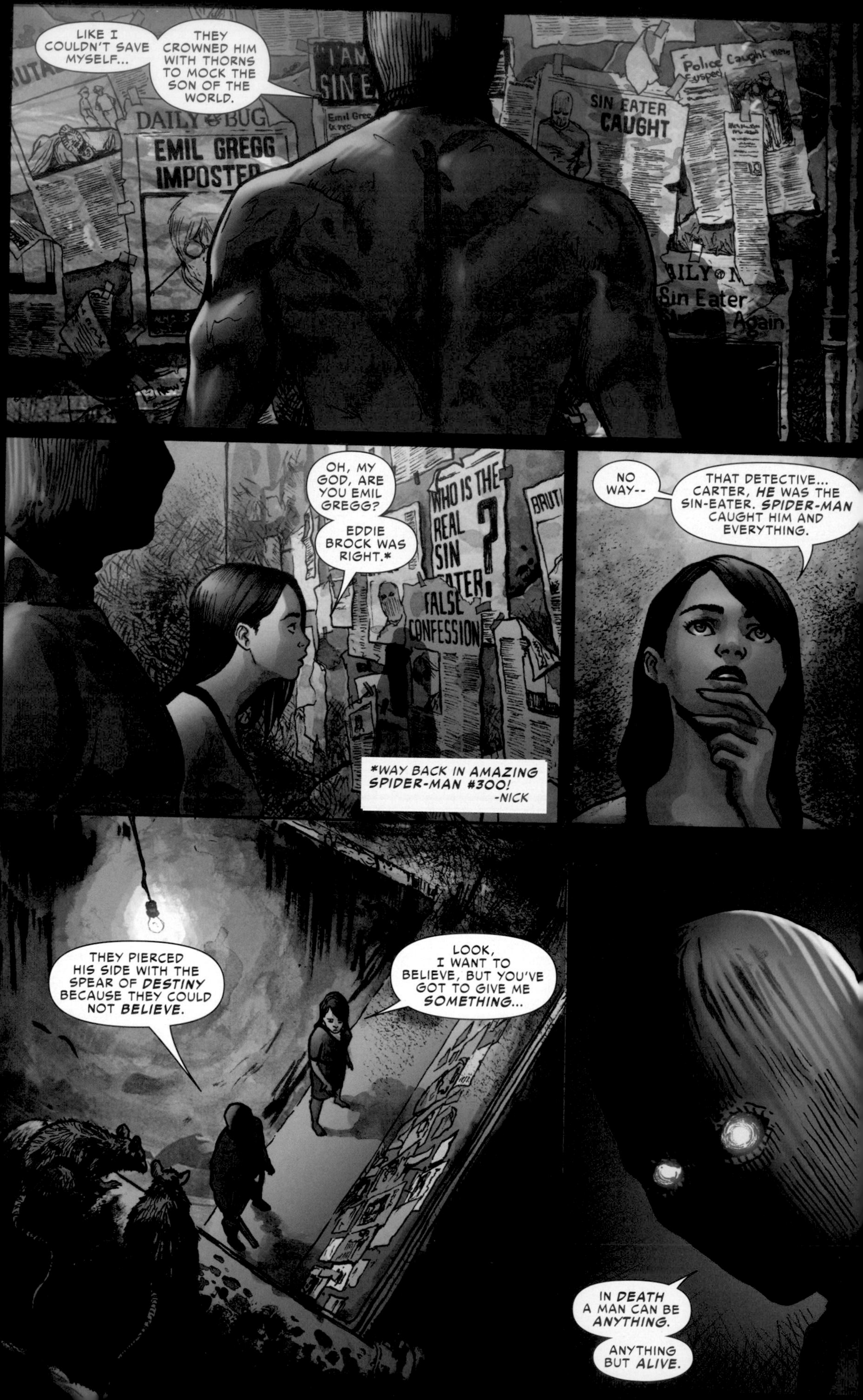
LIKE I COULDN'T SAVE MYSELF...
THEY CROWNED HIM WITH THORNS TO MOCK THE SON OF THE WORLD.
DAILY BUG
EMIL GREGG IMPOSTER
SIN EATER CAUGHT
Police Caught
Sin Eater
Again
OH, MY GOD, ARE YOU EMIL GREGG?
EDDIE BROCK WAS RIGHT.*
WHO IS THE REAL SIN EATER?
FALSE CONFESSION
*WAY BACK IN AMAZING SPIDER-MAN #300! -NICK
NO WAY--
THAT DETECTIVE... CARTER, HE WAS THE SIN-EATER. SPIDER-MAN CAUGHT HIM AND EVERYTHING.
THEY PIERCED HIS SIDE WITH THE SPEAR OF DESTINY BECAUSE THEY COULD NOT BELIEVE.
LOOK, I WANT TO BELIEVE, BUT YOU'VE GOT TO GIVE ME SOMETHING...
IN DEATH A MAN CAN BE ANYTHING.
ANYTHING BUT ALIVE.

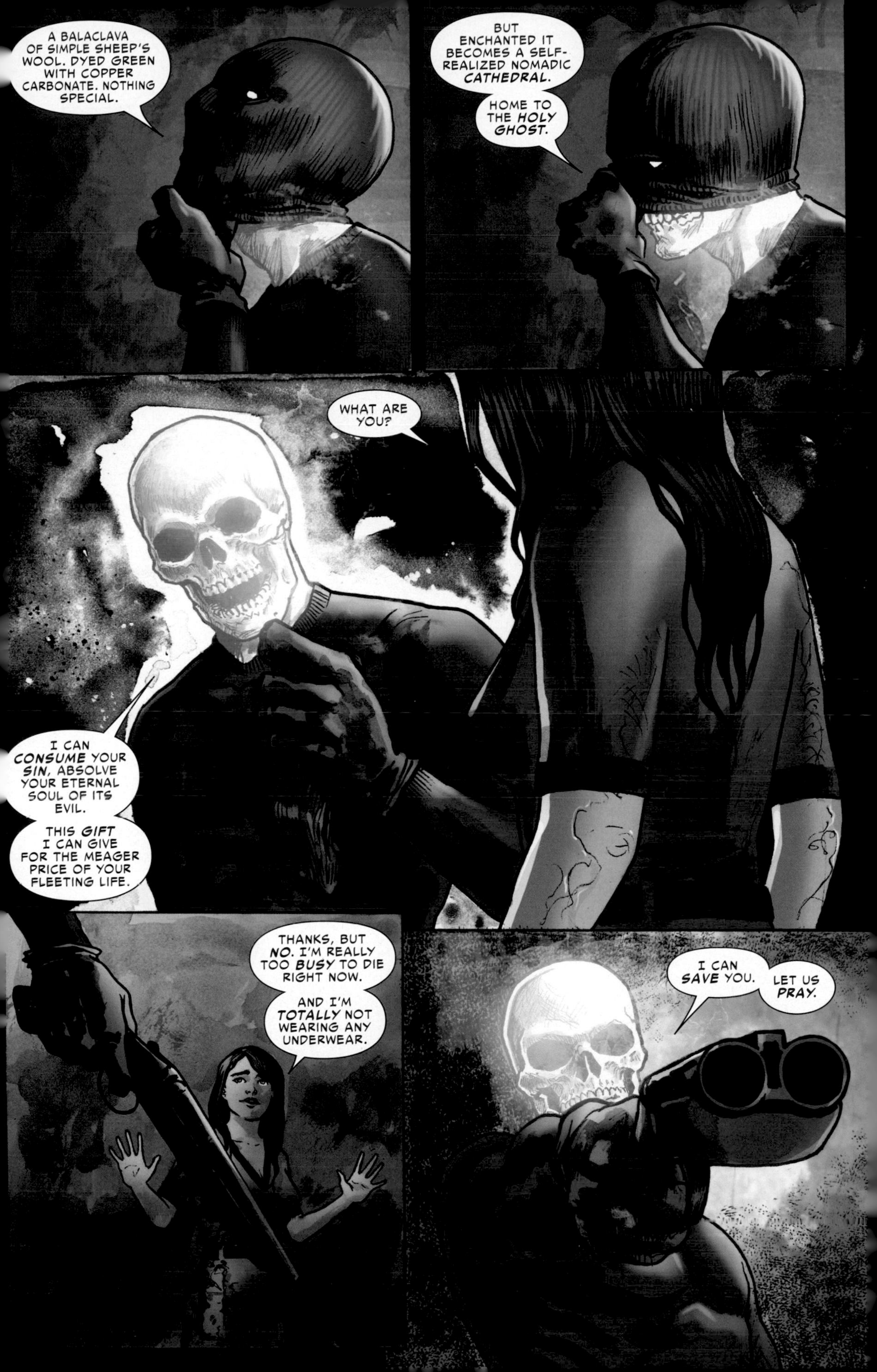
A BALACLAVA OF SIMPLE SHEEP'S WOOL. DYED GREEN WITH COPPER CARBONATE. NOTHING SPECIAL.
BUT ENCHANTED IT BECOMES A SELF-REALIZED NOMADIC CATHEDRAL.
HOME TO THE HOLY GHOST.
WHAT ARE YOU?
I CAN CONSUME YOUR SIN, ABSOLVE YOUR ETERNAL SOUL OF ITS EVIL.
THIS GIFT I CAN GIVE FOR THE MEAGER PRICE OF YOUR FLEETING LIFE.
THANKS, BUT NO. I'M REALLY TOO BUSY TO DIE RIGHT NOW.
AND I'M TOTALLY NOT WEARING ANY UNDERWEAR.
I CAN SAVE YOU.
LET US PRAY.

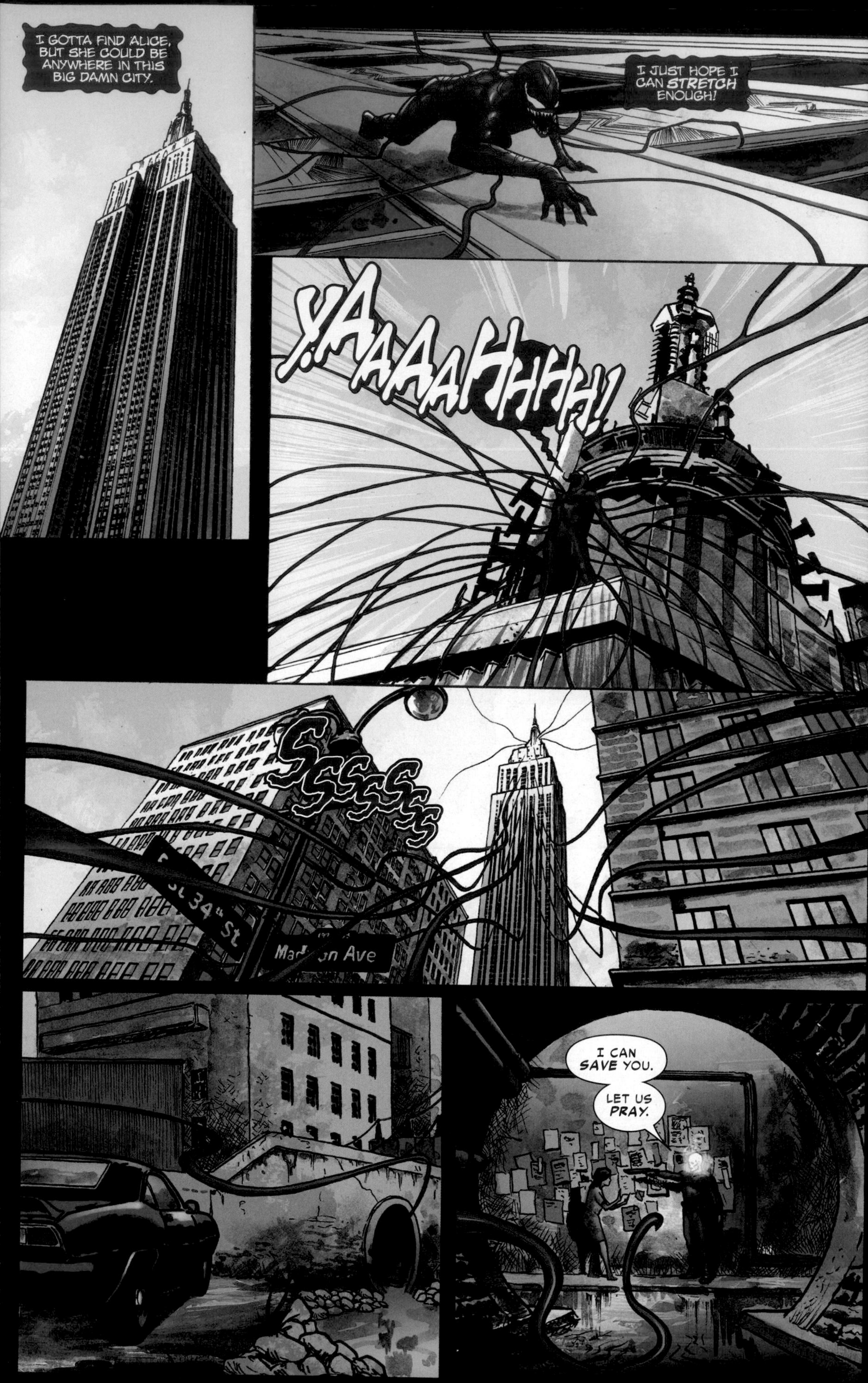
I GOTTA FIND ALICE, BUT SHE COULD BE ANYWHERE IN THIS BIG DAMN CITY.
I JUST HOPE I CAN STRETCH ENOUGH!
YAAAAAHHHH!
SSSSSSS
St 34th St
Madison Ave
I CAN SAVE YOU.
LET US PRAY.

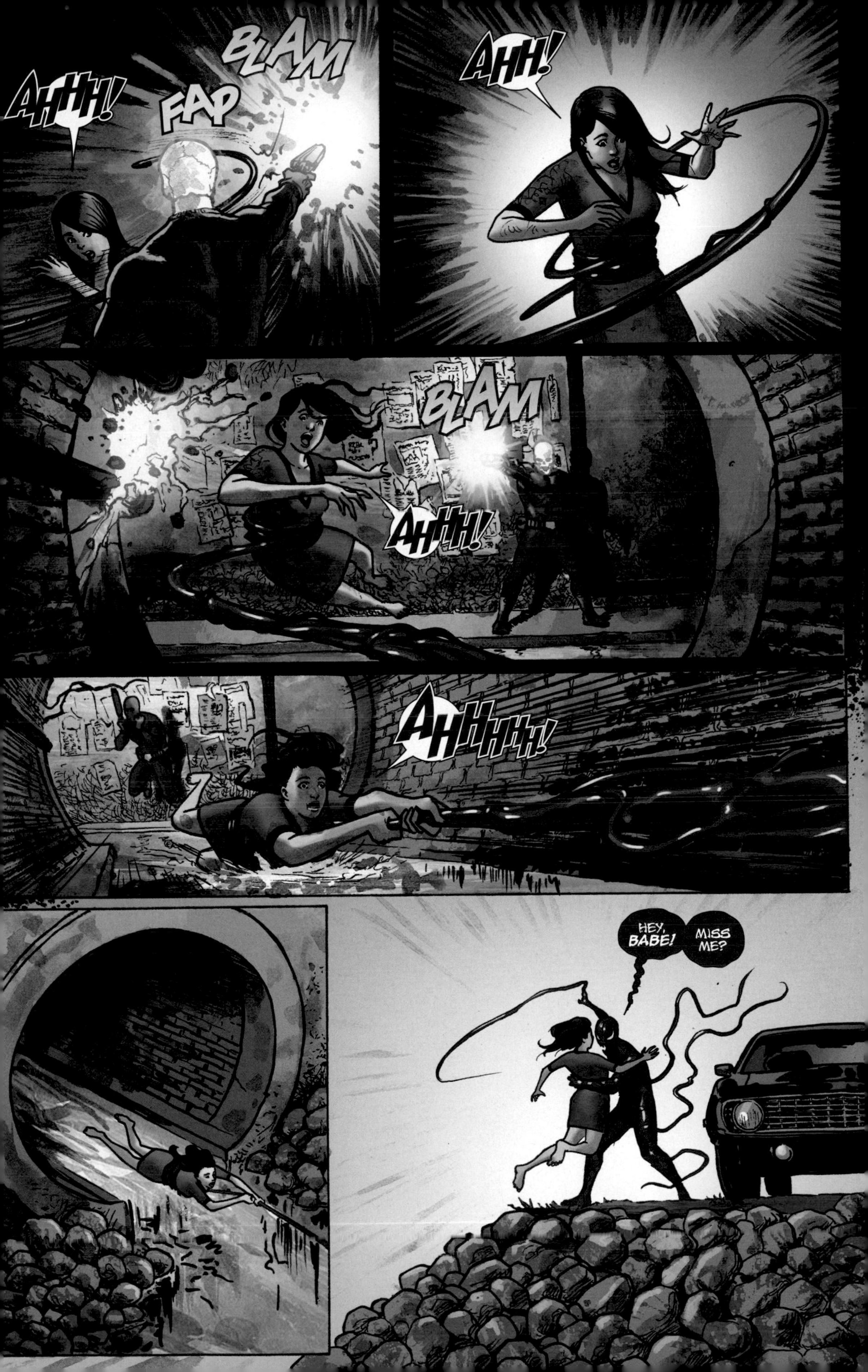
AHHH!
FAP
BLAM
AHH!
BLAM
AHHH!
AHHHHH!
HEY, BABE!
MISS ME?

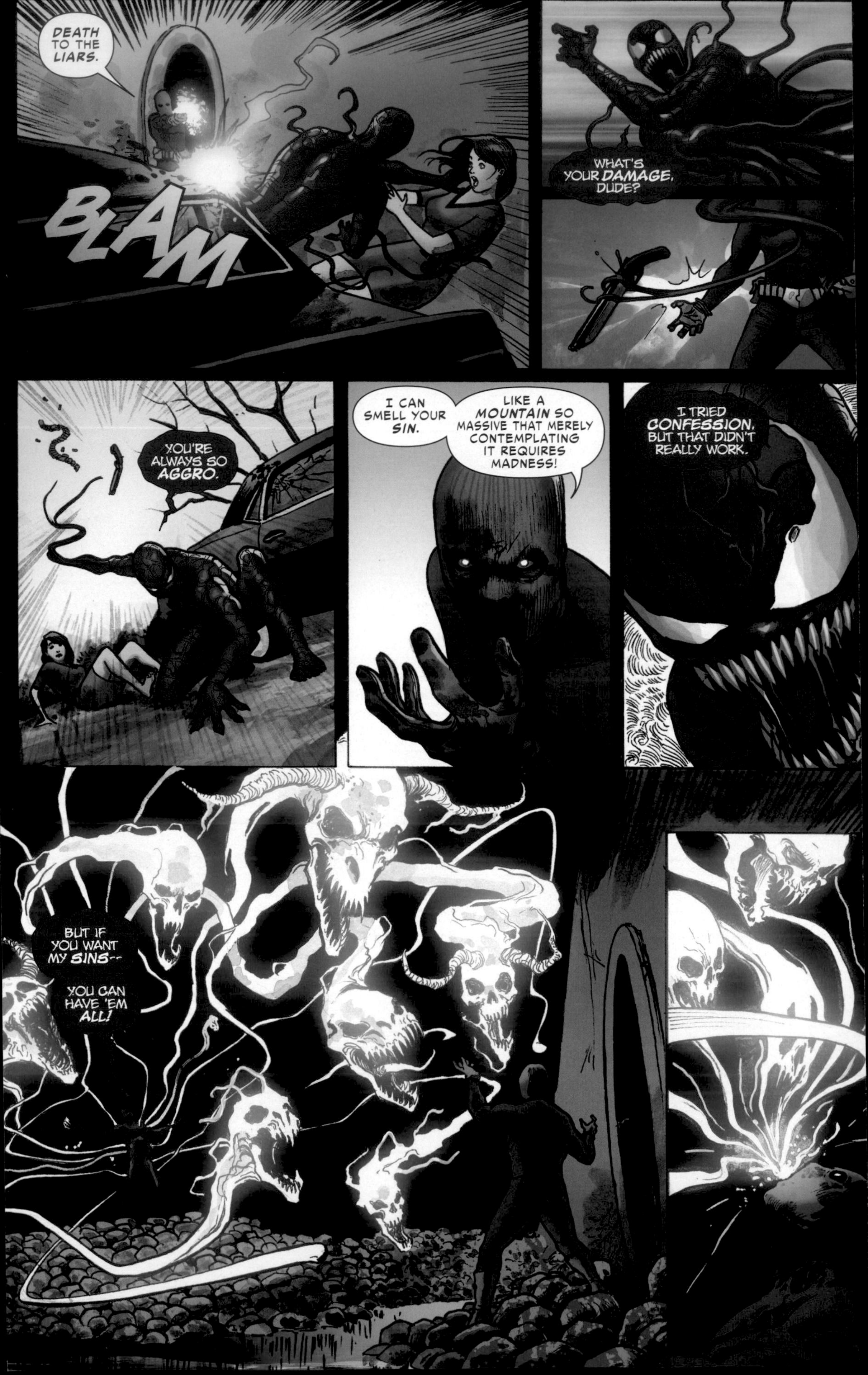
DEATH TO THE LIARS.
BLAM
WHAT'S YOUR DAMAGE, DUDE?
YOU'RE ALWAYS SO AGGRO.
I CAN SMELL YOUR SIN.
LIKE A MOUNTAIN SO MASSIVE THAT MERELY CONTEMPLATING IT REQUIRES MADNESS!
I TRIED CONFESSION, BUT THAT DIDN'T REALLY WORK.
BUT IF YOU WANT MY SINS--
YOU CAN HAVE 'EM ALL!

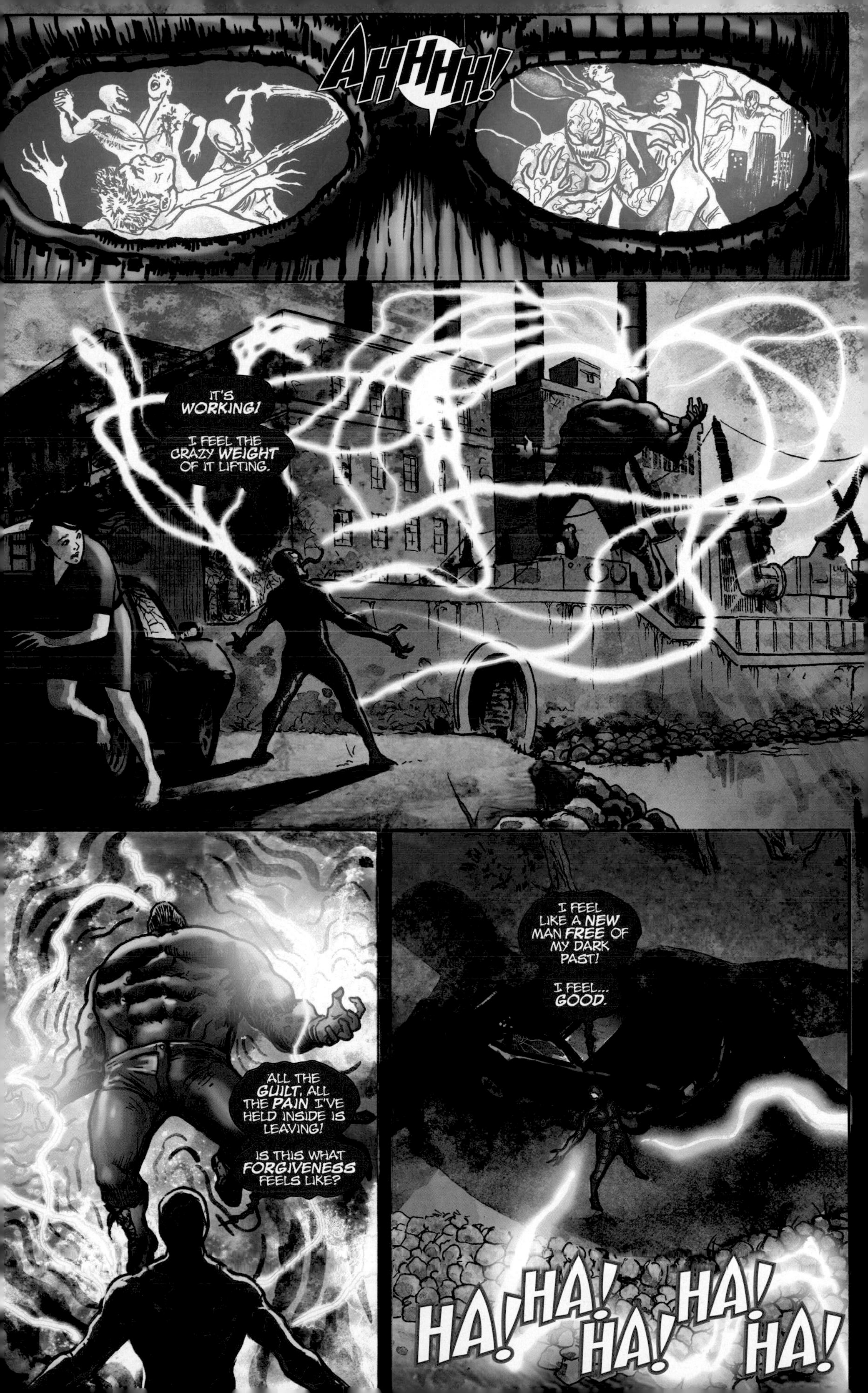
AHHHH!
IT'S WORKING!
I FEEL THE CRAZY WEIGHT OF IT LIFTING.
ALL THE GUILT, ALL THE PAIN I'VE HELD INSIDE IS LEAVING!
IS THIS WHAT FORGIVENESS FEELS LIKE?
I FEEL LIKE A NEW MAN FREE OF MY DARK PAST!
I FEEL... GOOD.
HA! HA! HA! HA! HA! HA!

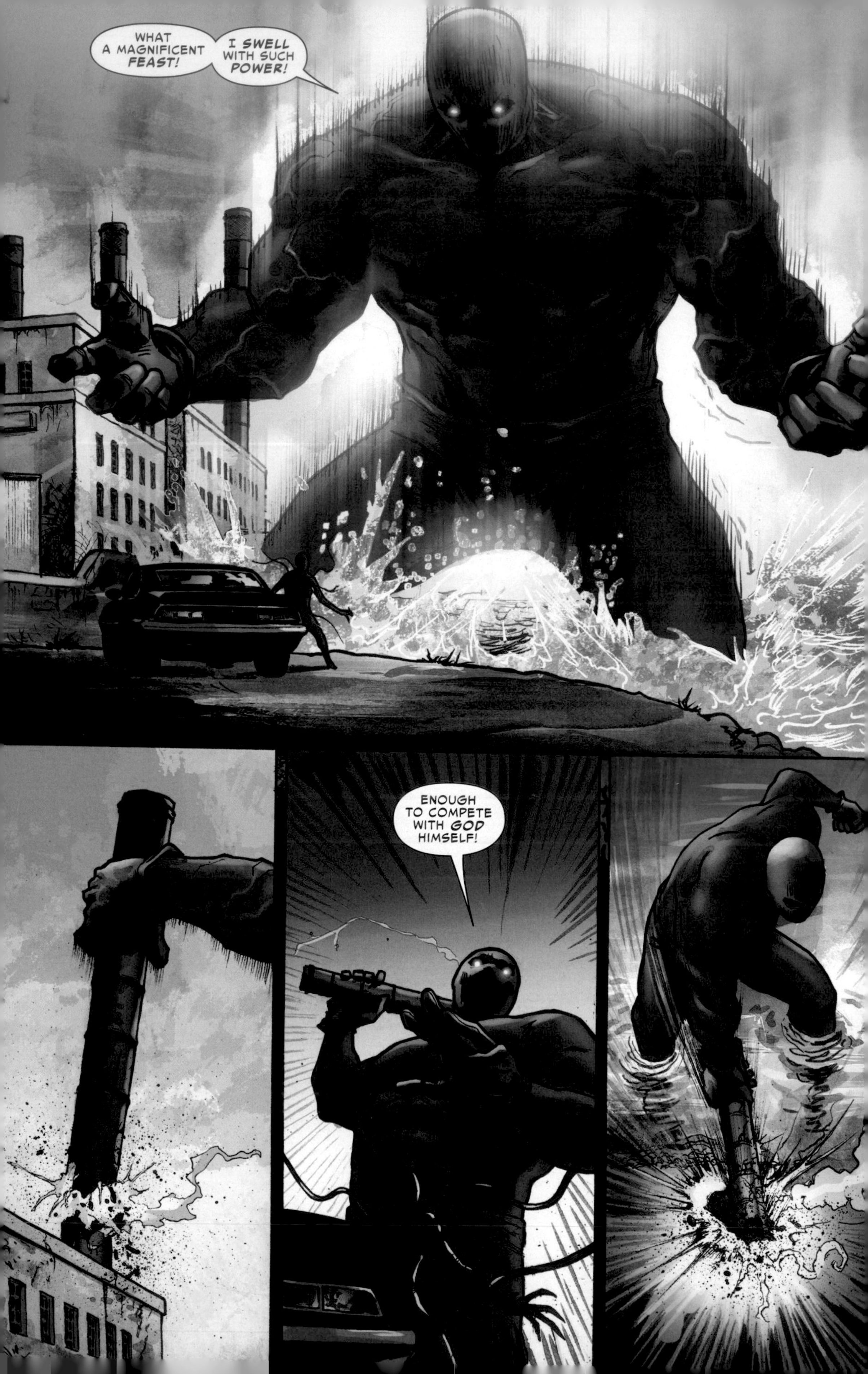
WHAT A MAGNIFICENT FEAST!
I SWELL WITH SUCH POWER!
ENOUGH TO COMPETE WITH GOD HIMSELF!

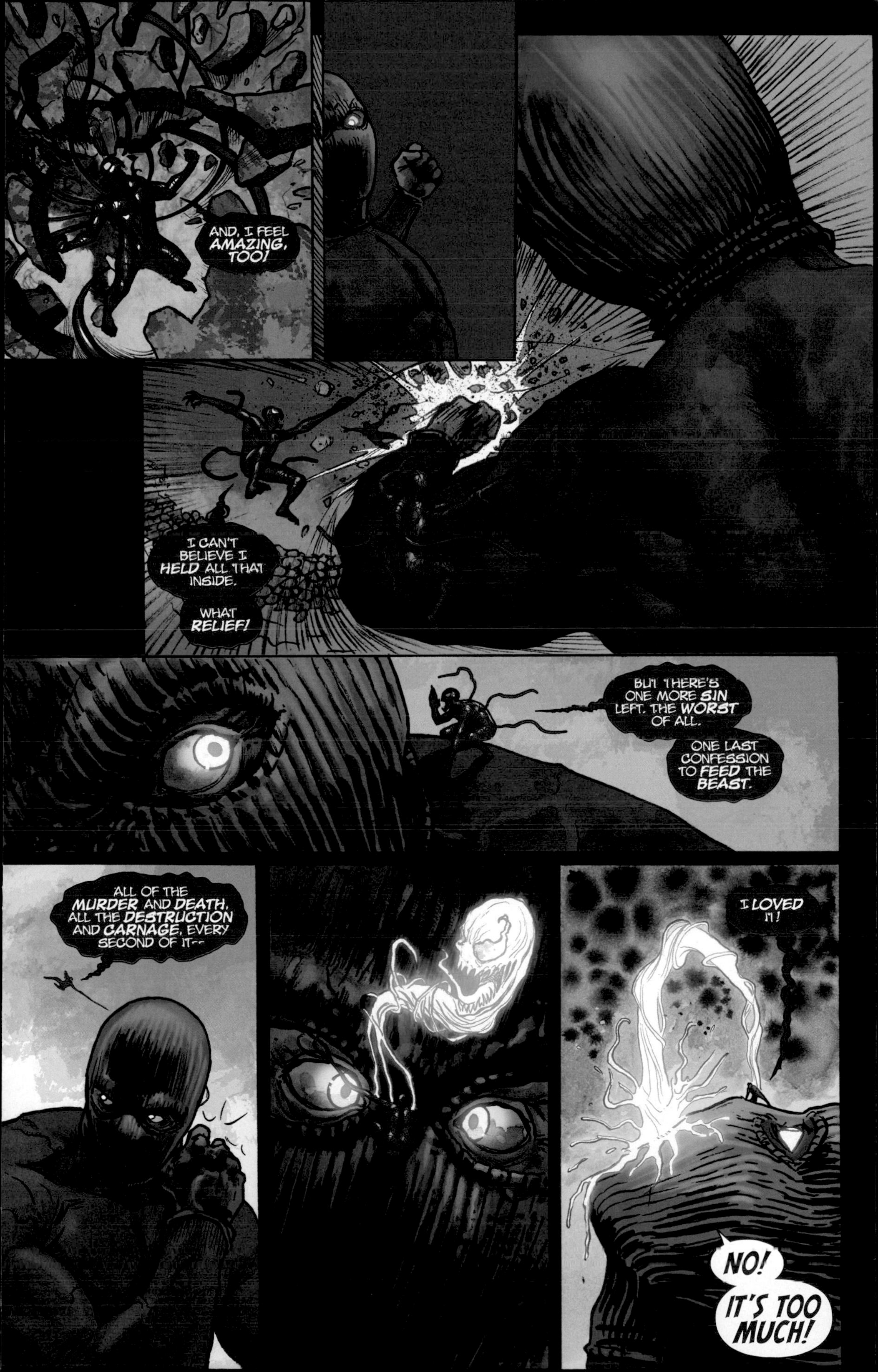
AND, I FEEL AMAZING, TOO!
I CAN'T BELIEVE I HELD ALL THAT INSIDE.
WHAT RELIEF!
BUT THERE'S ONE MORE SIN LEFT. THE WORST OF ALL.
ONE LAST CONFESSION TO FEED THE BEAST.
ALL OF THE MURDER AND DEATH, ALL THE DESTRUCTION AND CARNAGE, EVERY SECOND OF IT--
I LOVED IT!
NO!
IT'S TOO MUCH!

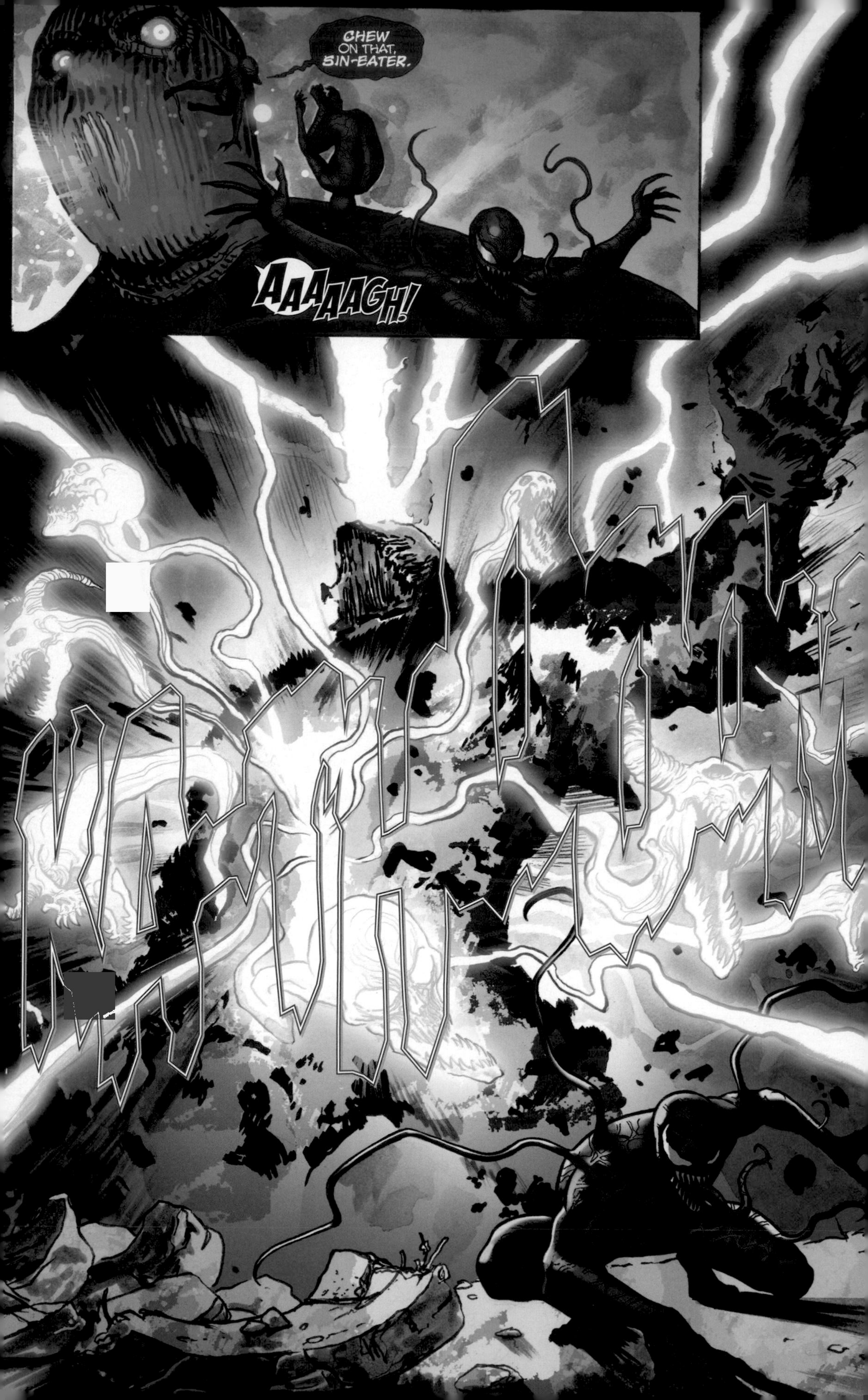
CHEW ON THAT, SIN-EATER.
AAAAAGH!

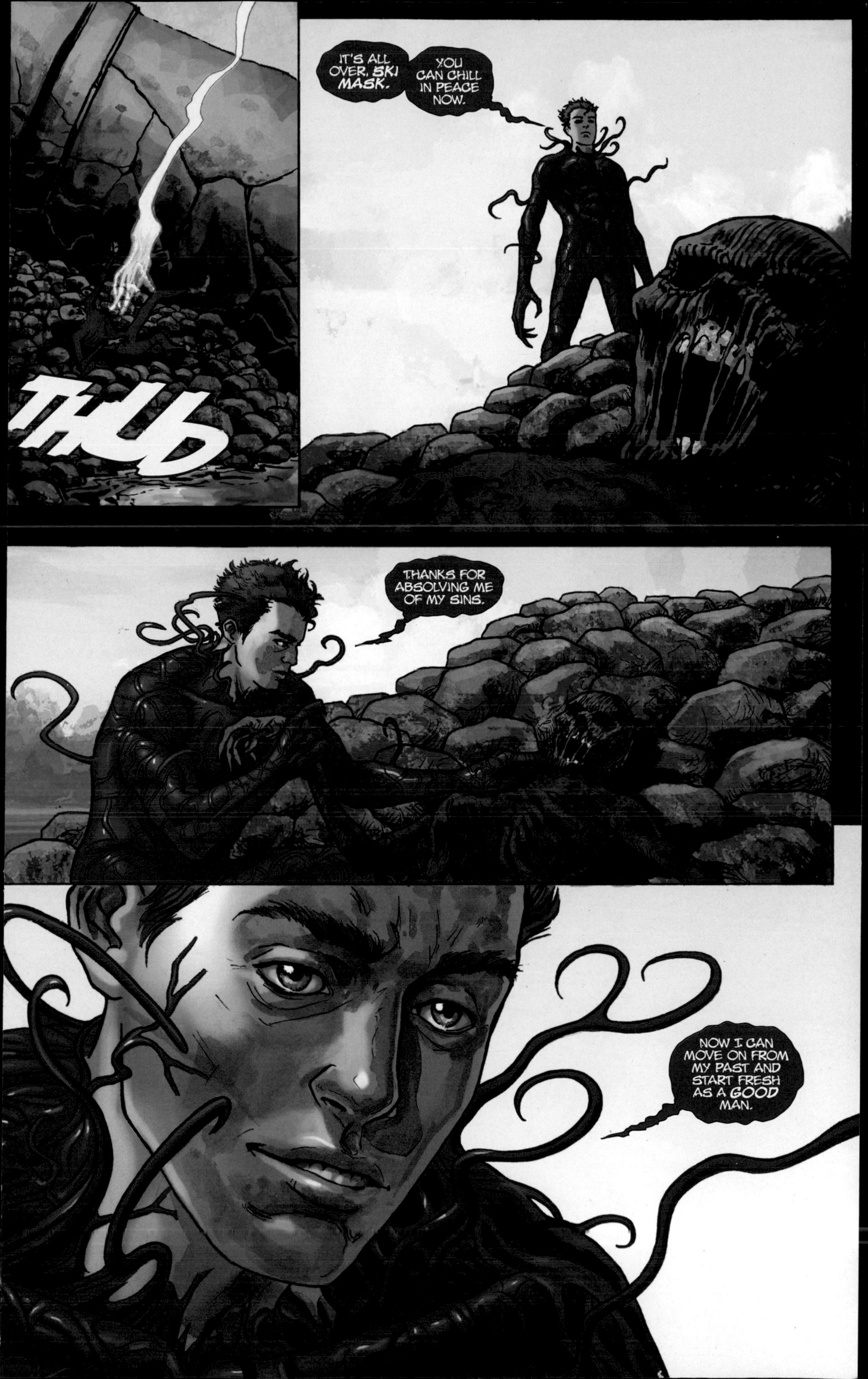
THUD
IT'S ALL OVER, SKI MASK.
YOU CAN CHILL IN PEACE NOW.
THANKS FOR ABSOLVING ME OF MY SINS.
NOW I CAN MOVE ON FROM MY PAST AND START FRESH AS A GOOD MAN.

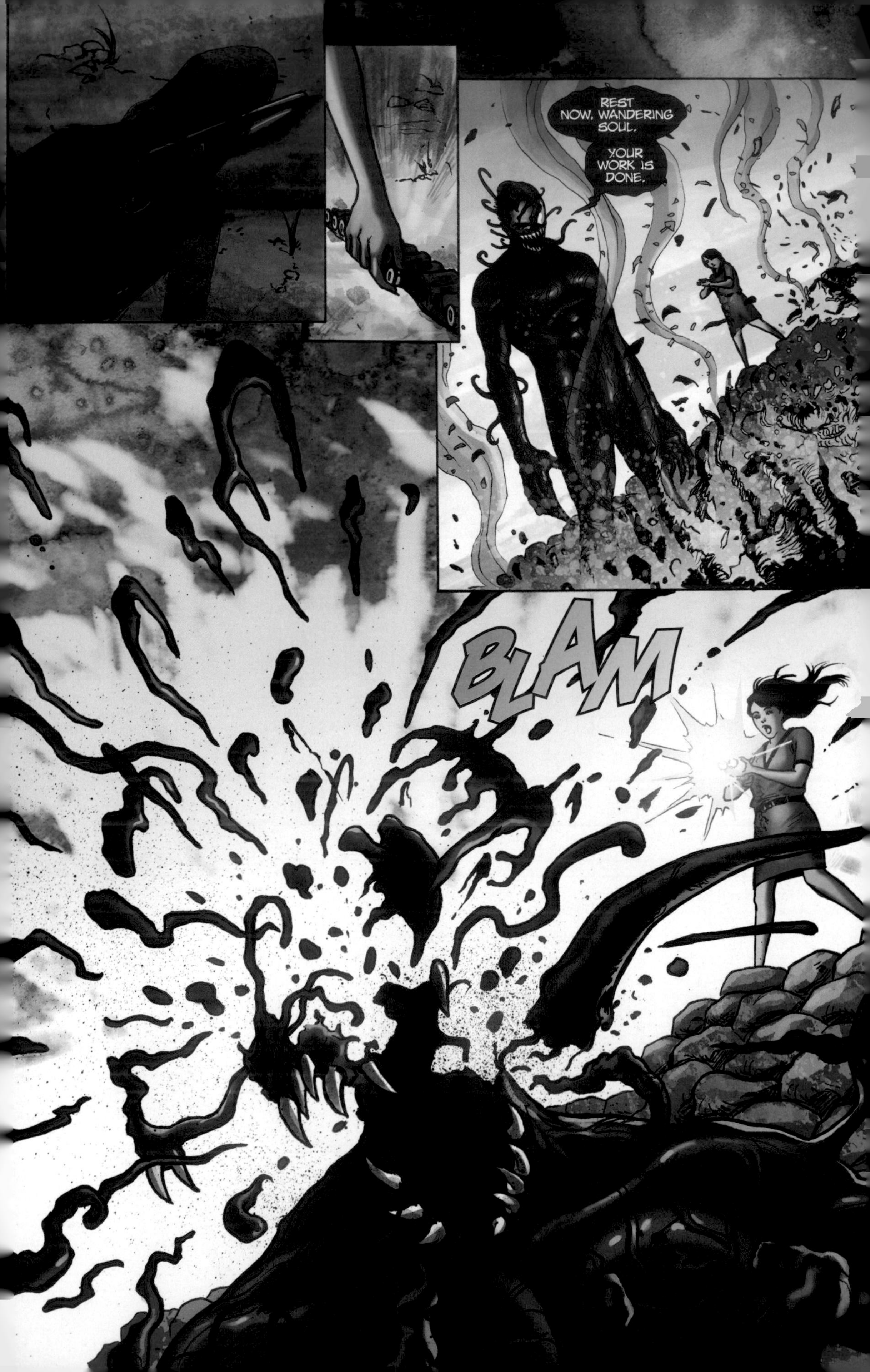
REST NOW, WANDERING SOUL.
YOUR WORK IS DONE.
BLAM

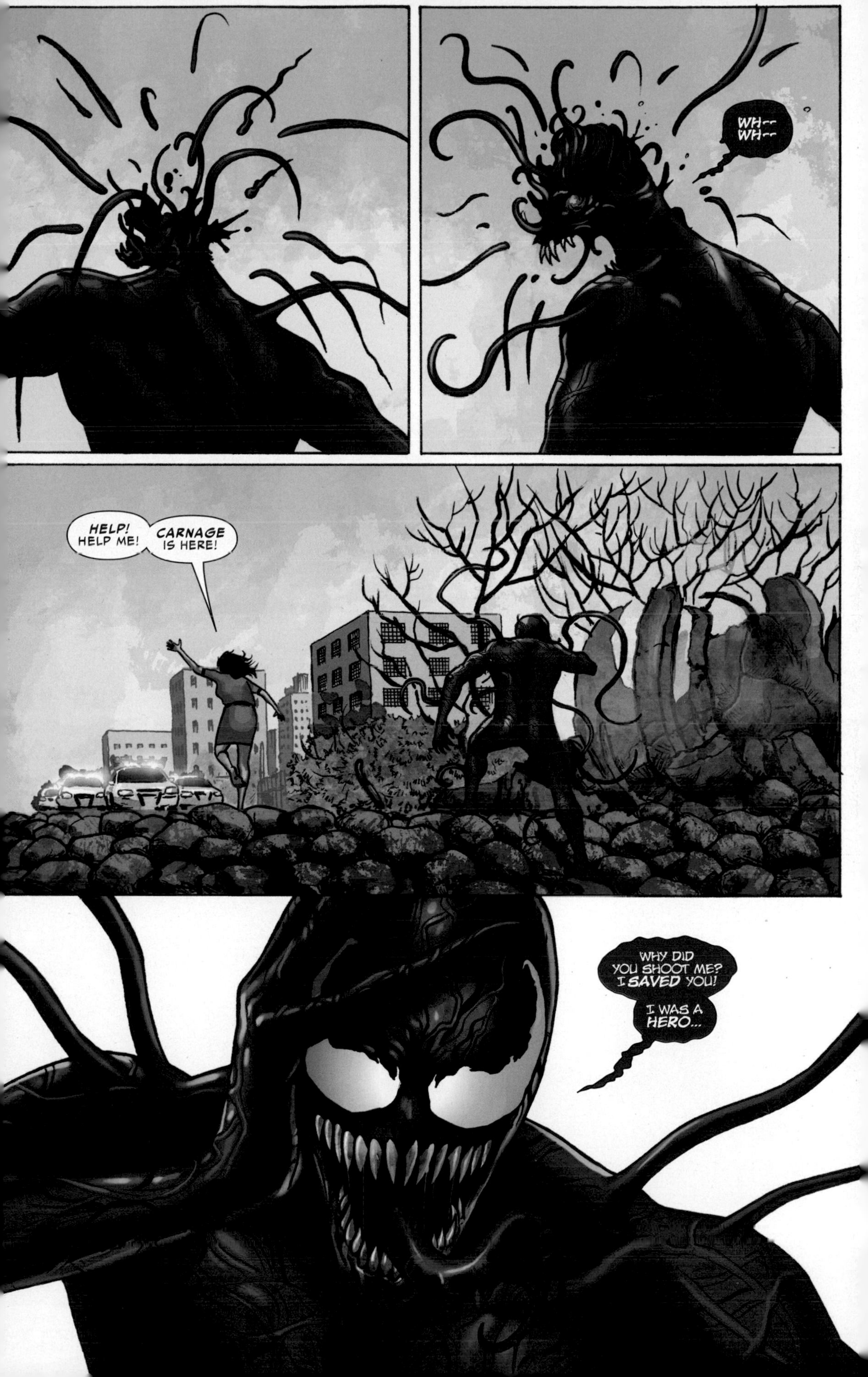
WH-- WH--
HELP! HELP ME!
CARNAGE IS HERE!
WHY DID YOU SHOOT ME? I SAVED YOU!
I WAS A HERO...

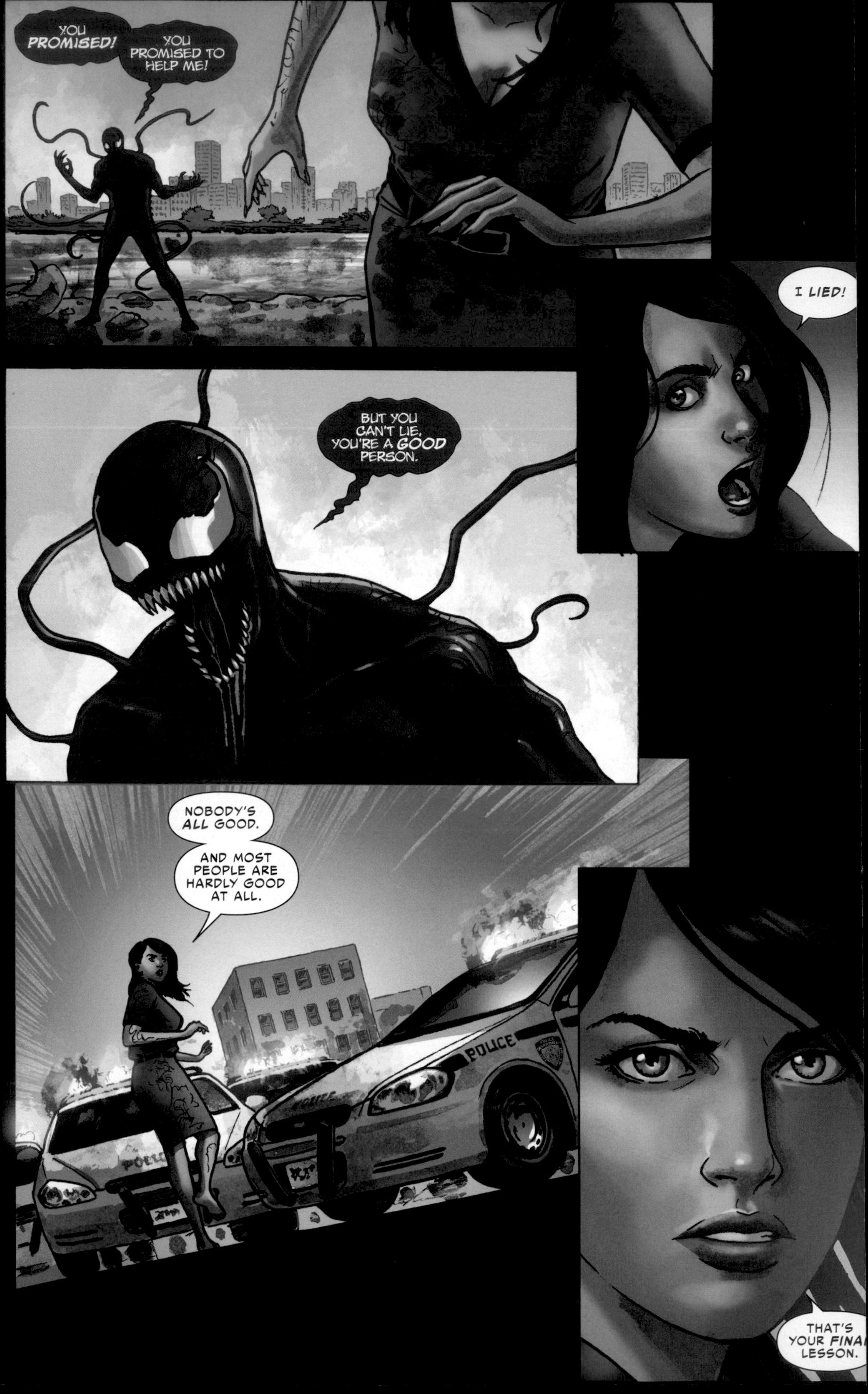
YOU PROMISED!
YOU PROMISED TO HELP ME!
I LIED!
BUT YOU CAN'T LIE, YOU'RE A GOOD PERSON.
NOBODY'S ALL GOOD.
AND MOST PEOPLE ARE HARDLY GOOD AT ALL.
POLICE
THAT'S YOUR FINAL LESSON.

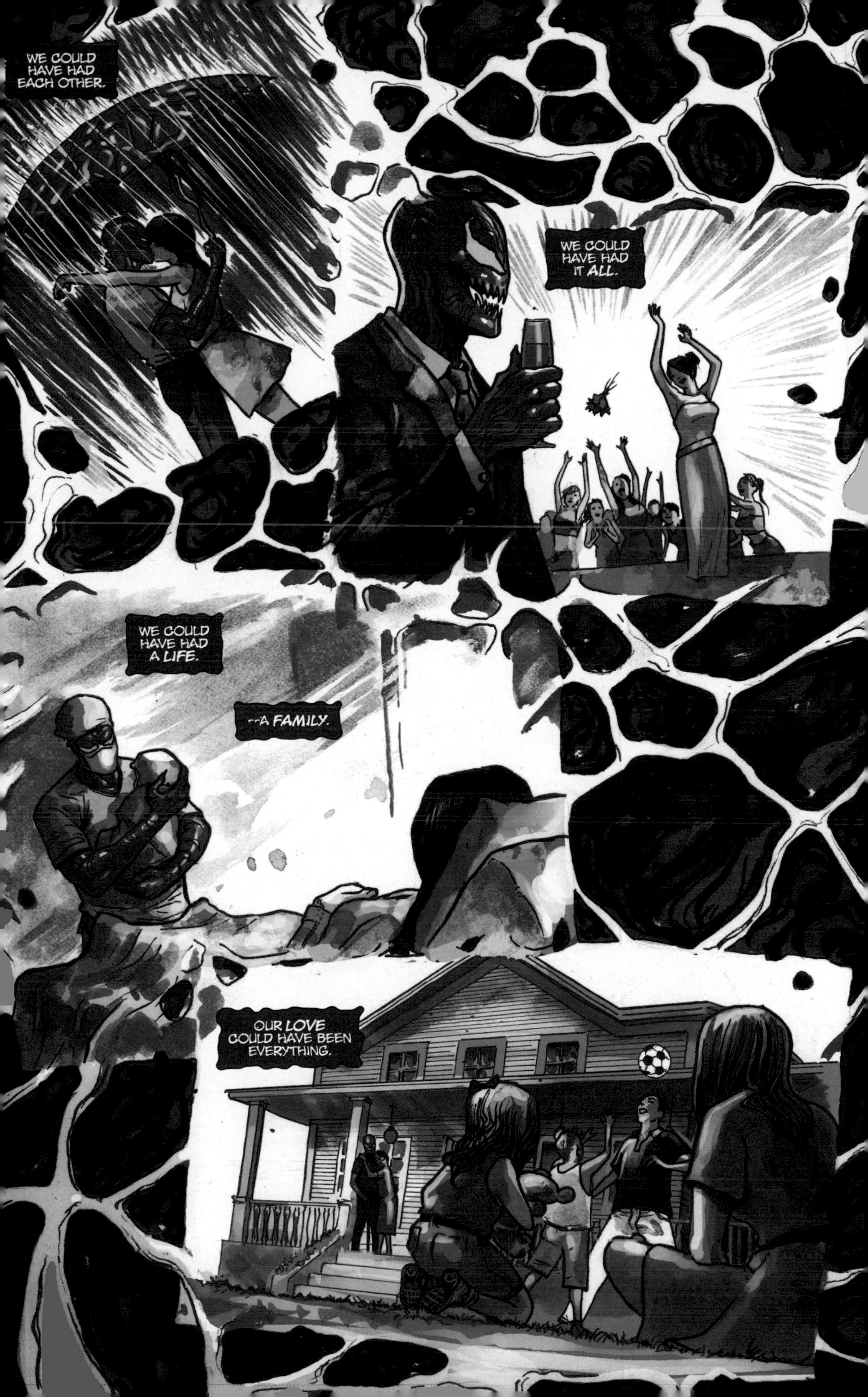
WE COULD HAVE HAD EACH OTHER.
WE COULD HAVE HAD IT ALL.
WE COULD HAVE HAD A LIFE.
--A FAMILY.
OUR LOVE COULD HAVE BEEN EVERYTHING.

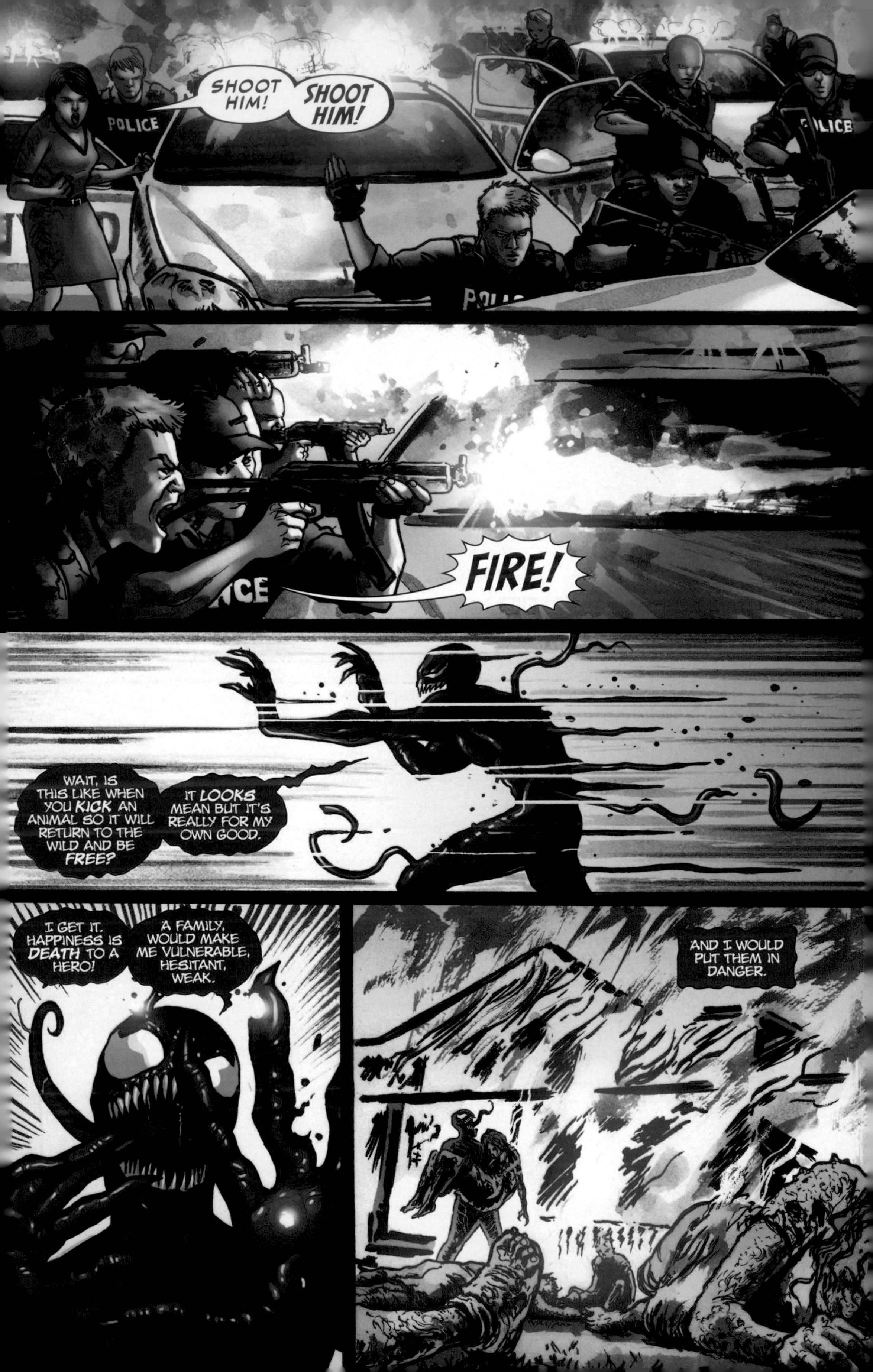
SHOOT HIM!
SHOOT HIM!
FIRE!
WAIT, IS THIS LIKE WHEN YOU KICK AN ANIMAL SO IT WILL RETURN TO THE WILD AND BE FREE?
IT LOOKS MEAN BUT IT'S REALLY FOR MY OWN GOOD.
I GET IT. HAPPINESS IS DEATH TO A HERO!
A FAMILY WOULD MAKE ME VULNERABLE, HESITANT, WEAK.
AND I WOULD PUT THEM IN DANGER.

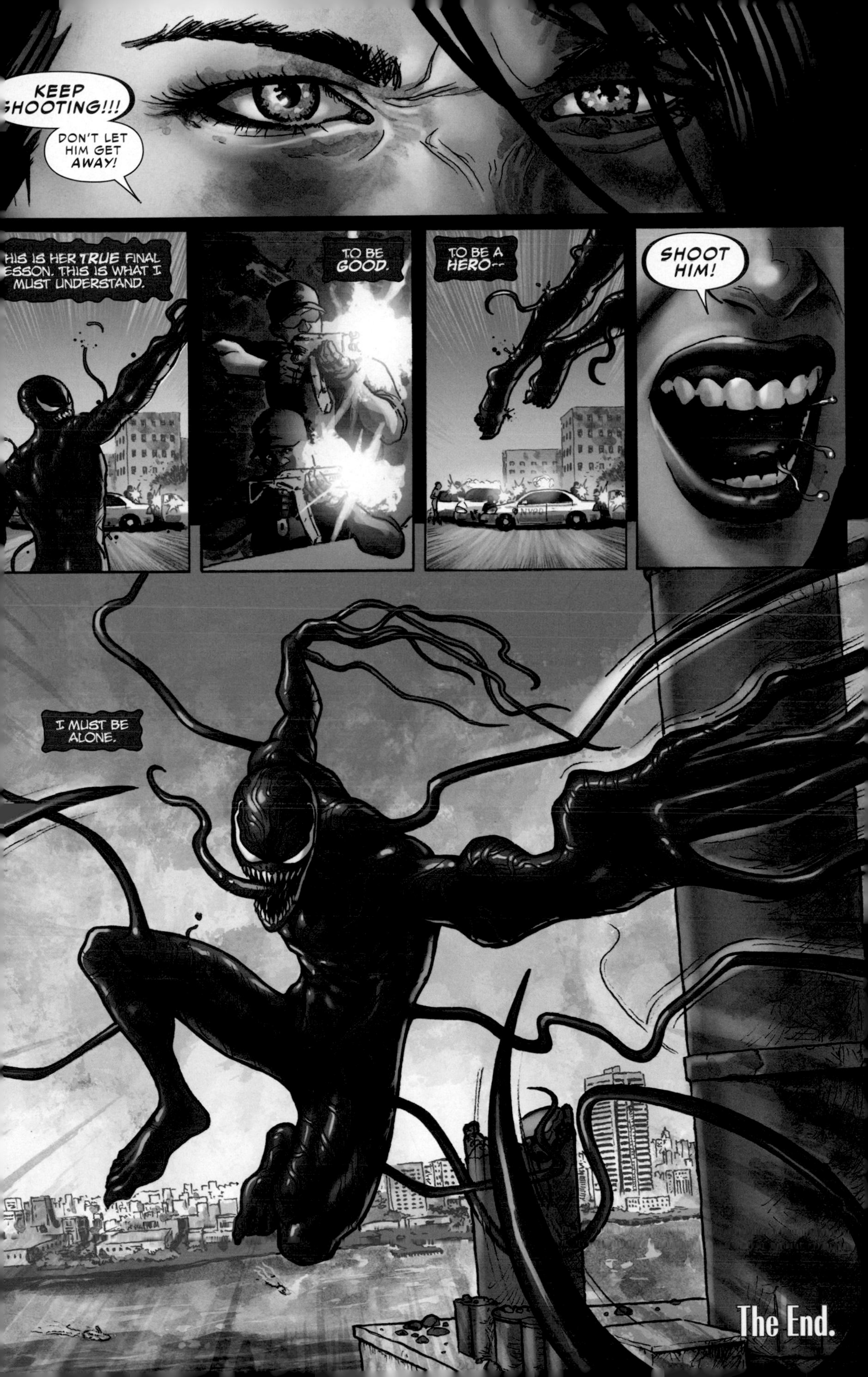
KEEP SHOOTING!!!
DON'T LET HIM GET AWAY!
HIS IS HER TRUE FINAL ESSON. THIS IS WHAT I MUST UNDERSTAND.
TO BE GOOD.
TO BE A HERO--
SHOOT HIM!
I MUST BE ALONE.
The End.

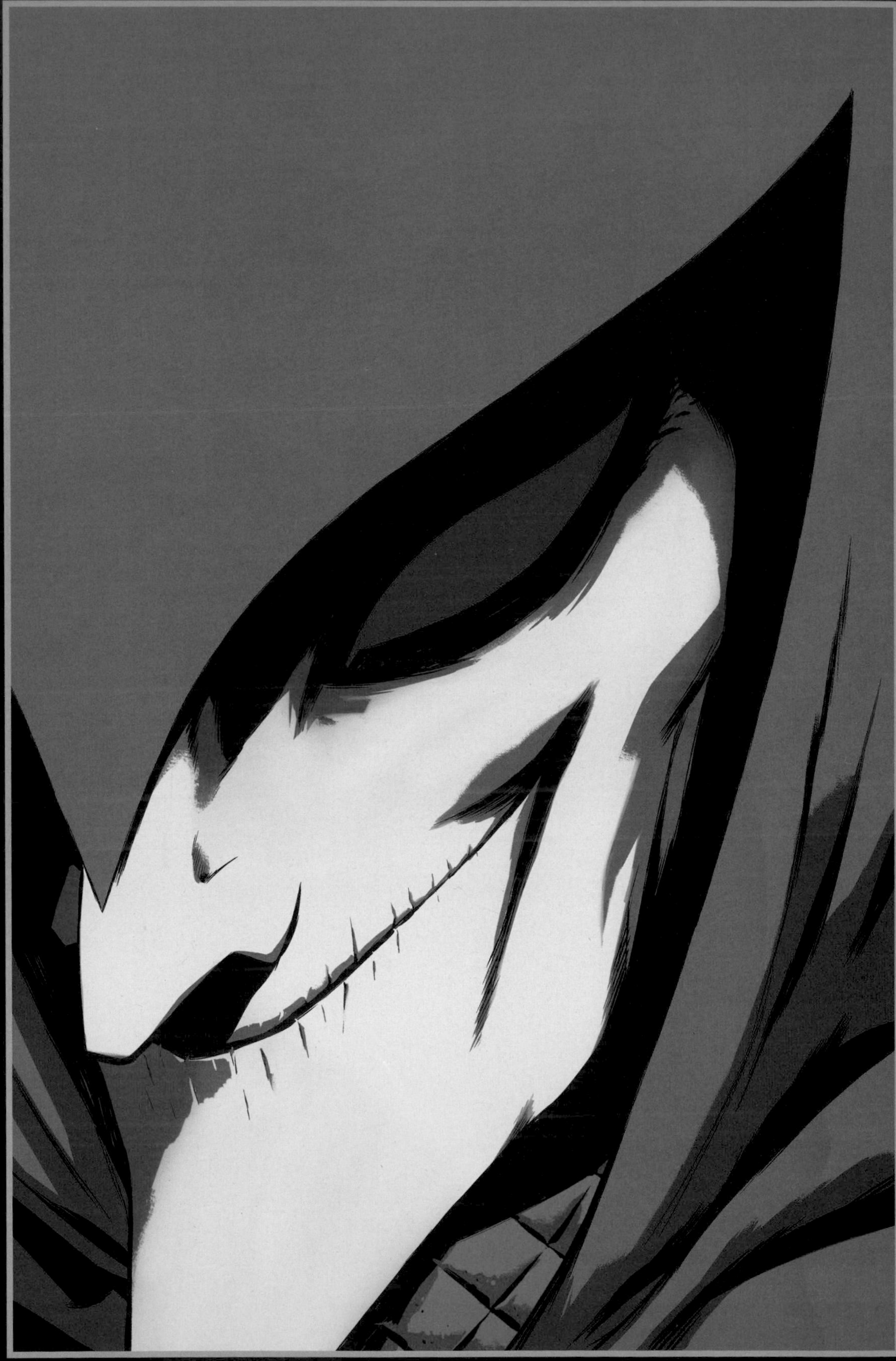

HOBGOBLIN #1

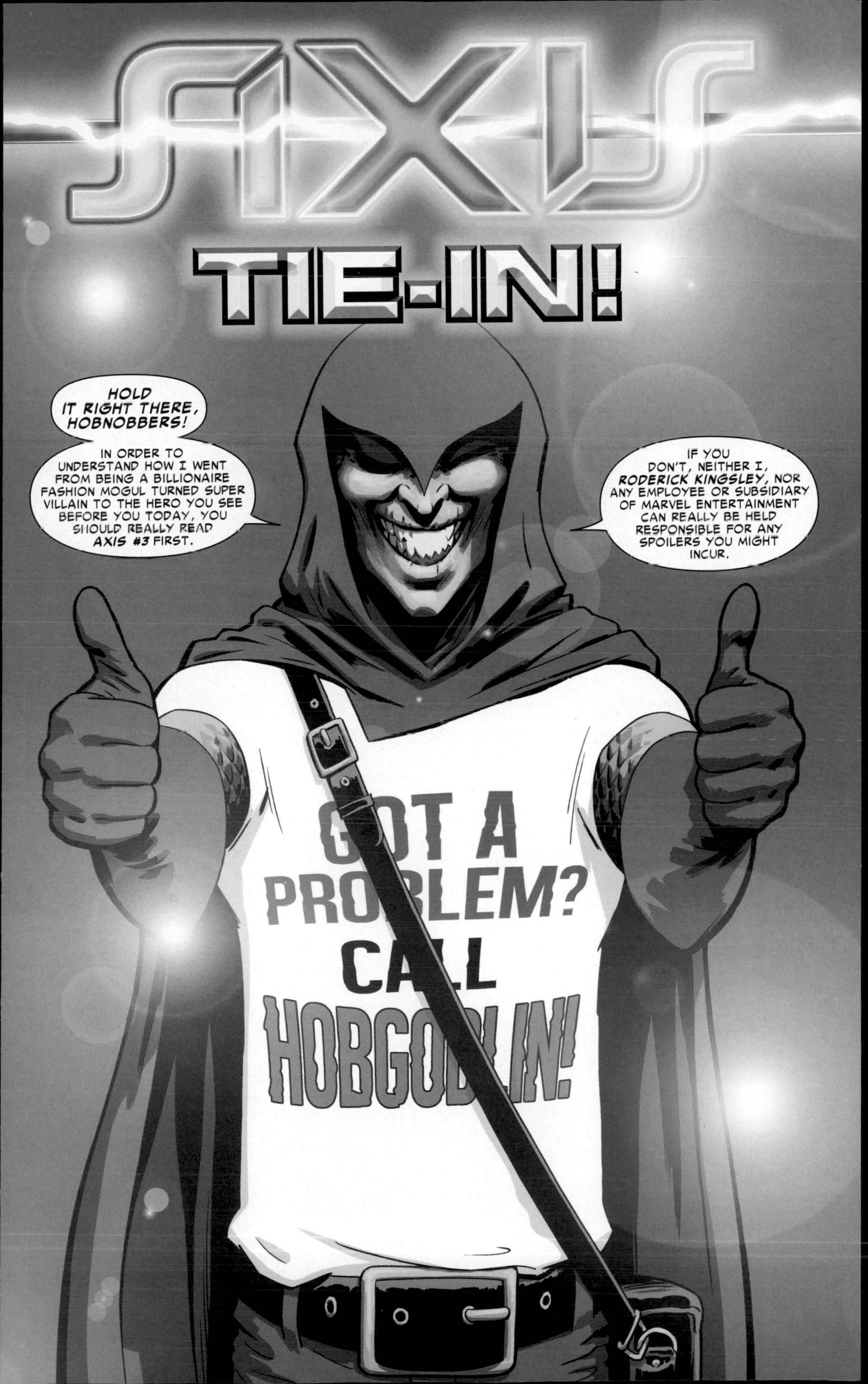
AXIS
TIE-IN!
HOLD IT RIGHT THERE, HOBNOBBERS!
IN ORDER TO UNDERSTAND HOW I WENT FROM BEING A BILLIONAIRE FASHION MOGUL TURNED SUPER VILLAIN TO THE HERO YOU SEE BEFORE YOU TODAY, YOU SHOULD REALLY READ AXIS #3 FIRST.
IF YOU DON'T, NEITHER I, RODERICK KINGSLEY, NOR ANY EMPLOYEE OR SUBSIDIARY OF MARVEL ENTERTAINMENT CAN REALLY BE HELD RESPONSIBLE FOR ANY SPOILERS YOU MIGHT INCUR.
GOT A PROBLEM? CALL HOBGOBLIN!

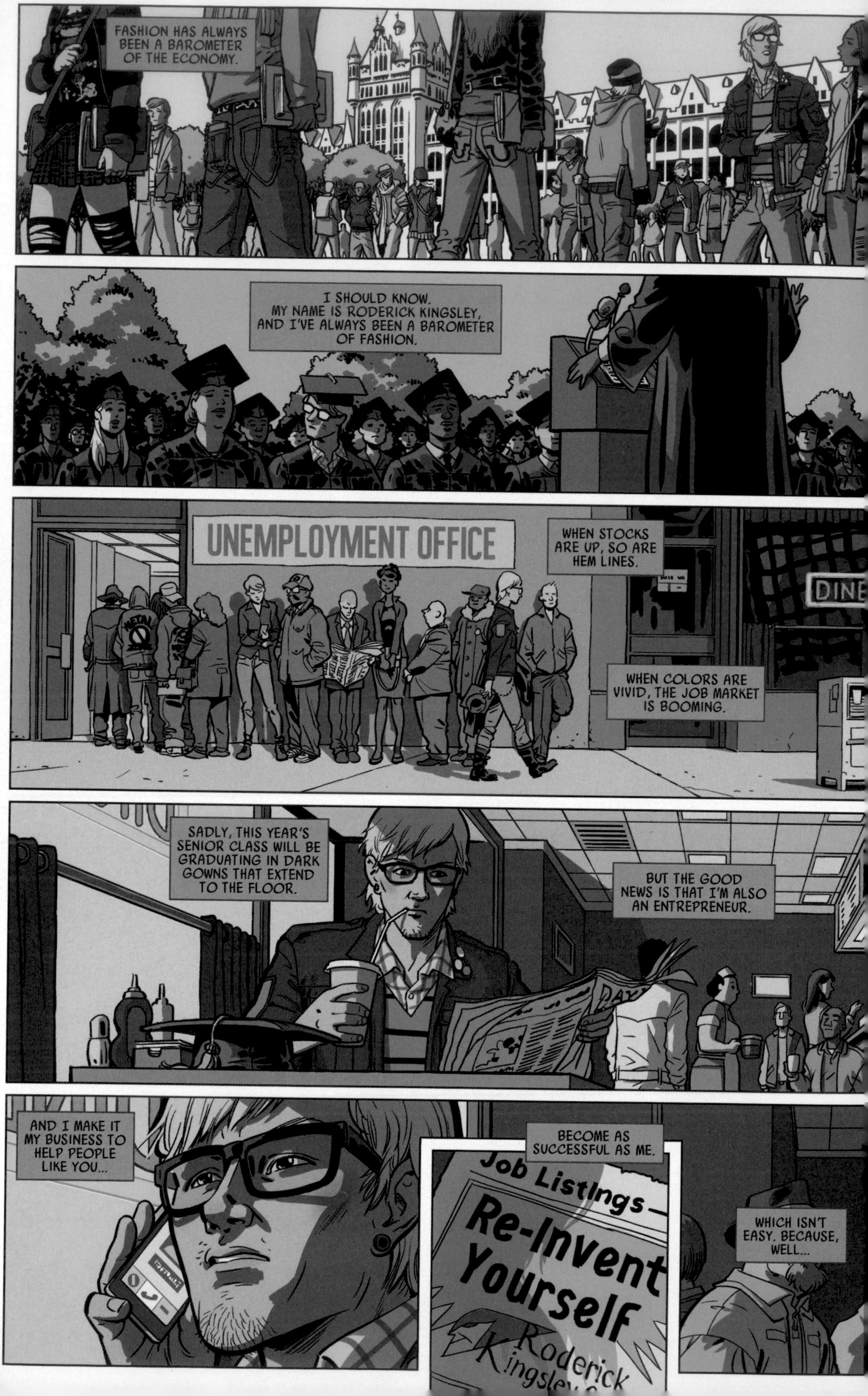
FASHION HAS ALWAYS BEEN A BAROMETER OF THE ECONOMY.
I SHOULD KNOW. MY NAME IS RODERICK KINGSLEY, AND I'VE ALWAYS BEEN A BAROMETER OF FASHION.
UNEMPLOYMENT OFFICE
WHEN STOCKS ARE UP, SO ARE HEM LINES.
DINE
WHEN COLORS ARE VIVID, THE JOB MARKET IS BOOMING.
SADLY, THIS YEAR'S SENIOR CLASS WILL BE GRADUATING IN DARK GOWNS THAT EXTEND TO THE FLOOR.
BUT THE GOOD NEWS IS THAT I'M ALSO AN ENTREPRENEUR.
AND I MAKE IT MY BUSINESS TO HELP PEOPLE LIKE YOU...
BECOME AS SUCCESSFUL AS ME.
Job Listings
Re-Invent Yourself
Roderick Kingsley
WHICH ISN'T EASY. BECAUSE, WELL...

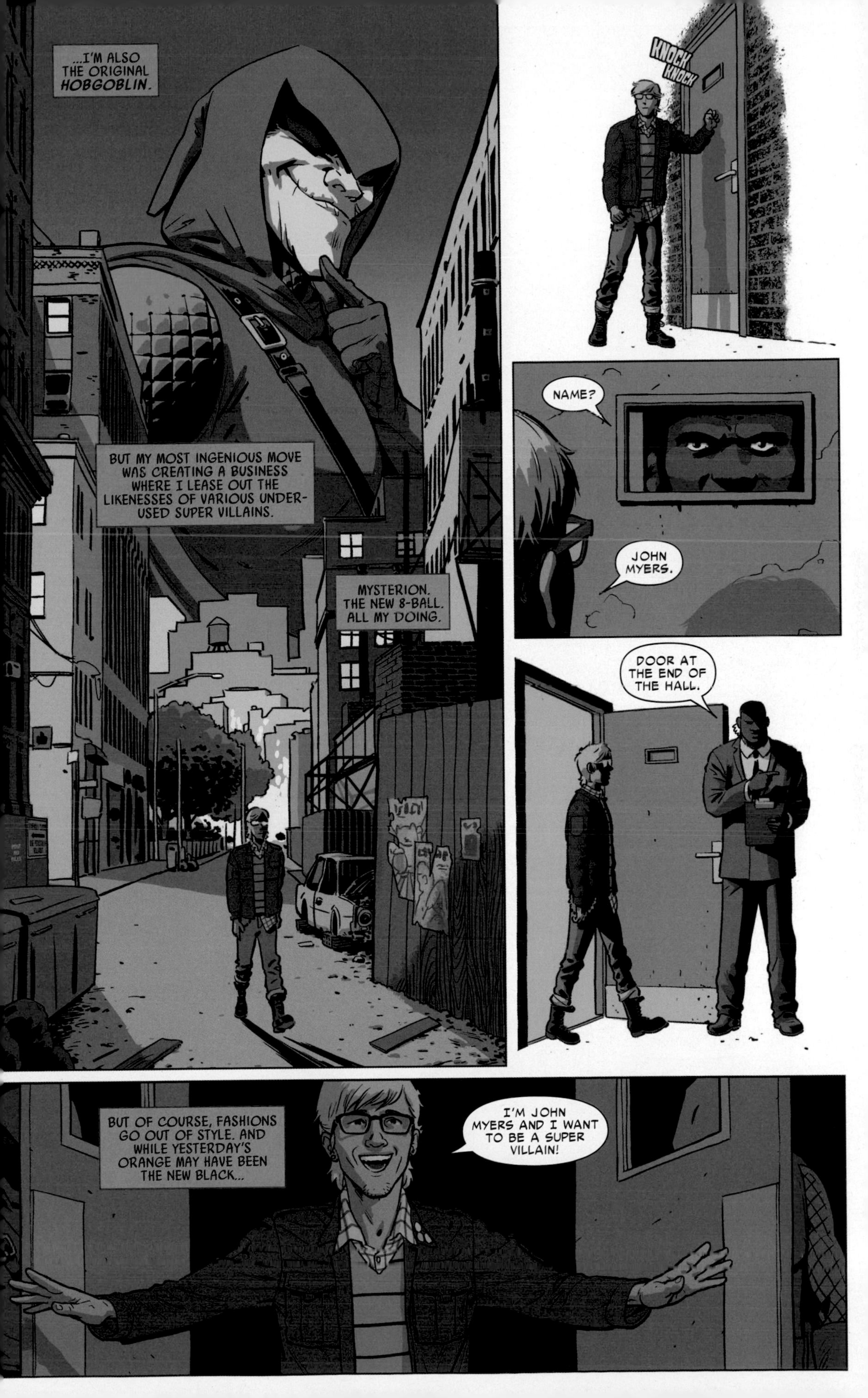

...I'M ALSO THE ORIGINAL HOBGOBLIN.
BUT MY MOST INGENIOUS MOVE WAS CREATING A BUSINESS WHERE I LEASE OUT THE LIKENESSES OF VARIOUS UNDER-USED SUPER VILLAINS.
MYSTERION. THE NEW 8-BALL. ALL MY DOING.
KNOCK KNOCK
NAME?
JOHN MYERS.
DOOR AT THE END OF THE HALL.
BUT OF COURSE, FASHIONS GO OUT OF STYLE. AND WHILE YESTERDAY'S ORANGE MAY HAVE BEEN THE NEW BLACK...
I'M JOHN MYERS AND I WANT TO BE A SUPER VILLAIN!

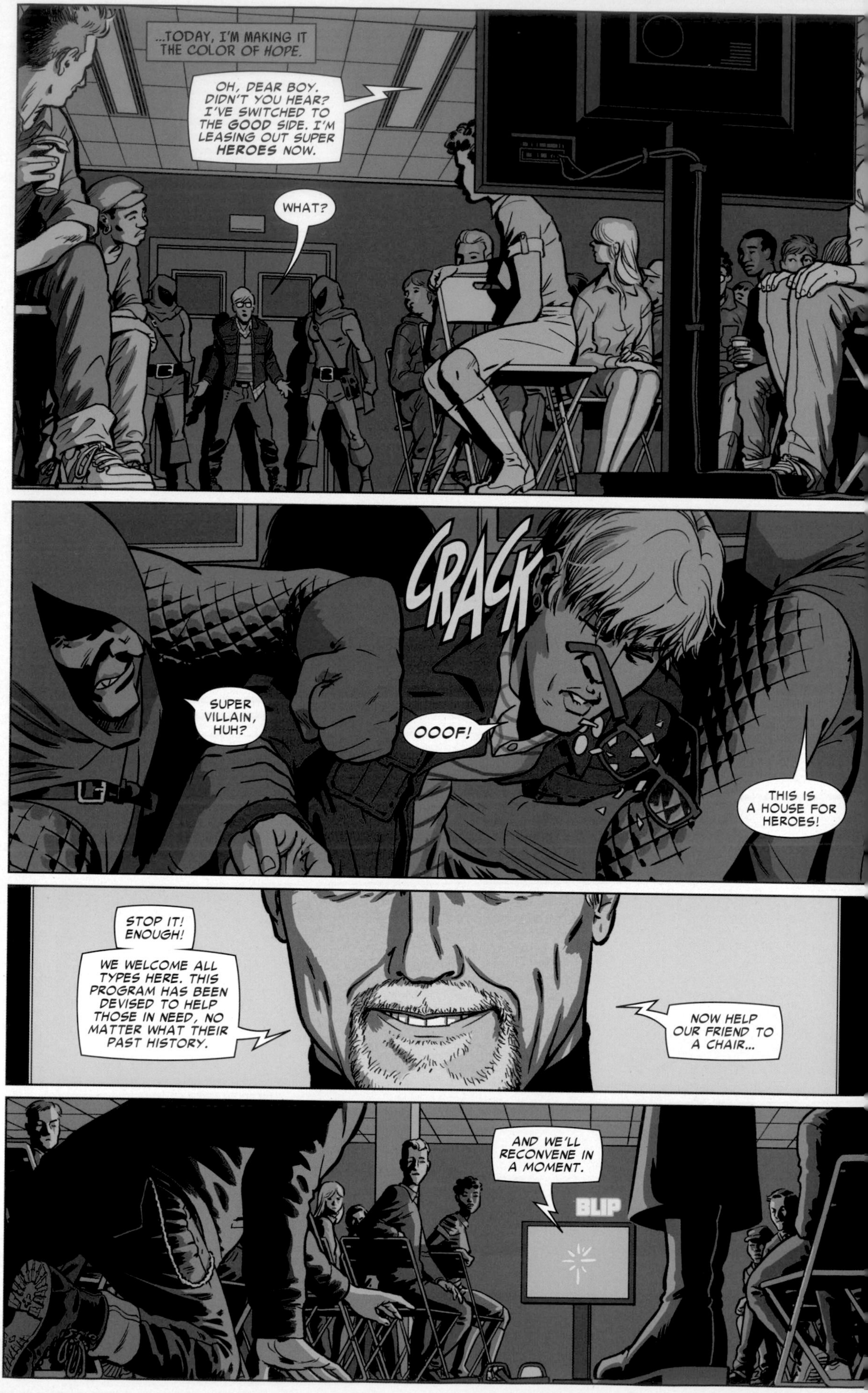
...TODAY, I'M MAKING IT THE COLOR OF HOPE.
OH, DEAR BOY. DIDN'T YOU HEAR? I'VE SWITCHED TO THE GOOD SIDE. I'M LEASING OUT SUPER HEROES NOW.
WHAT?
CRACK
SUPER VILLAIN, HUH?
OOOF!
THIS IS A HOUSE FOR HEROES!
STOP IT! ENOUGH!
WE WELCOME ALL TYPES HERE. THIS PROGRAM HAS BEEN DEVISED TO HELP THOSE IN NEED, NO MATTER WHAT THEIR PAST HISTORY.
NOW HELP OUR FRIEND TO A CHAIR...
AND WE'LL RECONVENE IN A MOMENT.
BLIP

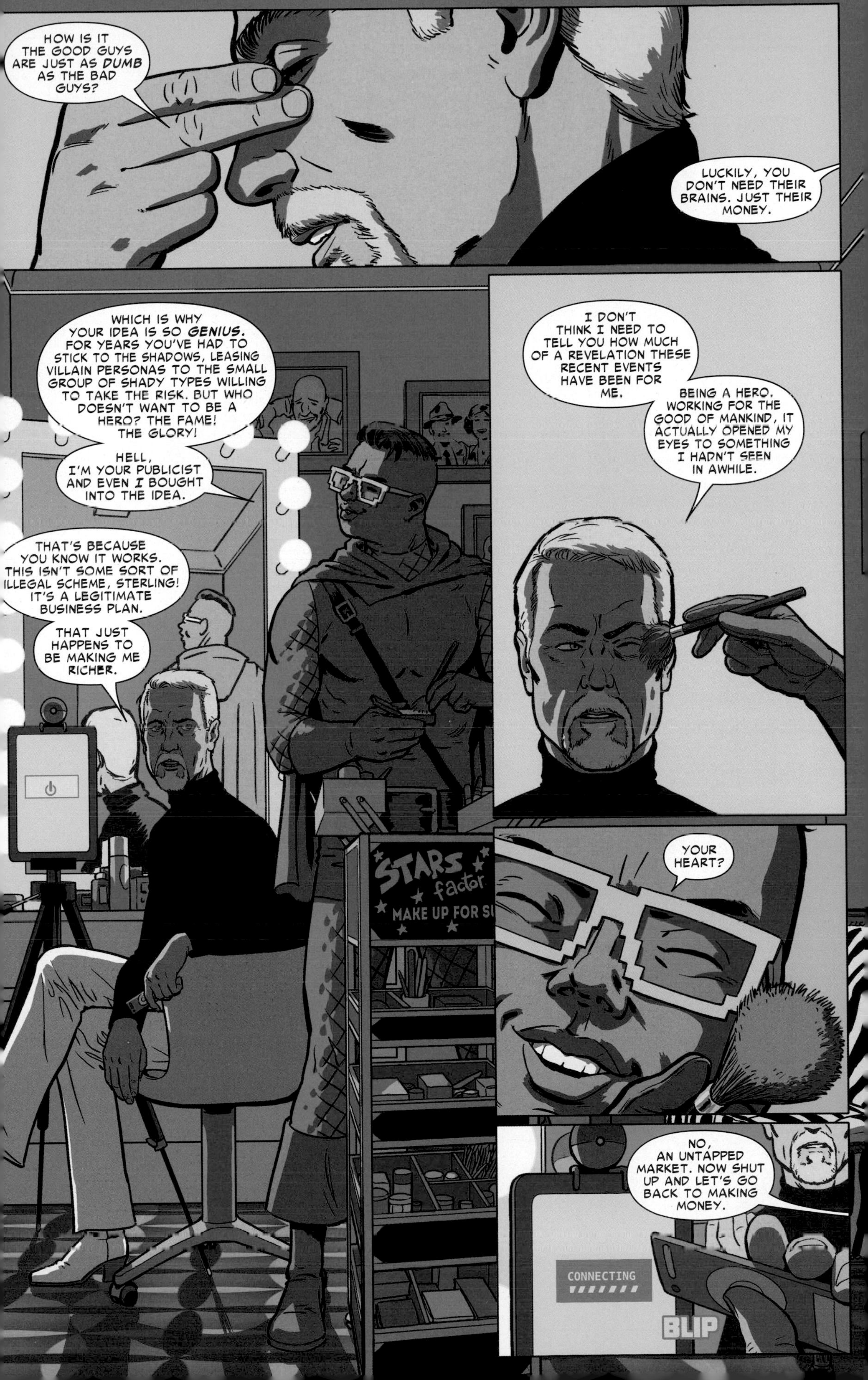
HOW IS IT THE GOOD GUYS ARE JUST AS DUMB AS THE BAD GUYS?
LUCKILY, YOU DON'T NEED THEIR BRAINS. JUST THEIR MONEY.
WHICH IS WHY YOUR IDEA IS SO GENIUS. FOR YEARS YOU'VE HAD TO STICK TO THE SHADOWS, LEASING VILLAIN PERSONAS TO THE SMALL GROUP OF SHADY TYPES WILLING TO TAKE THE RISK. BUT WHO DOESN'T WANT TO BE A HERO? THE FAME! THE GLORY!
HELL, I'M YOUR PUBLICIST AND EVEN I BOUGHT INTO THE IDEA.
THAT'S BECAUSE YOU KNOW IT WORKS. THIS ISN'T SOME SORT OF ILLEGAL SCHEME, STERLING! IT'S A LEGITIMATE BUSINESS PLAN.
THAT JUST HAPPENS TO BE MAKING ME RICHER.
STARS factor
MAKE UP FOR SU
I DON'T THINK I NEED TO TELL YOU HOW MUCH OF A REVELATION THESE RECENT EVENTS HAVE BEEN FOR ME.
BEING A HERO. WORKING FOR THE GOOD OF MANKIND, IT ACTUALLY OPENED MY EYES TO SOMETHING I HADN'T SEEN IN AWHILE.
YOUR HEART?
NO, AN UNTAPPED MARKET. NOW SHUT UP AND LET'S GO BACK TO MAKING MONEY.
CONNECTING
BLIP

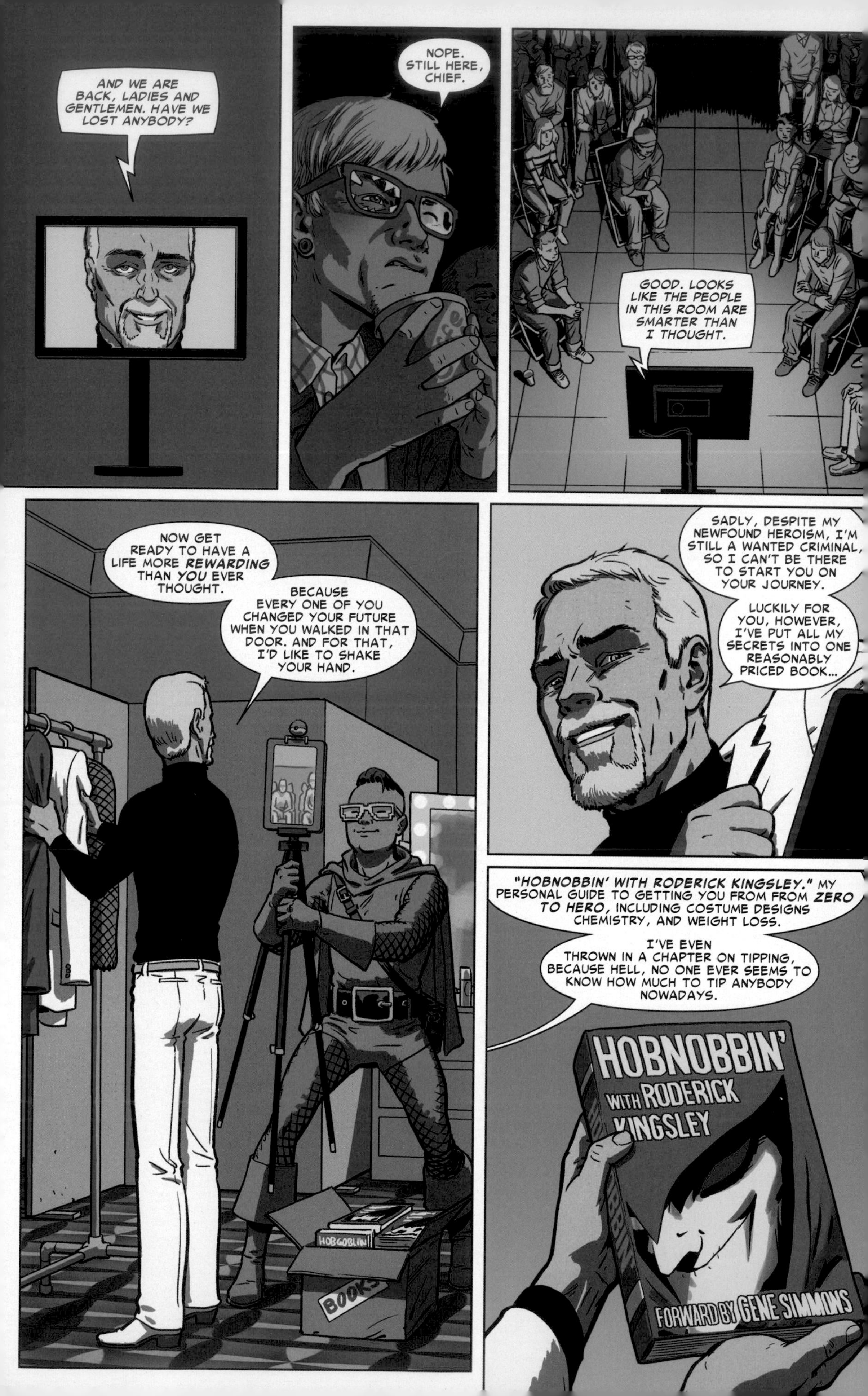
AND WE ARE BACK, LADIES AND GENTLEMEN. HAVE WE LOST ANYBODY?
NOPE. STILL HERE, CHIEF.
GOOD. LOOKS LIKE THE PEOPLE IN THIS ROOM ARE SMARTER THAN I THOUGHT.
NOW GET READY TO HAVE A LIFE MORE REWARDING THAN YOU EVER THOUGHT.
BECAUSE EVERY ONE OF YOU CHANGED YOUR FUTURE WHEN YOU WALKED IN THAT DOOR. AND FOR THAT, I'D LIKE TO SHAKE YOUR HAND.
HOBGOBLIN
BOOKS
SADLY, DESPITE MY NEWFOUND HEROISM, I'M STILL A WANTED CRIMINAL, SO I CAN'T BE THERE TO START YOU ON YOUR JOURNEY.
LUCKILY FOR YOU, HOWEVER, I'VE PUT ALL MY SECRETS INTO ONE REASONABLY PRICED BOOK...
"HOBNOBBIN' WITH RODERICK KINGSLEY." MY PERSONAL GUIDE TO GETTING YOU FROM FROM ZERO TO HERO, INCLUDING COSTUME DESIGNS CHEMISTRY, AND WEIGHT LOSS.
I'VE EVEN THROWN IN A CHAPTER ON TIPPING, BECAUSE HELL, NO ONE EVER SEEMS TO KNOW HOW MUCH TO TIP ANYBODY NOWADAYS.
HOBNOBBIN' WITH RODERICK KINGSLEY
FORWARD BY GENE SIMMONS

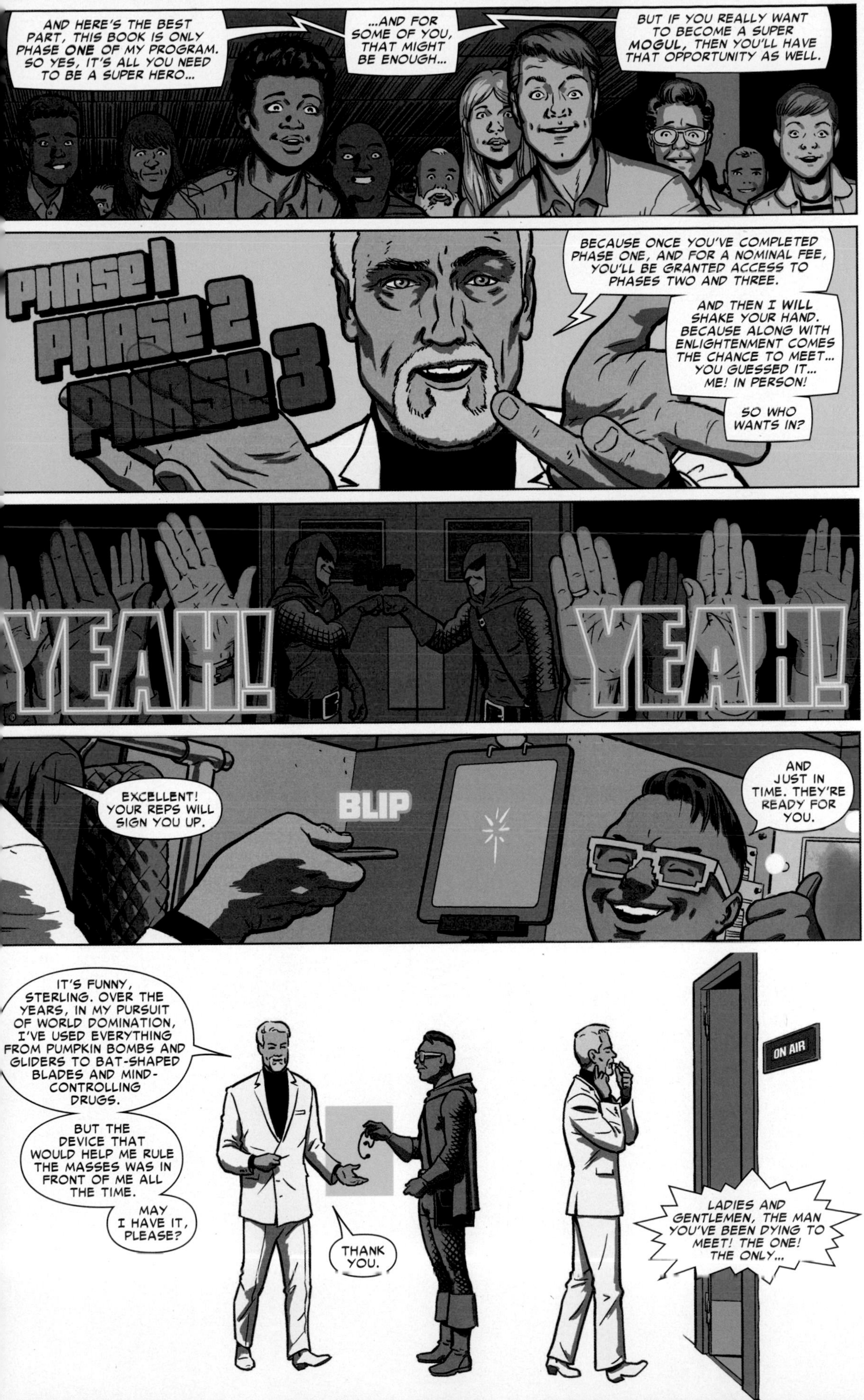
AND HERE'S THE BEST PART, THIS BOOK IS ONLY PHASE ONE OF MY PROGRAM. SO YES, IT'S ALL YOU NEED TO BE A SUPER HERO...
...AND FOR SOME OF YOU, THAT MIGHT BE ENOUGH...
BUT IF YOU REALLY WANT TO BECOME A SUPER MOGUL, THEN YOU'LL HAVE THAT OPPORTUNITY AS WELL.
PHASE 1
PHASE 2
PHASE 3
BECAUSE ONCE YOU'VE COMPLETED PHASE ONE, AND FOR A NOMINAL FEE, YOU'LL BE GRANTED ACCESS TO PHASES TWO AND THREE.
AND THEN I WILL SHAKE YOUR HAND. BECAUSE ALONG WITH ENLIGHTENMENT COMES THE CHANCE TO MEET... YOU GUESSED IT... ME! IN PERSON!
SO WHO WANTS IN?
YEAH!
YEAH!
EXCELLENT! YOUR REPS WILL SIGN YOU UP.
BLIP
AND JUST IN TIME. THEY'RE READY FOR YOU.
IT'S FUNNY, STERLING. OVER THE YEARS, IN MY PURSUIT OF WORLD DOMINATION, I'VE USED EVERYTHING FROM PUMPKIN BOMBS AND GLIDERS TO BAT-SHAPED BLADES AND MIND-CONTROLLING DRUGS.
BUT THE DEVICE THAT WOULD HELP ME RULE THE MASSES WAS IN FRONT OF ME ALL THE TIME.
MAY I HAVE IT, PLEASE?
THANK YOU.
ON AIR
LADIES AND GENTLEMEN, THE MAN YOU'VE BEEN DYING TO MEET! THE ONE! THE ONLY...

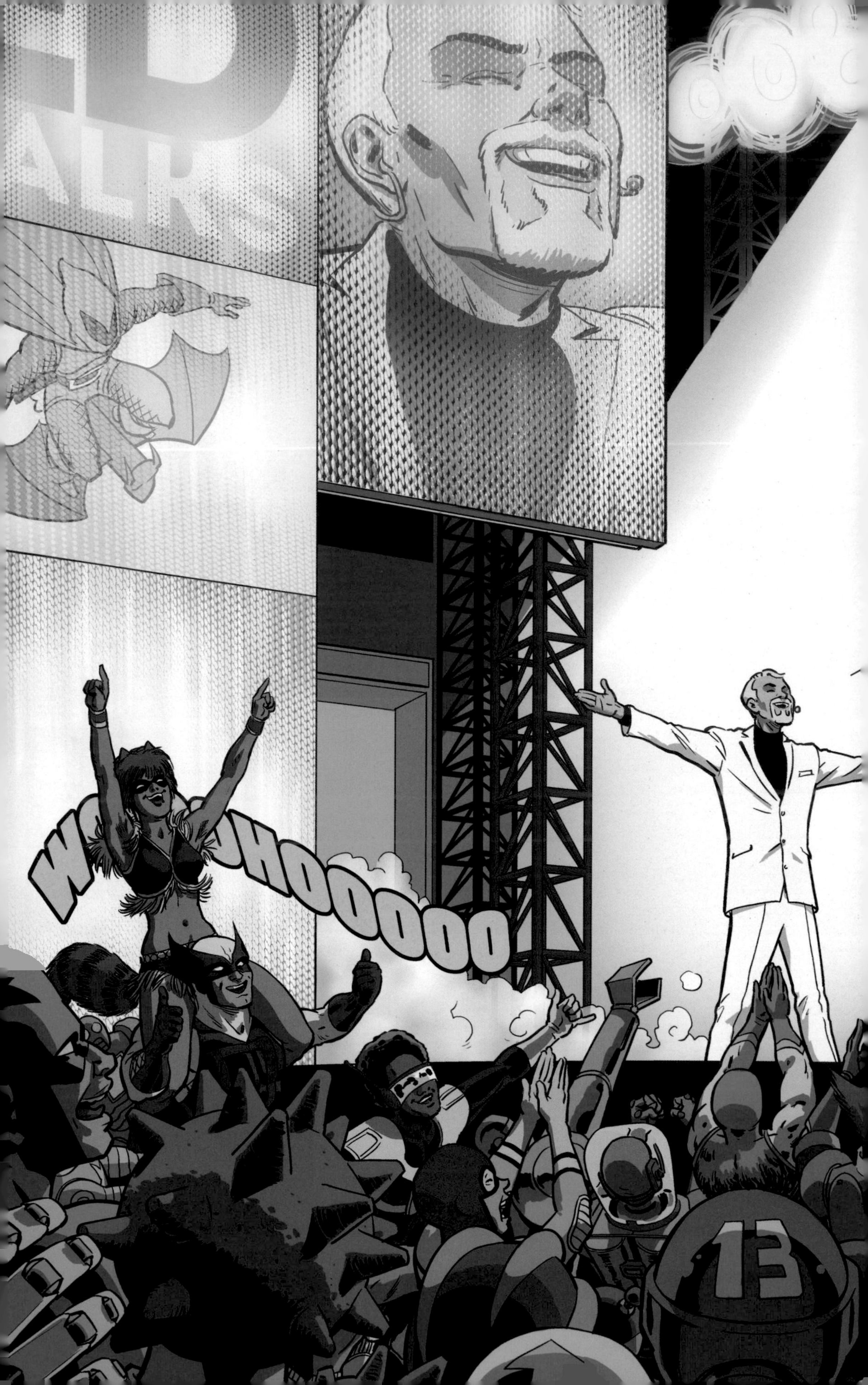
WOOOHOOOOOO

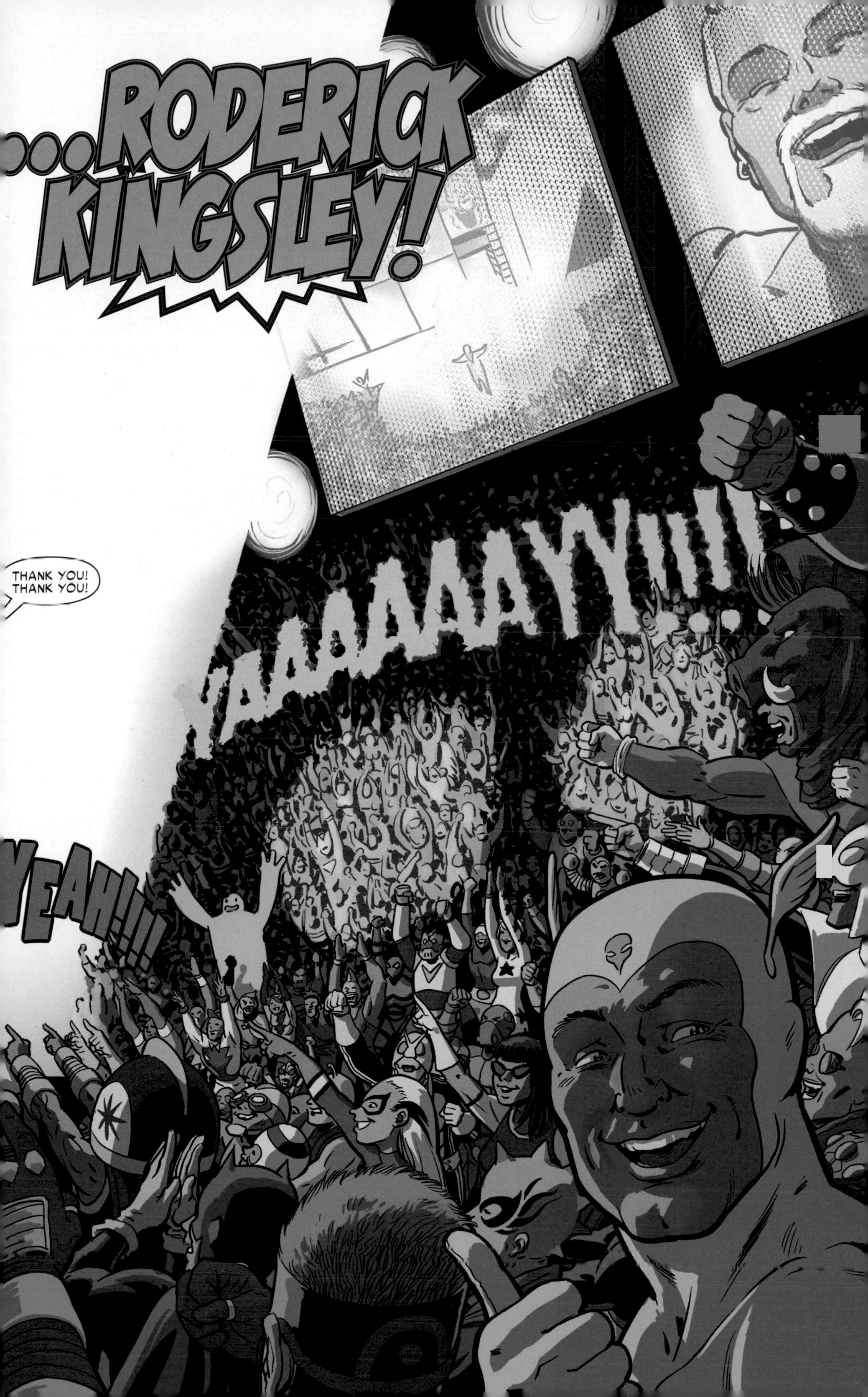
...RODERICK KINGSLEY!
THANK YOU! THANK YOU!
YAAAAAYY!!!!
YEAH!!!!

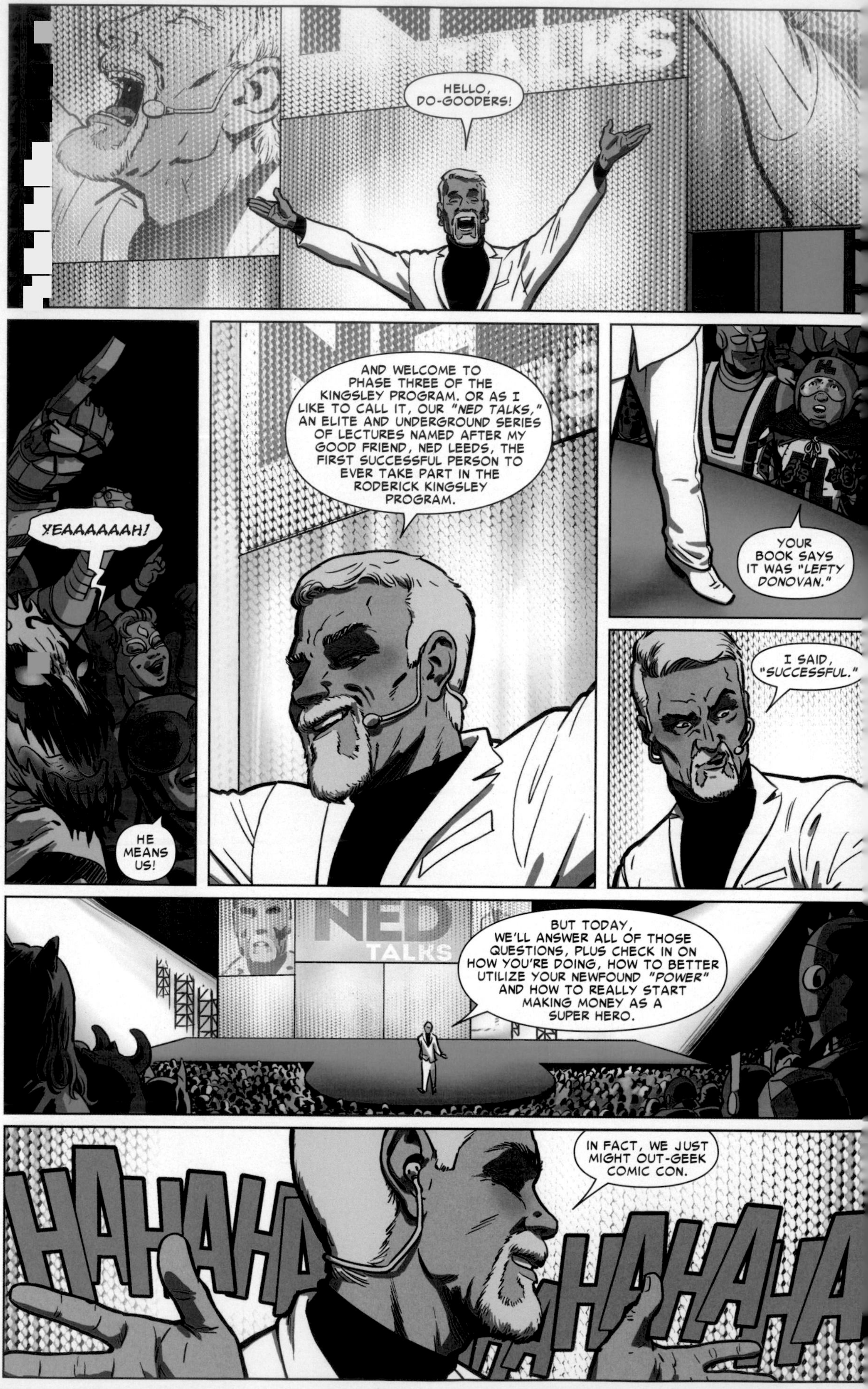
HELLO, DO-GOODERS!
YEAAAAAAH!
HE MEANS US!
AND WELCOME TO PHASE THREE OF THE KINGSLEY PROGRAM. OR AS I LIKE TO CALL IT, OUR "NED TALKS," AN ELITE AND UNDERGROUND SERIES OF LECTURES NAMED AFTER MY GOOD FRIEND, NED LEEDS, THE FIRST SUCCESSFUL PERSON TO EVER TAKE PART IN THE RODERICK KINGSLEY PROGRAM.
YOUR BOOK SAYS IT WAS "LEFTY DONOVAN."
I SAID, "SUCCESSFUL."
NED TALKS
BUT TODAY, WE'LL ANSWER ALL OF THOSE QUESTIONS, PLUS CHECK IN ON HOW YOU'RE DOING, HOW TO BETTER UTILIZE YOUR NEWFOUND "POWER" AND HOW TO REALLY START MAKING MONEY AS A SUPER HERO.
IN FACT, WE JUST MIGHT OUT-GEEK COMIC CON.
HAHAHA
HAHAHAHA

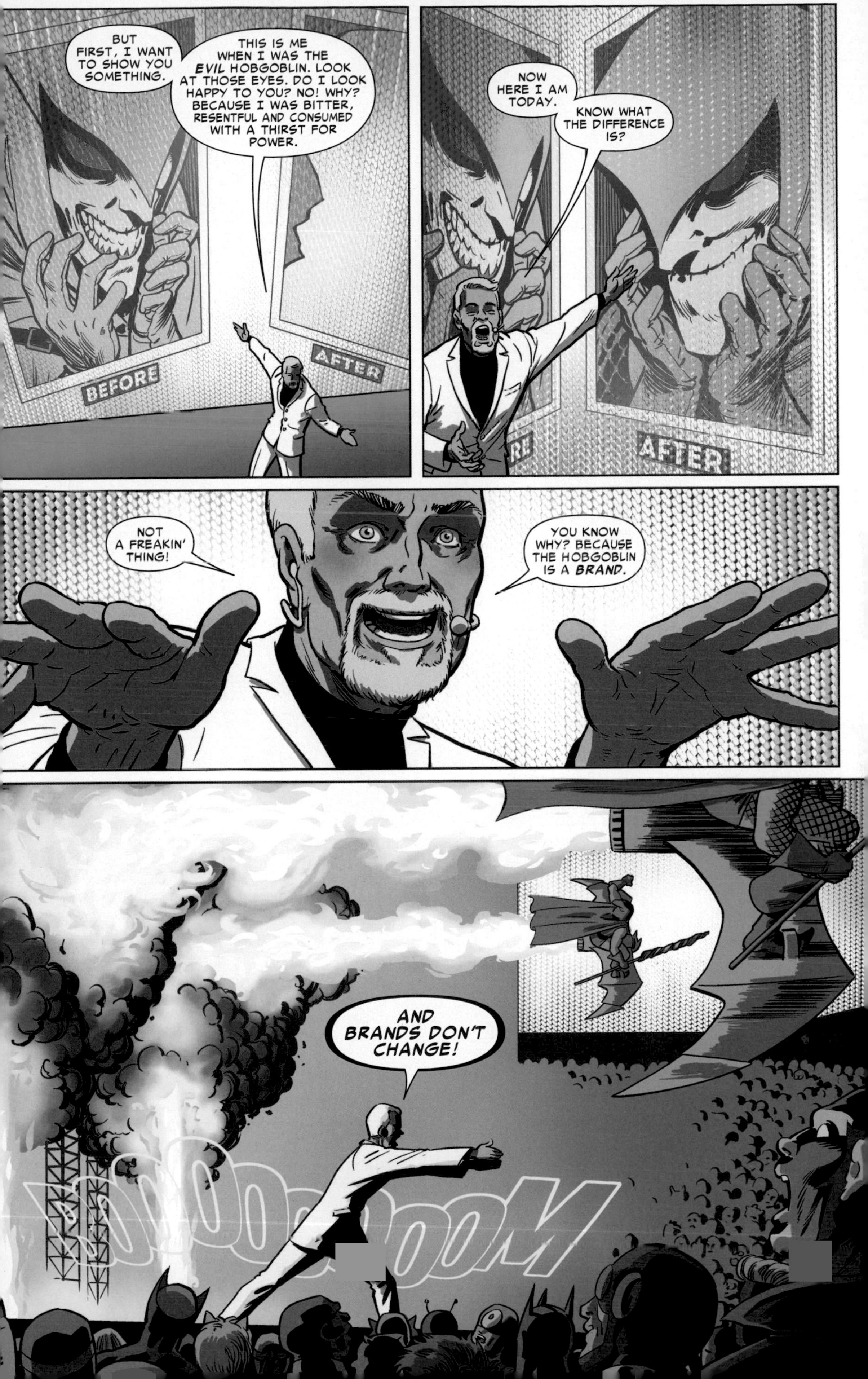
BUT FIRST, I WANT TO SHOW YOU SOMETHING.
THIS IS ME WHEN I WAS THE *EVIL* HOBGOBLIN. LOOK AT THOSE EYES. DO I LOOK HAPPY TO YOU? NO! WHY? BECAUSE I WAS BITTER, RESENTFUL AND CONSUMED WITH A THIRST FOR POWER.
BEFORE
AFTER
NOW HERE I AM TODAY.
KNOW WHAT THE DIFFERENCE IS?
AFTER
NOT A FREAKIN' THING!
YOU KNOW WHY? BECAUSE THE HOBGOBLIN IS A *BRAND*.
AND BRANDS DON'T CHANGE!

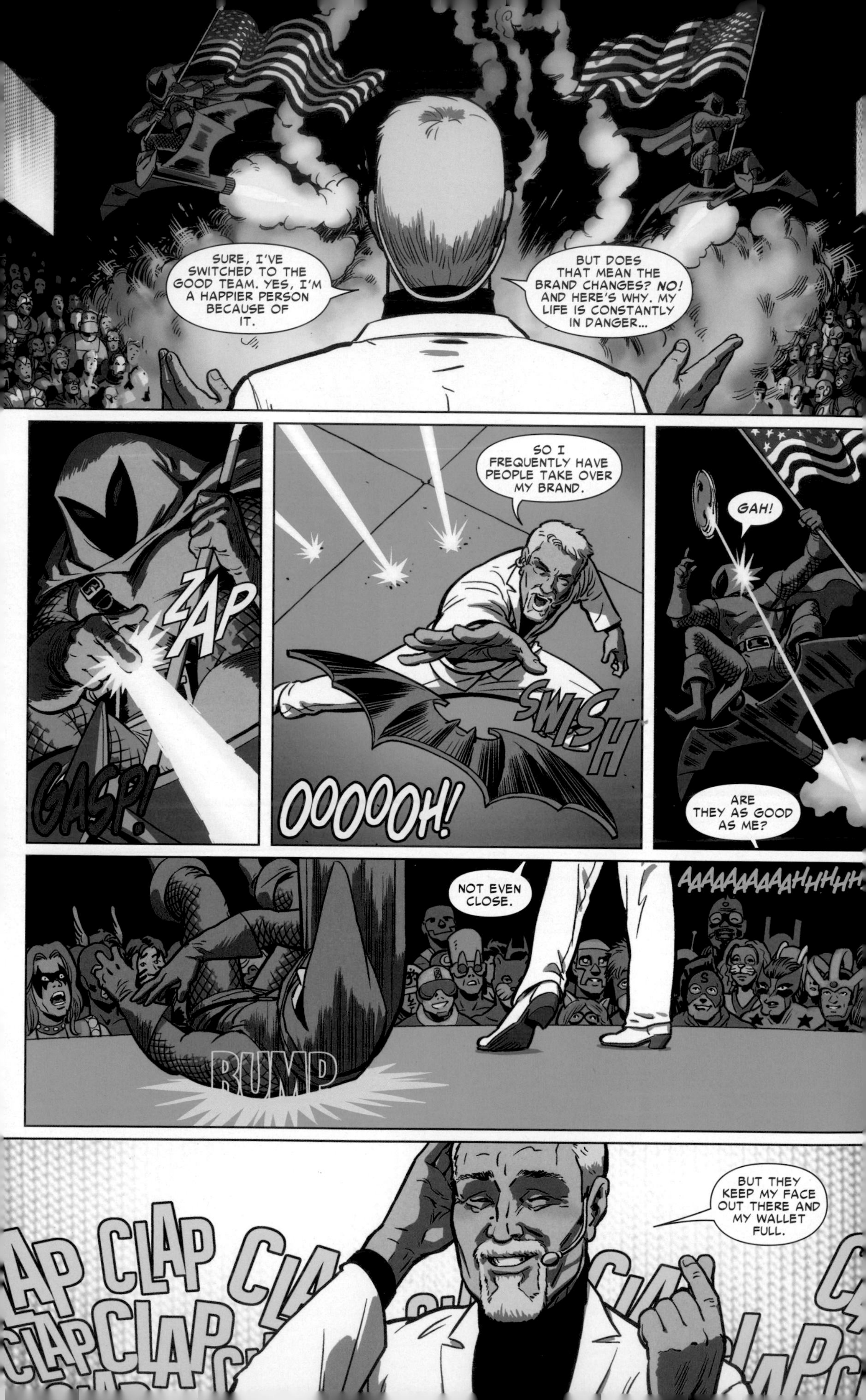
SURE, I'VE SWITCHED TO THE GOOD TEAM. YES, I'M A HAPPIER PERSON BECAUSE OF IT.
BUT DOES THAT MEAN THE BRAND CHANGES? NO! AND HERE'S WHY. MY LIFE IS CONSTANTLY IN DANGER...
ZAP
GASP!
SO I FREQUENTLY HAVE PEOPLE TAKE OVER MY BRAND.
SWISH
OOOOOH!
GAH!
ARE THEY AS GOOD AS ME?
NOT EVEN CLOSE.
AAAAAAAAAAHHHHH
BUMP
BUT THEY KEEP MY FACE OUT THERE AND MY WALLET FULL.
CLAP CLAP CLAP CLAP

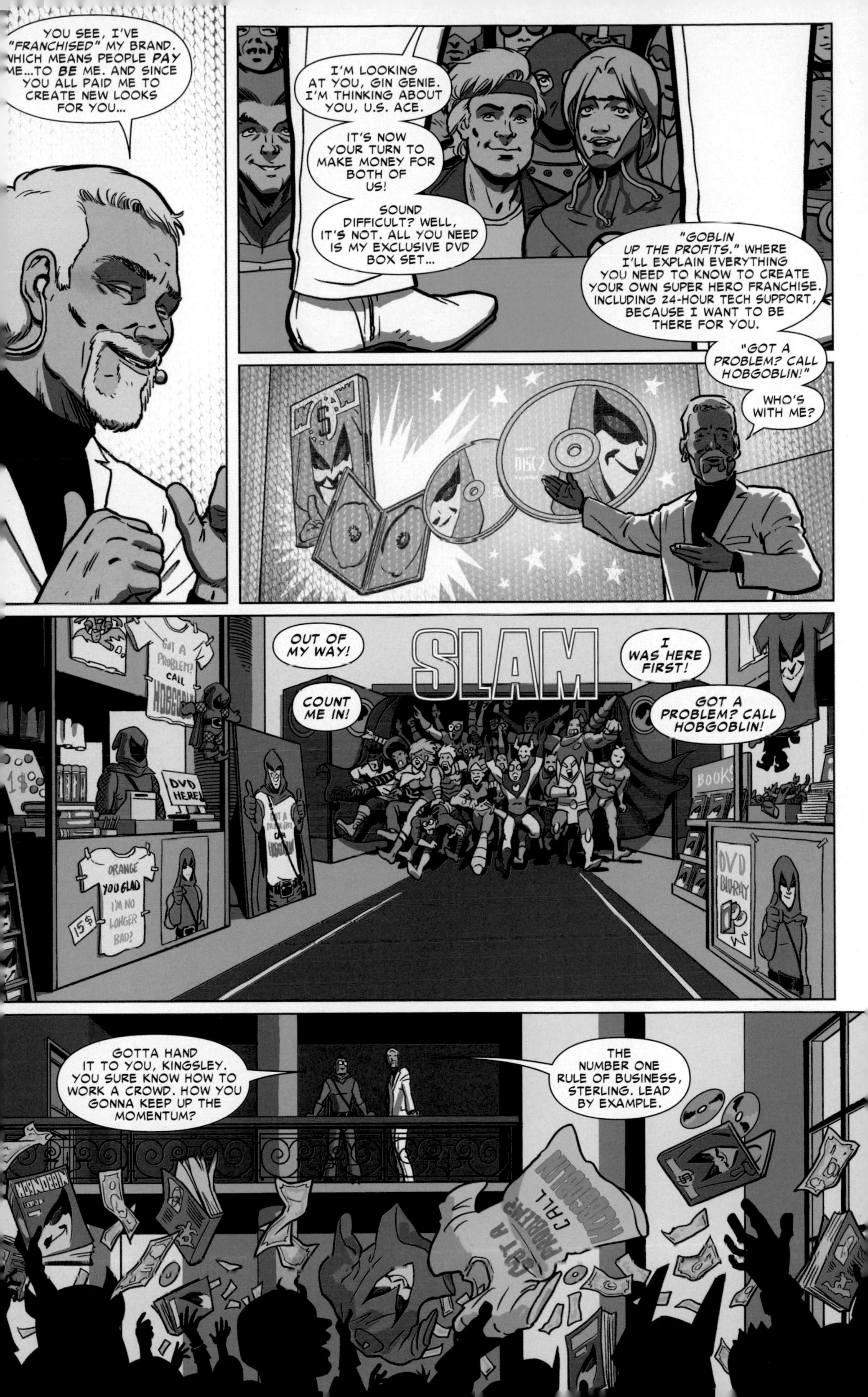
YOU SEE, I'VE "FRANCHISED" MY BRAND. WHICH MEANS PEOPLE PAY ME...TO BE ME. AND SINCE YOU ALL PAID ME TO CREATE NEW LOOKS FOR YOU...
I'M LOOKING AT YOU, GIN GENIE. I'M THINKING ABOUT YOU, U.S. ACE.
IT'S NOW YOUR TURN TO MAKE MONEY FOR BOTH OF US!
SOUND DIFFICULT? WELL, IT'S NOT. ALL YOU NEED IS MY EXCLUSIVE DVD BOX SET...
"GOBLIN UP THE PROFITS." WHERE I'LL EXPLAIN EVERYTHING YOU NEED TO KNOW TO CREATE YOUR OWN SUPER HERO FRANCHISE. INCLUDING 24-HOUR TECH SUPPORT, BECAUSE I WANT TO BE THERE FOR YOU.
"GOT A PROBLEM? CALL HOBGOBLIN!"
WHO'S WITH ME?
DISC 2
SLAM
OUT OF MY WAY!
I WAS HERE FIRST!
COUNT ME IN!
GOT A PROBLEM? CALL HOBGOBLIN!
GOT A PROBLEM? CALL HOBGOBLIN
1$
DVD HERE!
ORANGE YOU GLAD I'M NO LONGER BAD?
15$
BOOKS
DVD BLURAY
GOTTA HAND IT TO YOU, KINGSLEY. YOU SURE KNOW HOW TO WORK A CROWD. HOW YOU GONNA KEEP UP THE MOMENTUM?
THE NUMBER ONE RULE OF BUSINESS, STERLING. LEAD BY EXAMPLE.

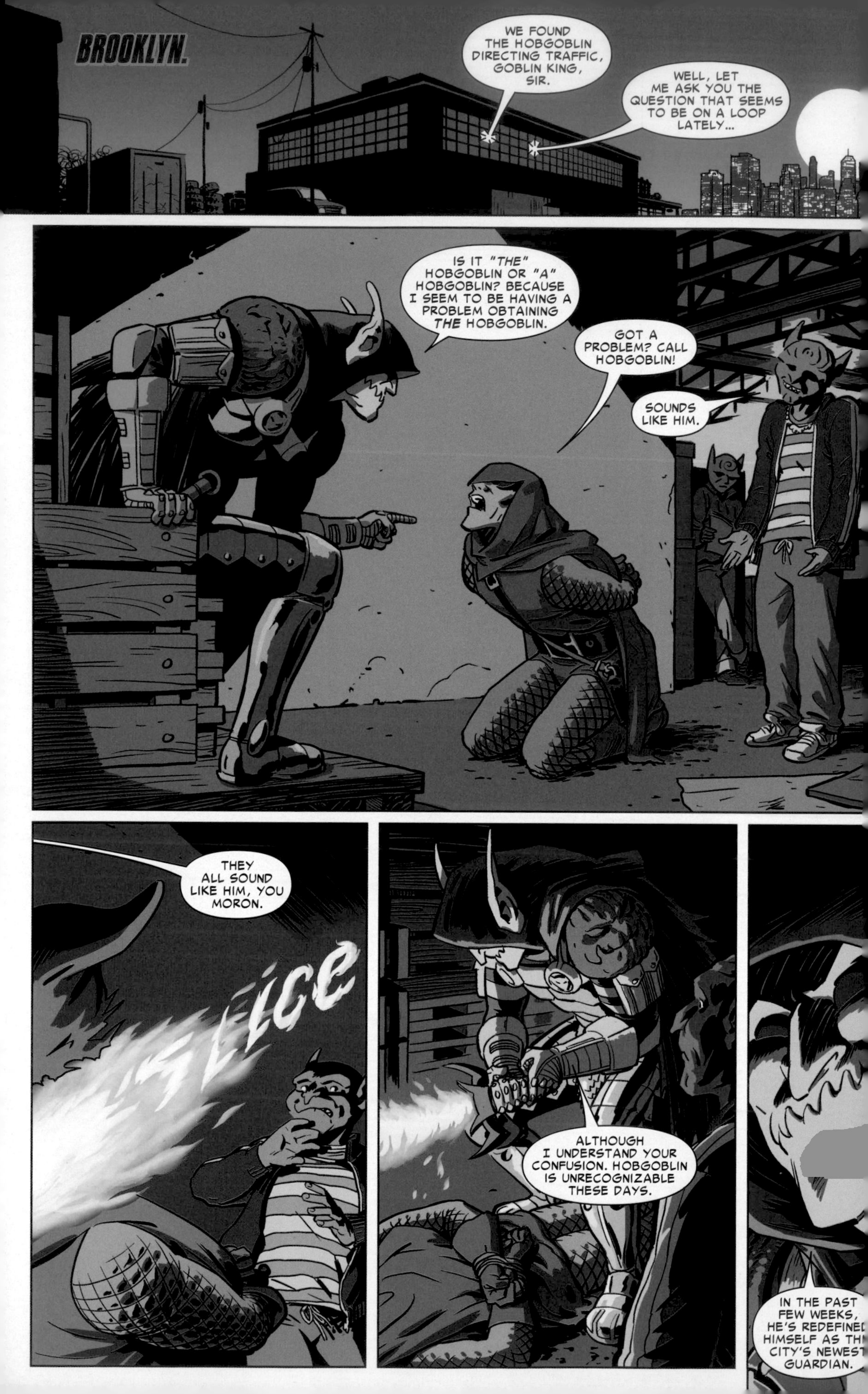
BROOKLYN.
WE FOUND THE HOBGOBLIN DIRECTING TRAFFIC, GOBLIN KING, SIR.
WELL, LET ME ASK YOU THE QUESTION THAT SEEMS TO BE ON A LOOP LATELY...
IS IT "THE" HOBGOBLIN OR "A" HOBGOBLIN? BECAUSE I SEEM TO BE HAVING A PROBLEM OBTAINING THE HOBGOBLIN.
GOT A PROBLEM? CALL HOBGOBLIN!
SOUNDS LIKE HIM.
THEY ALL SOUND LIKE HIM, YOU MORON.
ALTHOUGH I UNDERSTAND YOUR CONFUSION. HOBGOBLIN IS UNRECOGNIZABLE THESE DAYS.
IN THE PAST FEW WEEKS, HE'S REDEFINE HIMSELF AS TH CITY'S NEWEST GUARDIAN.

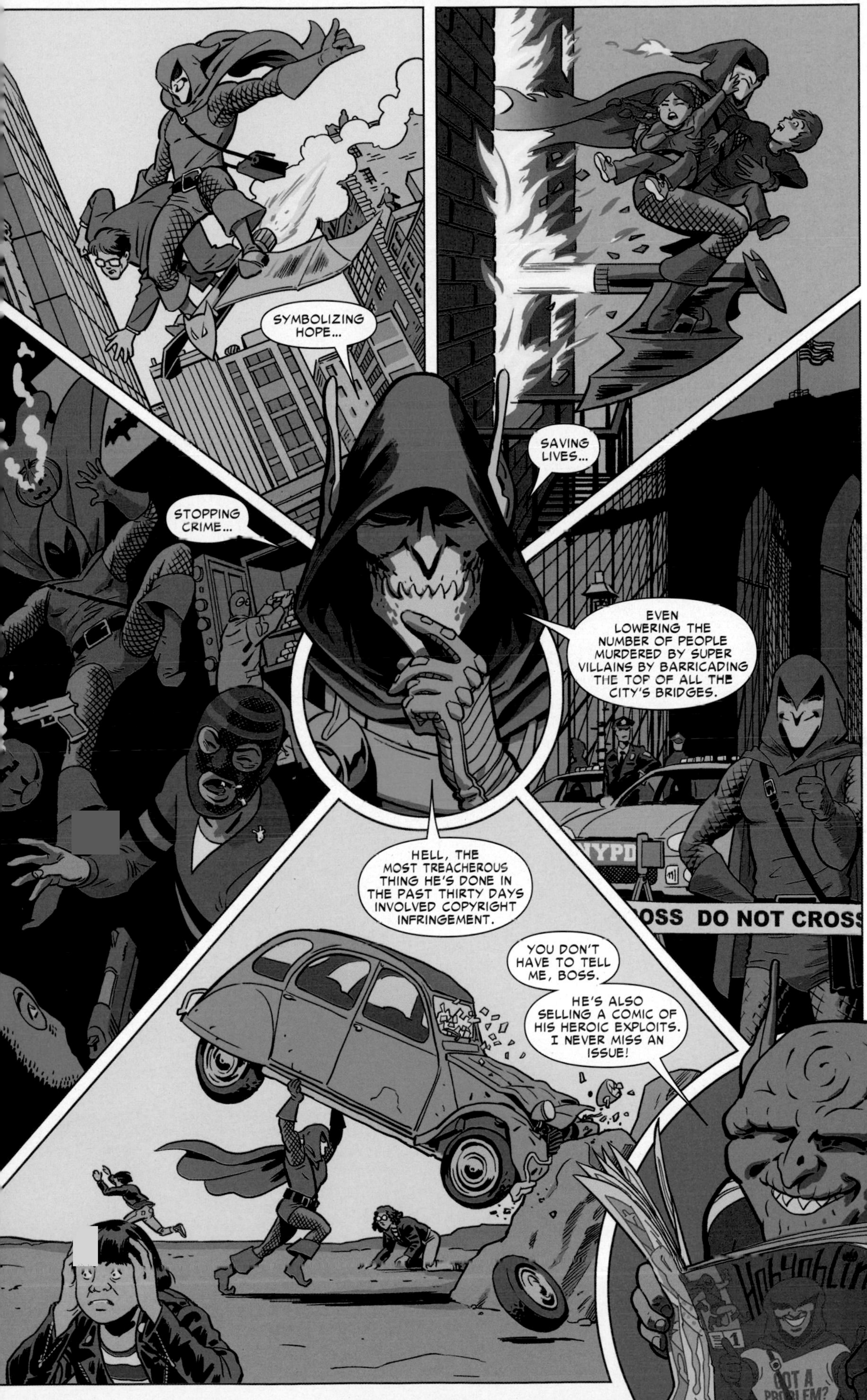
SYMBOLIZING HOPE...
SAVING LIVES...
STOPPING CRIME...
EVEN LOWERING THE NUMBER OF PEOPLE MURDERED BY SUPER VILLAINS BY BARRICADING THE TOP OF ALL THE CITY'S BRIDGES.
NYPD
DO NOT CROSS
HELL, THE MOST TREACHEROUS THING HE'S DONE IN THE PAST THIRTY DAYS INVOLVED COPYRIGHT INFRINGEMENT.
YOU DON'T HAVE TO TELL ME, BOSS.
HE'S ALSO SELLING A COMIC OF HIS HEROIC EXPLOITS. I NEVER MISS AN ISSUE!
GOT A PROBLEM?

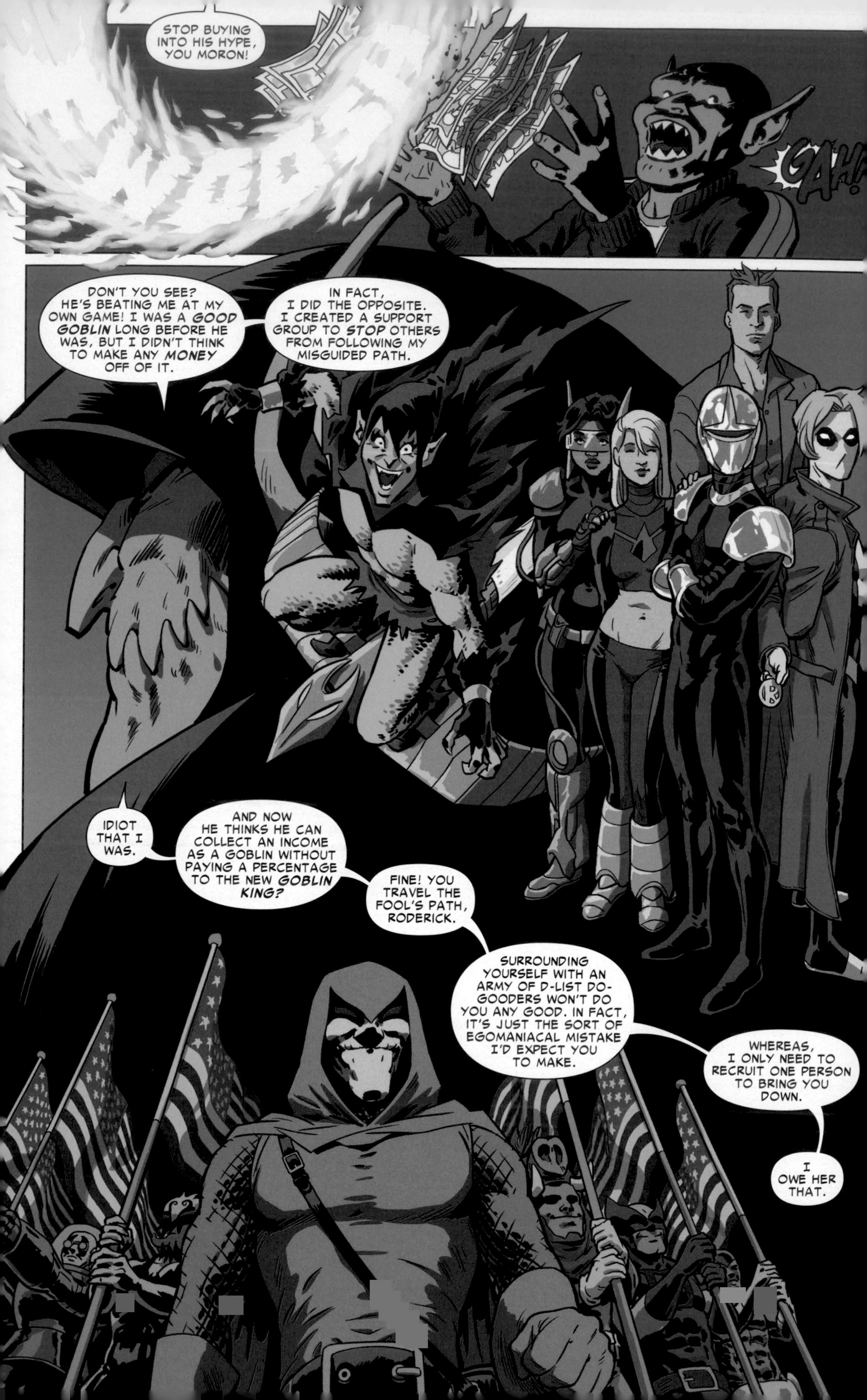
STOP BUYING INTO HIS HYPE, YOU MORON!
GAH!
DON'T YOU SEE? HE'S BEATING ME AT MY OWN GAME! I WAS A GOOD GOBLIN LONG BEFORE HE WAS, BUT I DIDN'T THINK TO MAKE ANY MONEY OFF OF IT.
IN FACT, I DID THE OPPOSITE. I CREATED A SUPPORT GROUP TO STOP OTHERS FROM FOLLOWING MY MISGUIDED PATH.
IDIOT THAT I WAS.
AND NOW HE THINKS HE CAN COLLECT AN INCOME AS A GOBLIN WITHOUT PAYING A PERCENTAGE TO THE NEW GOBLIN KING?
FINE! YOU TRAVEL THE FOOL'S PATH, RODERICK.
SURROUNDING YOURSELF WITH AN ARMY OF D-LIST DO-GOODERS WON'T DO YOU ANY GOOD. IN FACT, IT'S JUST THE SORT OF EGOMANIACAL MISTAKE I'D EXPECT YOU TO MAKE.
WHEREAS, I ONLY NEED TO RECRUIT ONE PERSON TO BRING YOU DOWN.
I OWE HER THAT.

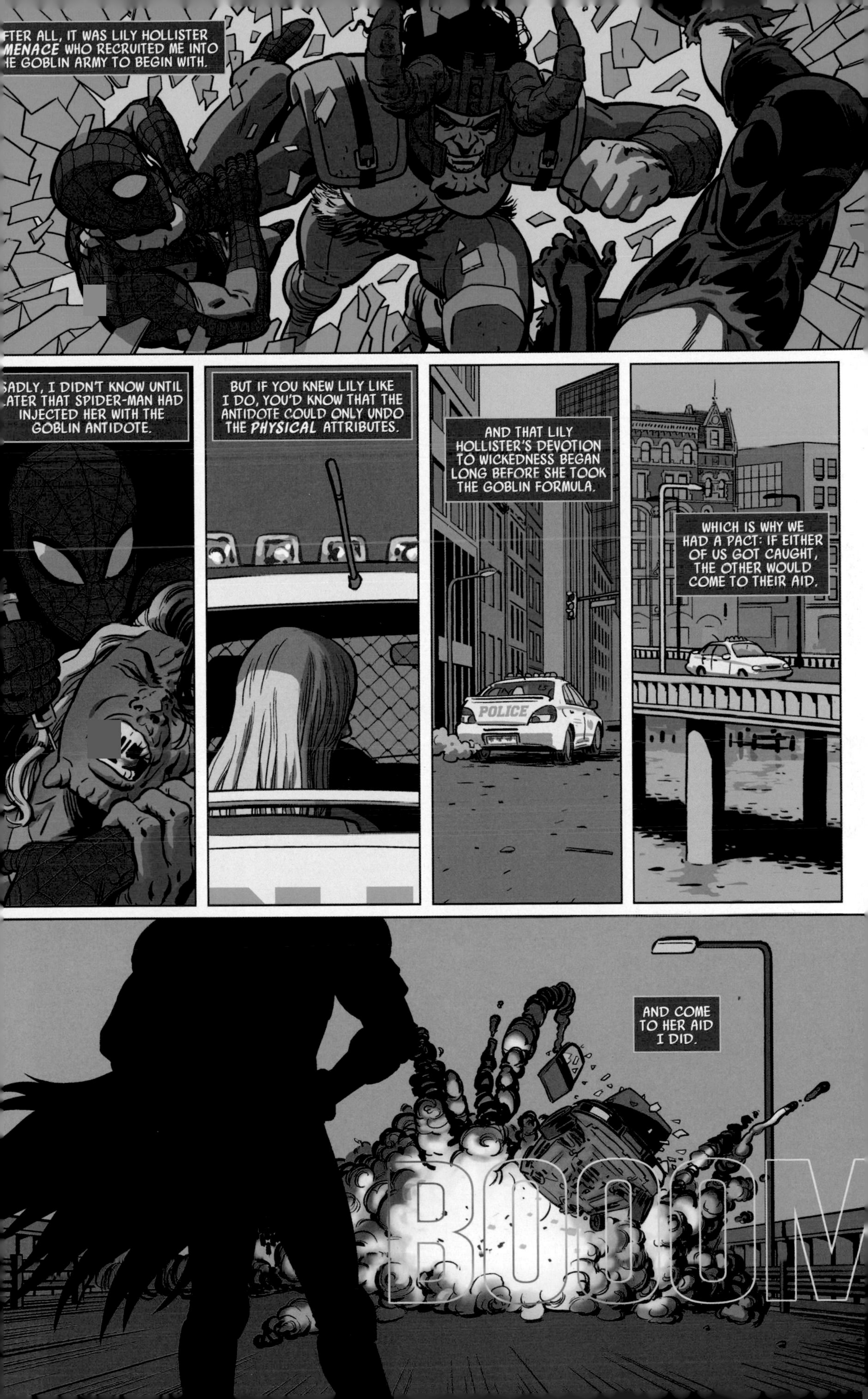

FTER ALL, IT WAS LILY HOLLISTER
MENACE WHO RECRUITED ME INTO
HE GOBLIN ARMY TO BEGIN WITH.
SADLY, I DIDN'T KNOW UNTIL
LATER THAT SPIDER-MAN HAD
INJECTED HER WITH THE
GOBLIN ANTIDOTE.
BUT IF YOU KNEW LILY LIKE I DO, YOU'D KNOW THAT THE ANTIDOTE COULD ONLY UNDO THE *PHYSICAL* ATTRIBUTES.
AND THAT LILY HOLLISTER'S DEVOTION TO WICKEDNESS BEGAN LONG BEFORE SHE TOOK THE GOBLIN FORMULA.
POLICE
WHICH IS WHY WE HAD A PACT: IF EITHER OF US GOT CAUGHT, THE OTHER WOULD COME TO THEIR AID.
AND COME TO HER AID I DID.
BOOOM

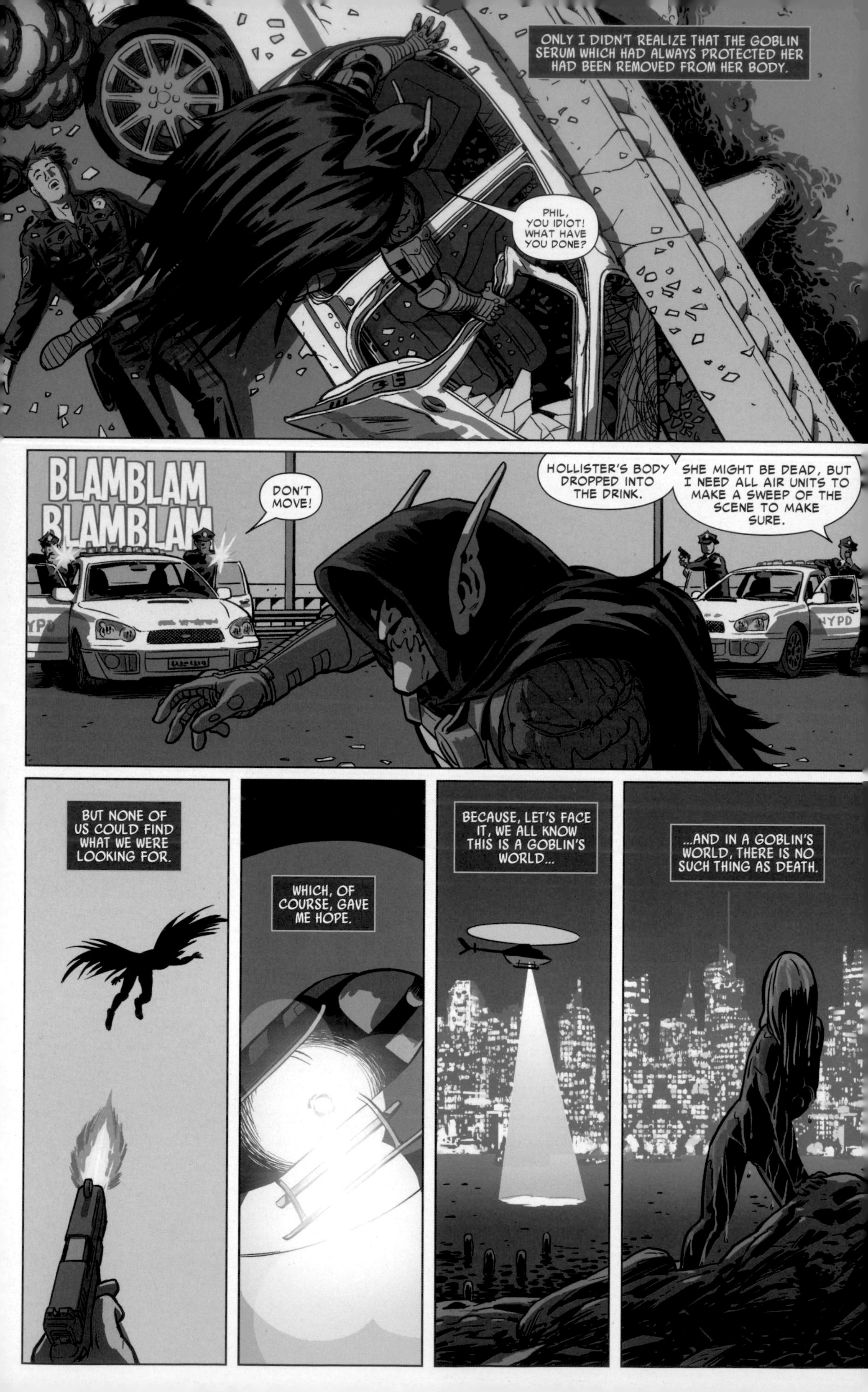
ONLY I DIDN'T REALIZE THAT THE GOBLIN SERUM WHICH HAD ALWAYS PROTECTED HER HAD BEEN REMOVED FROM HER BODY.
PHIL, YOU IDIOT! WHAT HAVE YOU DONE?
BLAMBLAM BLAMBLAM
DON'T MOVE!
HOLLISTER'S BODY DROPPED INTO THE DRINK.
SHE MIGHT BE DEAD, BUT I NEED ALL AIR UNITS TO MAKE A SWEEP OF THE SCENE TO MAKE SURE.
NYPD
NYPD
BUT NONE OF US COULD FIND WHAT WE WERE LOOKING FOR.
WHICH, OF COURSE, GAVE ME HOPE.
BECAUSE, LET'S FACE IT, WE ALL KNOW THIS IS A GOBLIN'S WORLD...
...AND IN A GOBLIN'S WORLD, THERE IS NO SUCH THING AS DEATH.

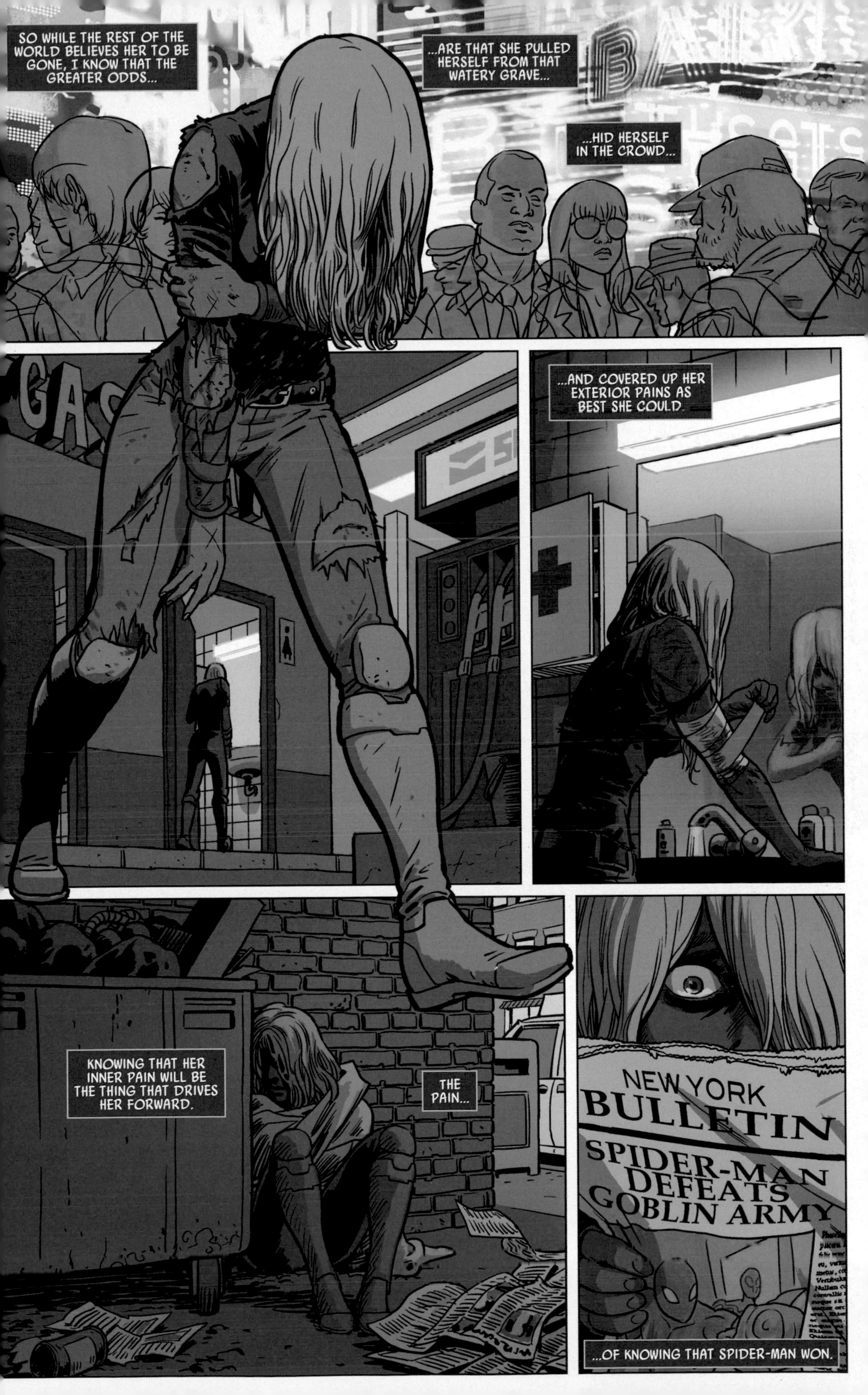
SO WHILE THE REST OF THE WORLD BELIEVES HER TO BE GONE, I KNOW THAT THE GREATER ODDS...
...ARE THAT SHE PULLED HERSELF FROM THAT WATERY GRAVE...
...HID HERSELF IN THE CROWD...
GAS
...AND COVERED UP HER EXTERIOR PAINS AS BEST SHE COULD.
KNOWING THAT HER INNER PAIN WILL BE THE THING THAT DRIVES HER FORWARD.
THE PAIN...
NEW YORK BULLETIN
SPIDER-MAN DEFEATS GOBLIN ARMY
...OF KNOWING THAT SPIDER-MAN WON.

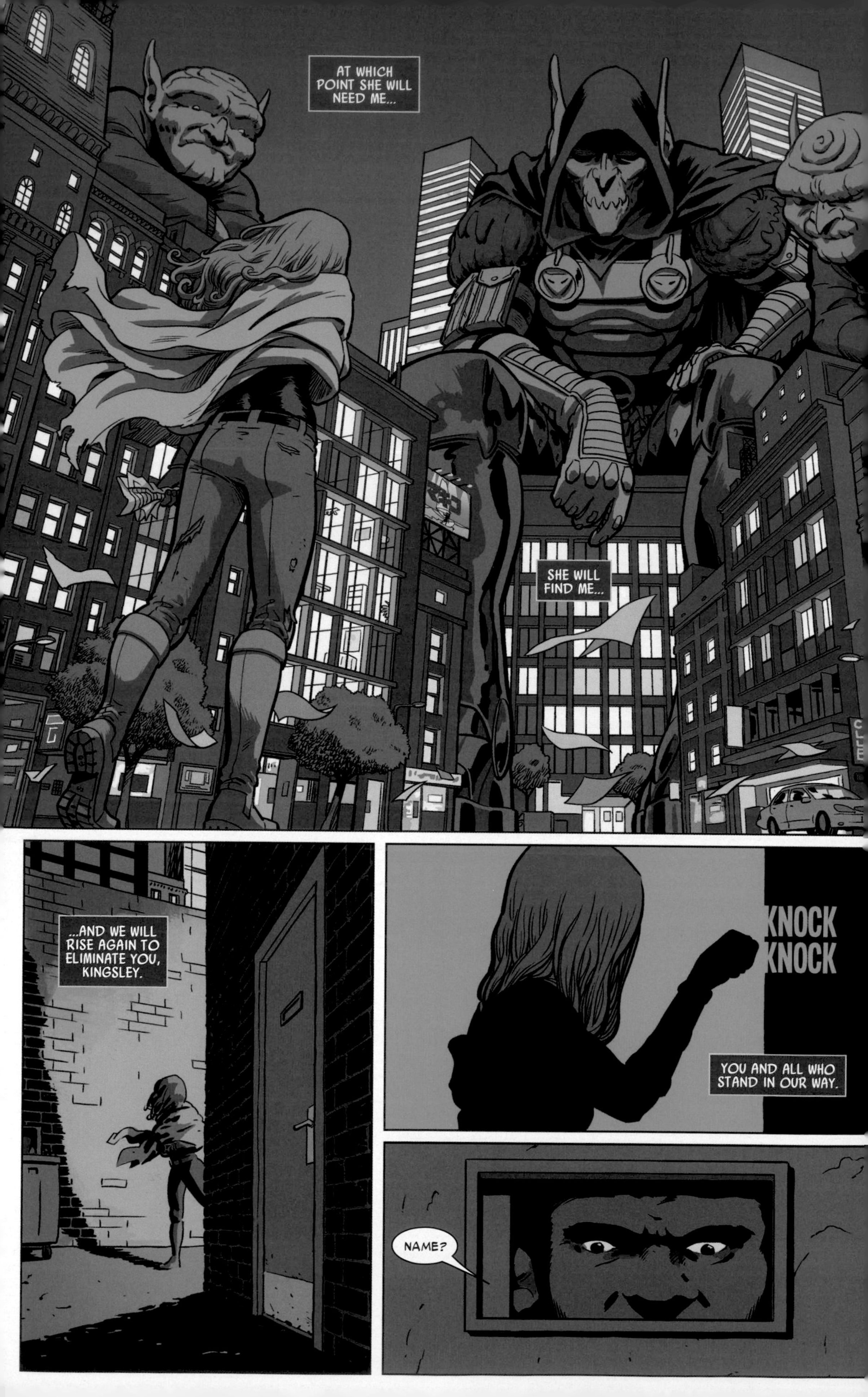
AT WHICH POINT SHE WILL NEED ME...
SHE WILL FIND ME...
...AND WE WILL RISE AGAIN TO ELIMINATE YOU, KINGSLEY.
KNOCK KNOCK
YOU AND ALL WHO STAND IN OUR WAY.
NAME?

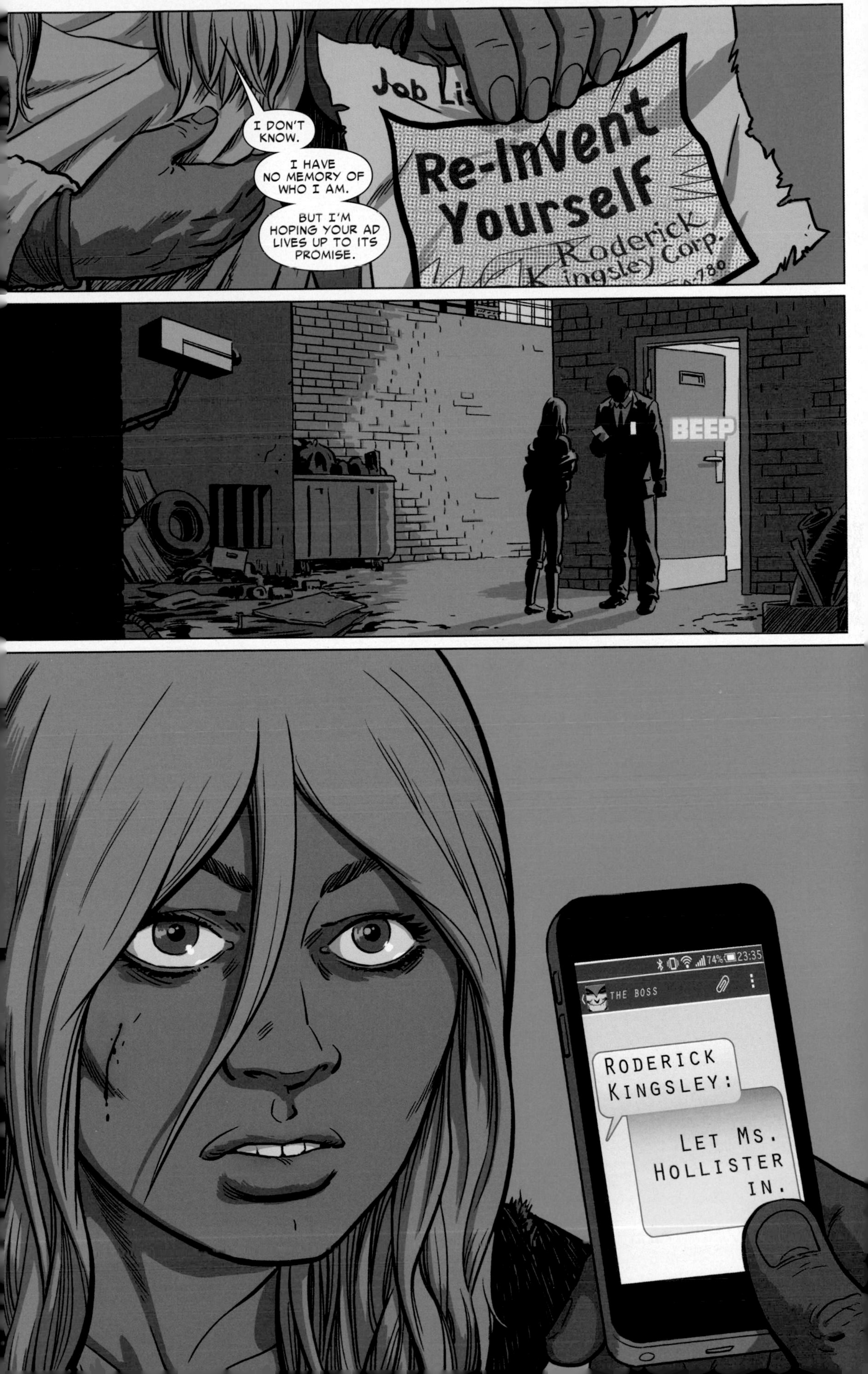
I DON'T KNOW.
I HAVE NO MEMORY OF WHO I AM.
BUT I'M HOPING YOUR AD LIVES UP TO ITS PROMISE.
Job Lis
Re-Invent Yourself
Roderick Kingsley Corp.
BEEP
THE BOSS
RODERICK KINGSLEY:
LET MS. HOLLISTER IN.

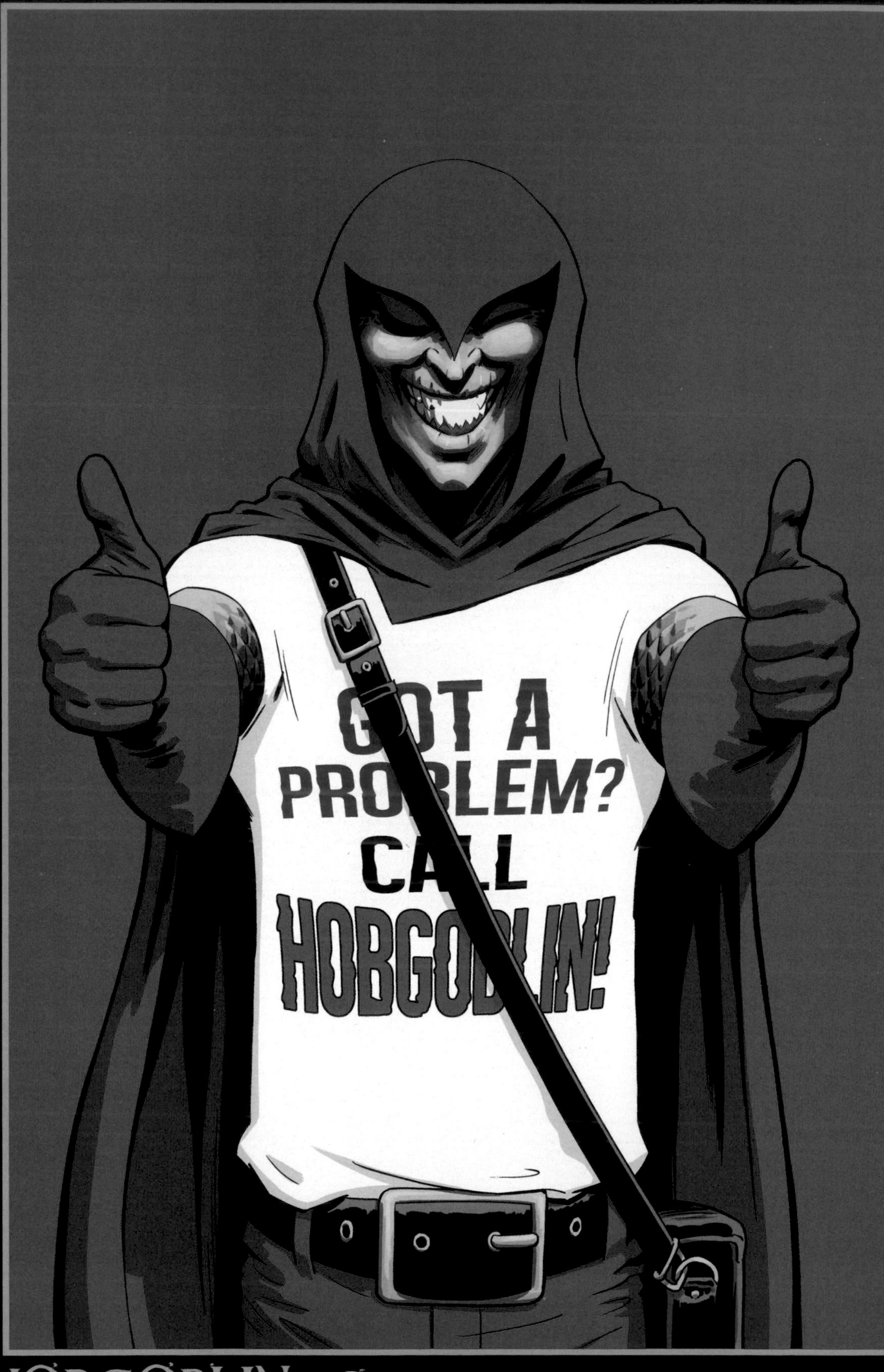
GOT A
PROBLEM?
CALL
HOBGOBLIN!

HOBGOBLIN #2

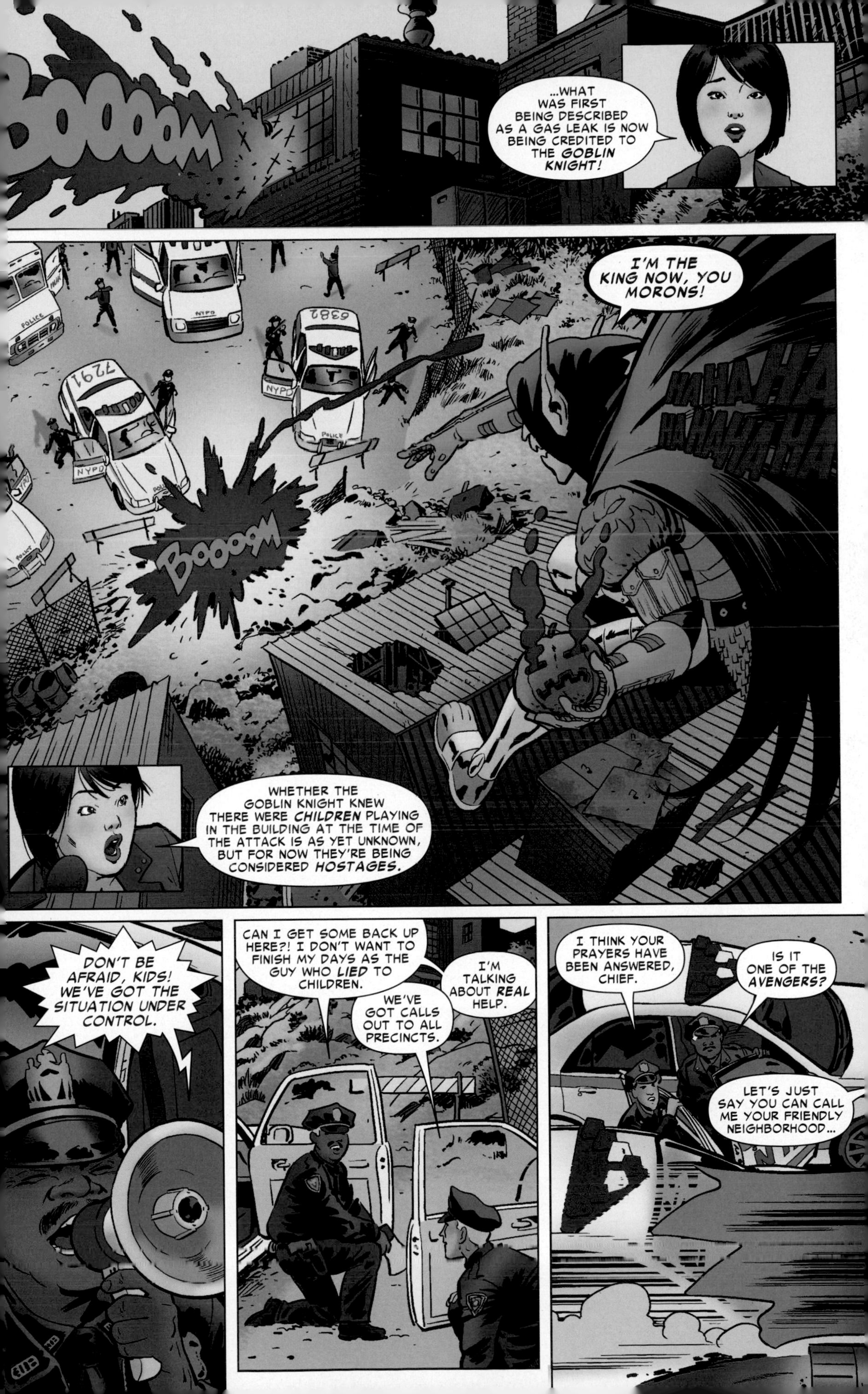
BOOOOOM
...WHAT WAS FIRST BEING DESCRIBED AS A GAS LEAK IS NOW BEING CREDITED TO THE GOBLIN KNIGHT!
I'M THE KING NOW, YOU MORONS!
HAHAHA HAHAHAHA
BOOOOM
WHETHER THE GOBLIN KNIGHT KNEW THERE WERE CHILDREN PLAYING IN THE BUILDING AT THE TIME OF THE ATTACK IS AS YET UNKNOWN, BUT FOR NOW THEY'RE BEING CONSIDERED HOSTAGES.
DON'T BE AFRAID, KIDS! WE'VE GOT THE SITUATION UNDER CONTROL.
CAN I GET SOME BACK UP HERE?! I DON'T WANT TO FINISH MY DAYS AS THE GUY WHO LIED TO CHILDREN.
WE'VE GOT CALLS OUT TO ALL PRECINCTS.
I'M TALKING ABOUT REAL HELP.
I THINK YOUR PRAYERS HAVE BEEN ANSWERED, CHIEF.
IS IT ONE OF THE AVENGERS?
LET'S JUST SAY YOU CAN CALL ME YOUR FRIENDLY NEIGHBORHOOD...

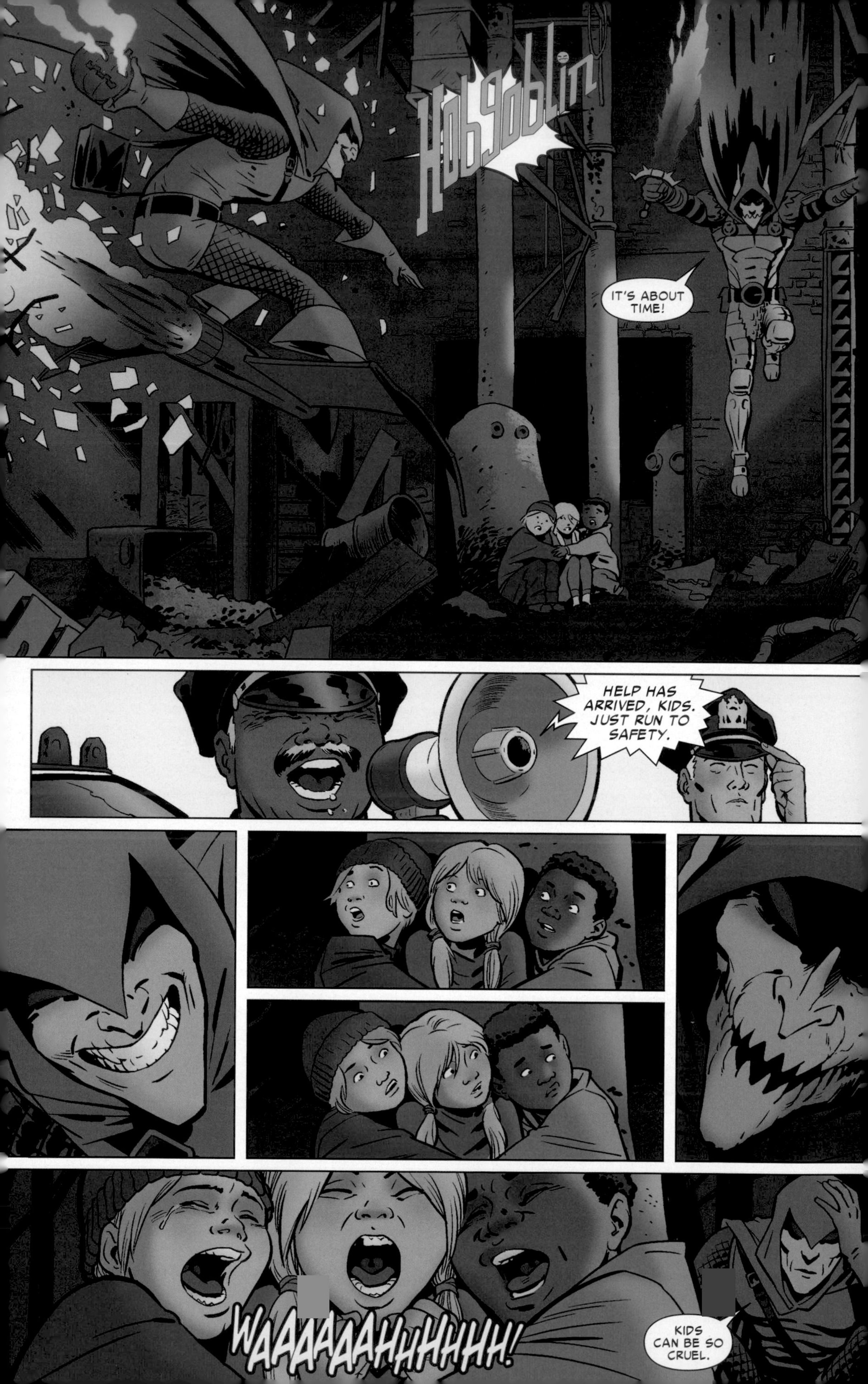
HOBGOBLIN
IT'S ABOUT TIME!
HELP HAS ARRIVED, KIDS. JUST RUN TO SAFETY.
WAAAAAAHHHHHH!
KIDS CAN BE SO CRUEL.

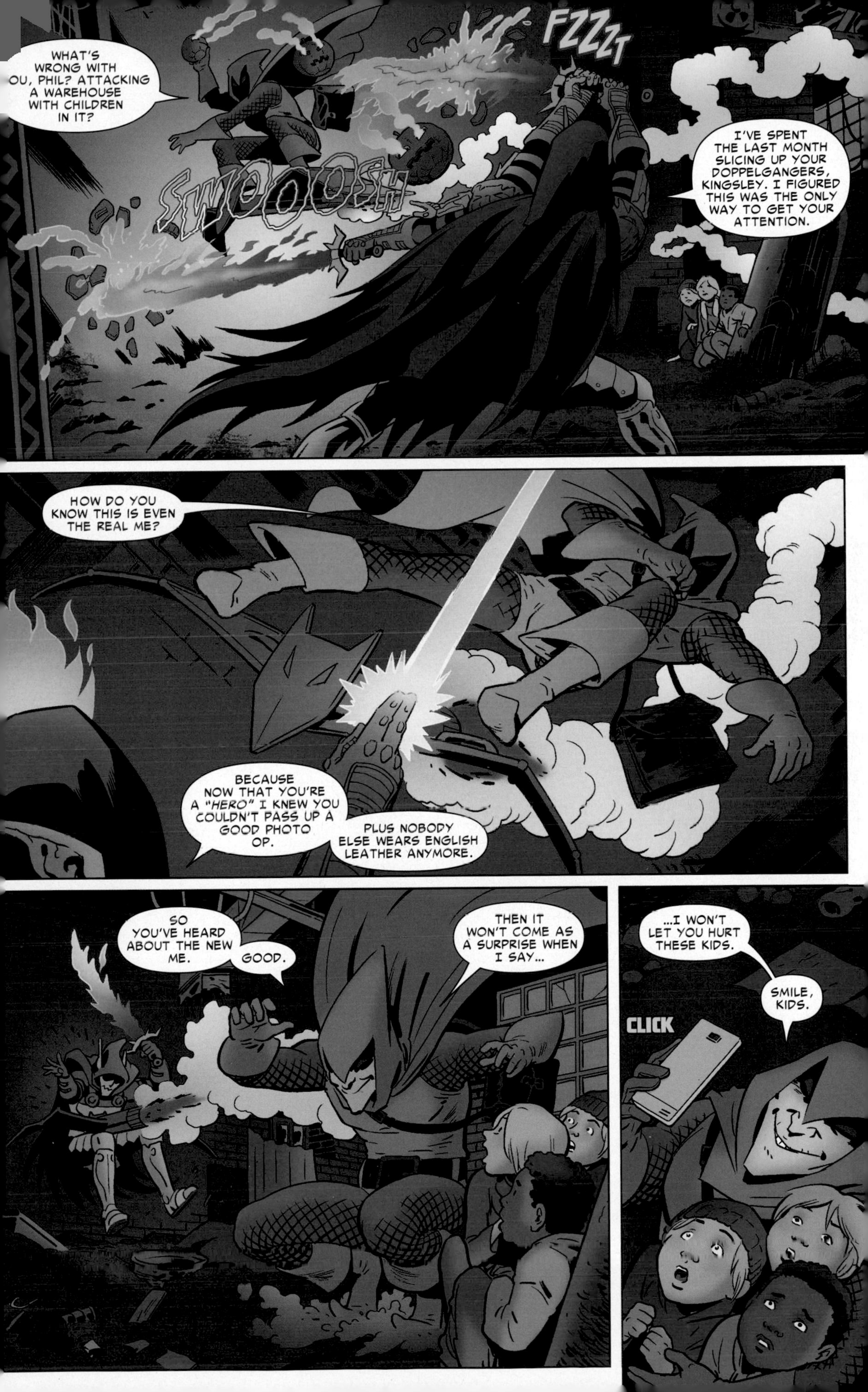

WHAT'S WRONG WITH OU, PHIL? ATTACKING A WAREHOUSE WITH CHILDREN IN IT?
FZZZT
SWOOOSH
I'VE SPENT THE LAST MONTH SLICING UP YOUR DOPPELGANGERS, KINGSLEY. I FIGURED THIS WAS THE ONLY WAY TO GET YOUR ATTENTION.
HOW DO YOU KNOW THIS IS EVEN THE REAL ME?
BECAUSE NOW THAT YOU'RE A "HERO" I KNEW YOU COULDN'T PASS UP A GOOD PHOTO OP.
PLUS NOBODY ELSE WEARS ENGLISH LEATHER ANYMORE.
SO YOU'VE HEARD ABOUT THE NEW ME.
GOOD.
THEN IT WON'T COME AS A SURPRISE WHEN I SAY...
...I WON'T LET YOU HURT THESE KIDS.
SMILE, KIDS.
CLICK

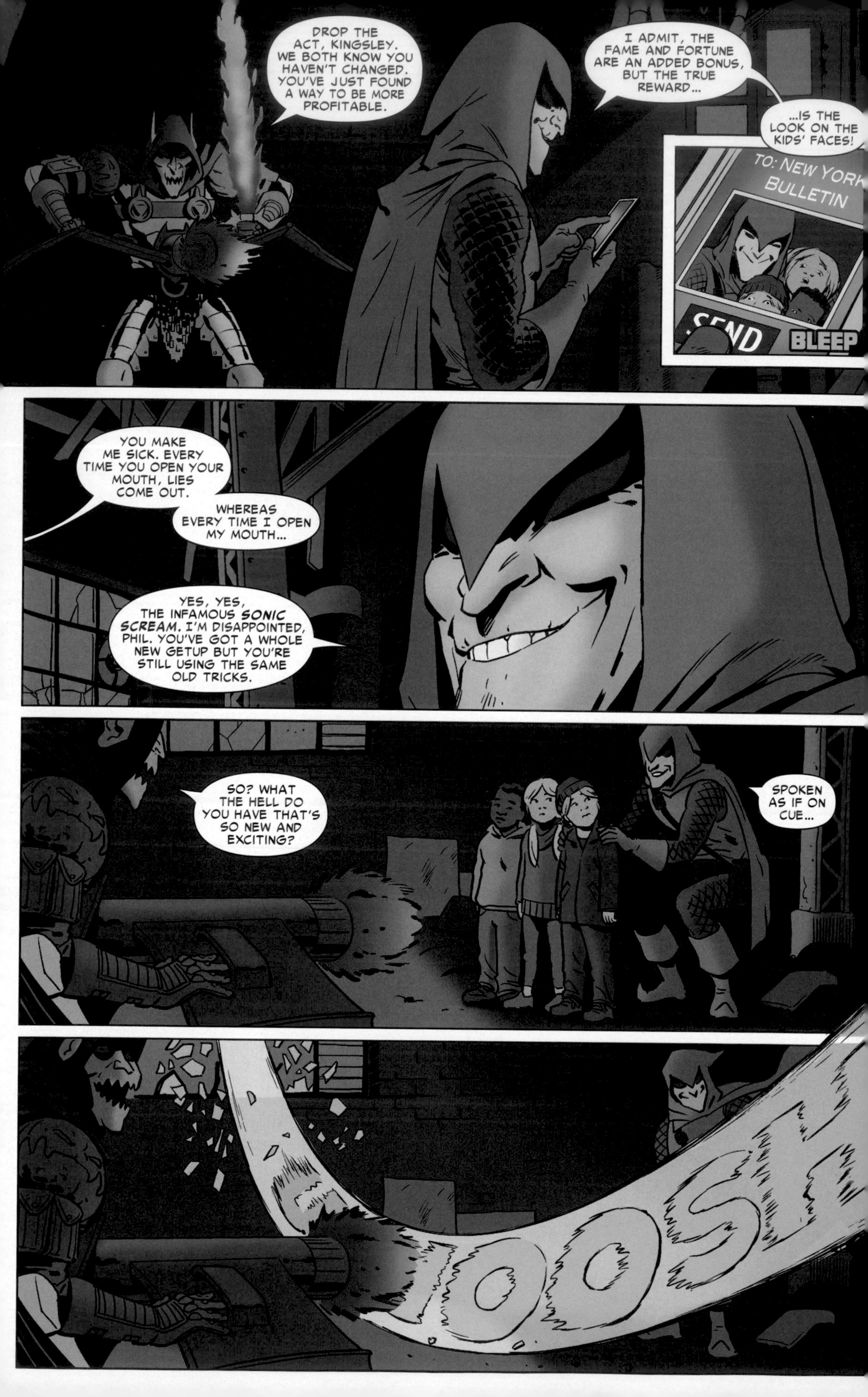
DROP THE ACT, KINGSLEY. WE BOTH KNOW YOU HAVEN'T CHANGED. YOU'VE JUST FOUND A WAY TO BE MORE PROFITABLE.
I ADMIT, THE FAME AND FORTUNE ARE AN ADDED BONUS, BUT THE TRUE REWARD...
...IS THE LOOK ON THE KIDS' FACES!
TO: NEW YORK BULLETIN
SEND
BLEEP
YOU MAKE ME SICK. EVERY TIME YOU OPEN YOUR MOUTH, LIES COME OUT.
WHEREAS EVERY TIME I OPEN MY MOUTH...
YES, YES, THE INFAMOUS **SONIC SCREAM**. I'M DISAPPOINTED, PHIL. YOU'VE GOT A WHOLE NEW GETUP BUT YOU'RE STILL USING THE SAME OLD TRICKS.
SO? WHAT THE HELL DO YOU HAVE THAT'S SO NEW AND EXCITING?
SPOKEN AS IF ON CUE...
WOOOSH

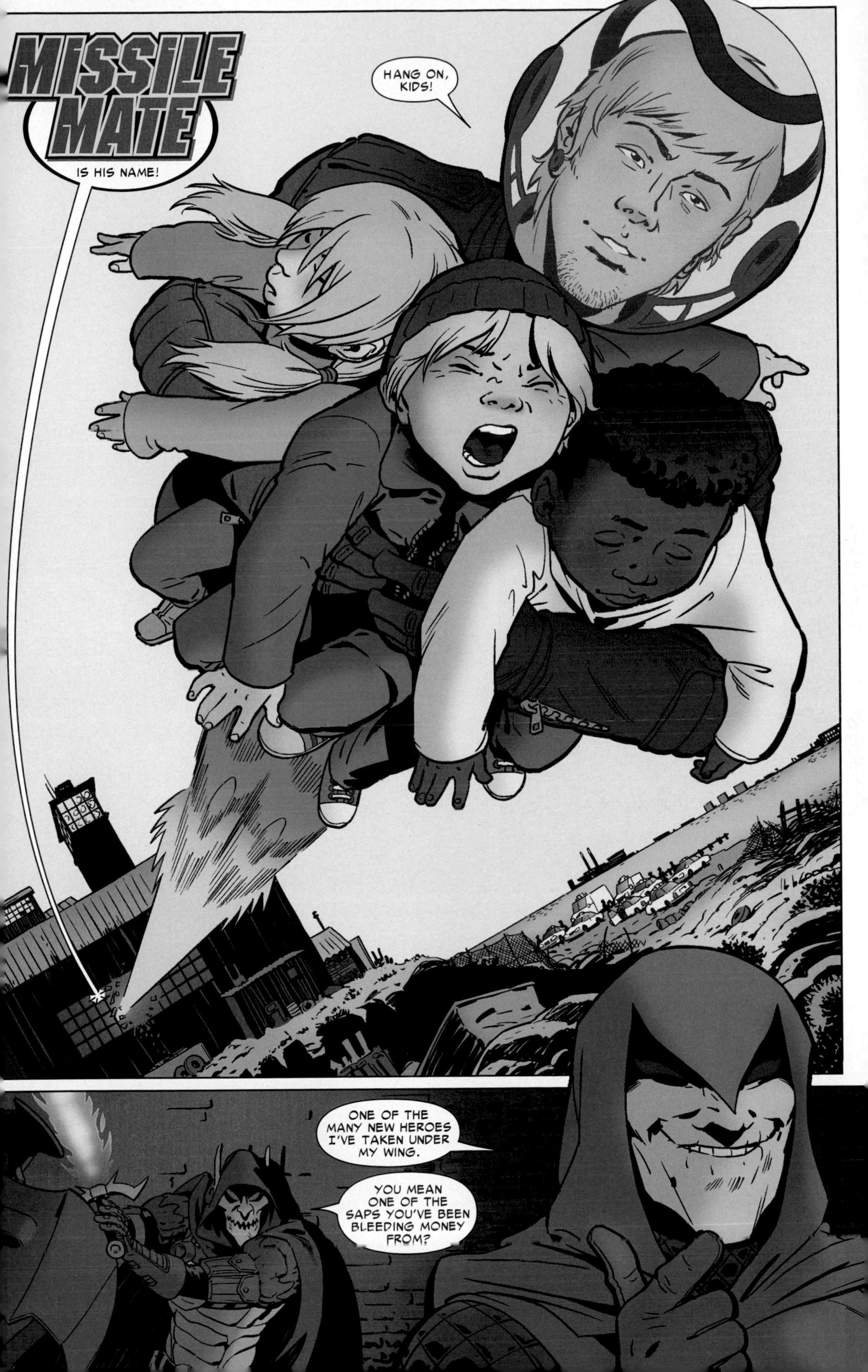
MISSILE MATE
IS HIS NAME!
HANG ON, KIDS!
ONE OF THE MANY NEW HEROES I'VE TAKEN UNDER MY WING.
YOU MEAN ONE OF THE SAPS YOU'VE BEEN BLEEDING MONEY FROM?

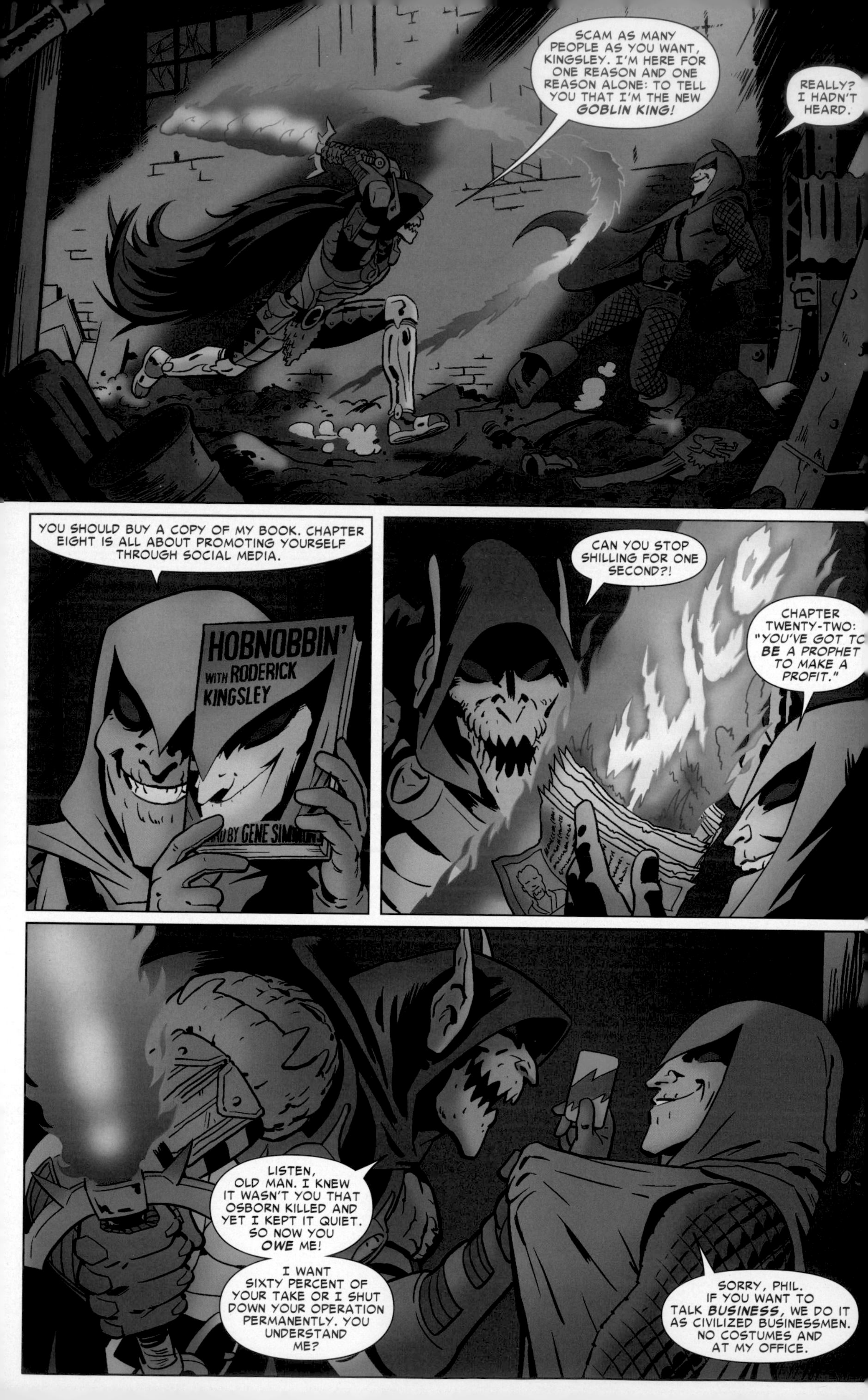
SCAM AS MANY PEOPLE AS YOU WANT, KINGSLEY. I'M HERE FOR ONE REASON AND ONE REASON ALONE: TO TELL YOU THAT I'M THE NEW GOBLIN KING!
REALLY? I HADN'T HEARD.
YOU SHOULD BUY A COPY OF MY BOOK. CHAPTER EIGHT IS ALL ABOUT PROMOTING YOURSELF THROUGH SOCIAL MEDIA.
HOBNOBBIN' WITH RODERICK KINGSLEY
CAN YOU STOP SHILLING FOR ONE SECOND?!
CHAPTER TWENTY-TWO: "YOU'VE GOT TO BE A PROPHET TO MAKE A PROFIT."
LISTEN, OLD MAN. I KNEW IT WASN'T YOU THAT OSBORN KILLED AND YET I KEPT IT QUIET. SO NOW YOU OWE ME!
I WANT SIXTY PERCENT OF YOUR TAKE OR I SHUT DOWN YOUR OPERATION PERMANENTLY. YOU UNDERSTAND ME?
SORRY, PHIL. IF YOU WANT TO TALK BUSINESS, WE DO IT AS CIVILIZED BUSINESSMEN. NO COSTUMES AND AT MY OFFICE.

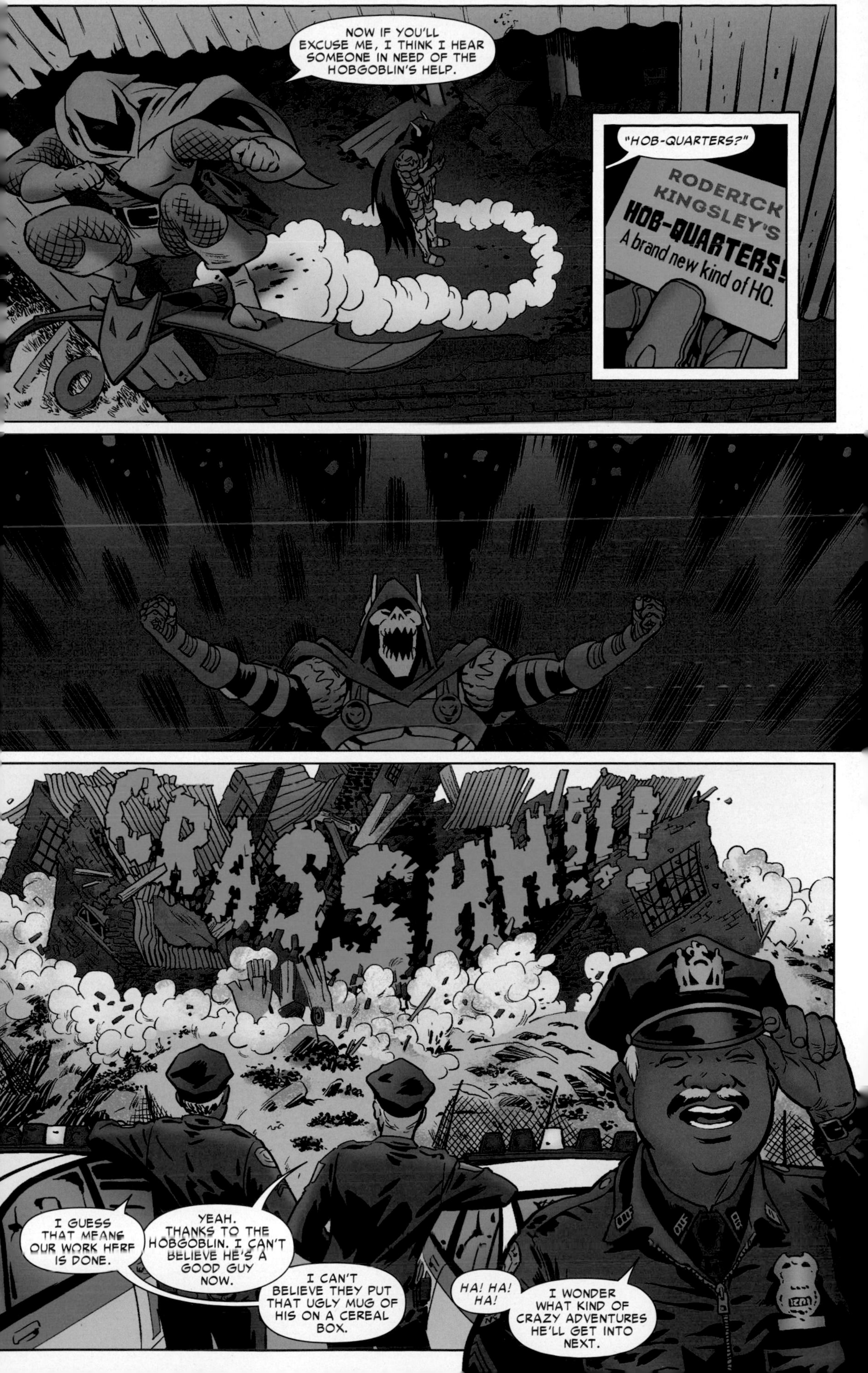

NOW IF YOU'LL EXCUSE ME, I THINK I HEAR SOMEONE IN NEED OF THE HOBGOBLIN'S HELP.
"HOB-QUARTERS?"
RODERICK KINGSLEY'S HOB-QUARTERS! A brand new kind of HQ.
CRASSH!!!
I GUESS THAT MEANS OUR WORK HERE IS DONE.
YEAH. THANKS TO THE HOBGOBLIN. I CAN'T BELIEVE HE'S A GOOD GUY NOW.
I CAN'T BELIEVE THEY PUT THAT UGLY MUG OF HIS ON A CEREAL BOX.
HA! HA! HA!
I WONDER WHAT KIND OF CRAZY ADVENTURES HE'LL GET INTO NEXT.

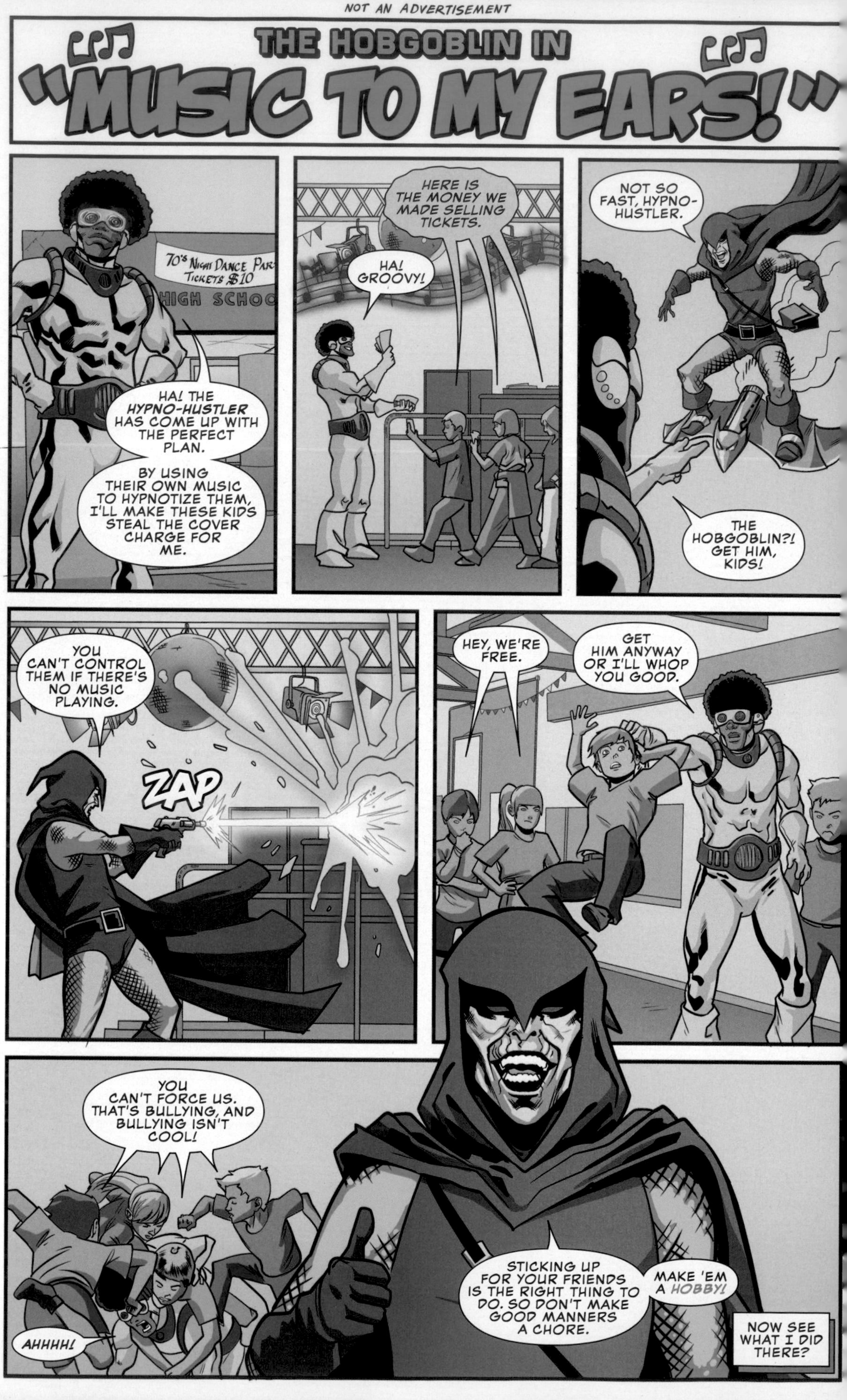
THE HOBGOBLIN IN
"MUSIC TO MY EARS!"
70's Night Dance Party Tickets $10
HIGH SCHOO
HA! THE HYPNO-HUSTLER HAS COME UP WITH THE PERFECT PLAN.
BY USING THEIR OWN MUSIC TO HYPNOTIZE THEM, I'LL MAKE THESE KIDS STEAL THE COVER CHARGE FOR ME.
HERE IS THE MONEY WE MADE SELLING TICKETS.
HA! GROOVY!
NOT SO FAST, HYPNO-HUSTLER.
THE HOBGOBLIN?! GET HIM, KIDS!
YOU CAN'T CONTROL THEM IF THERE'S NO MUSIC PLAYING.
ZAP
HEY, WE'RE FREE.
GET HIM ANYWAY OR I'LL WHOP YOU GOOD.
YOU CAN'T FORCE US. THAT'S BULLYING, AND BULLYING ISN'T COOL!
AHHHH!
STICKING UP FOR YOUR FRIENDS IS THE RIGHT THING TO DO. SO DON'T MAKE GOOD MANNERS A CHORE.
MAKE 'EM A HOBBY!
NOW SEE WHAT I DID THERE?

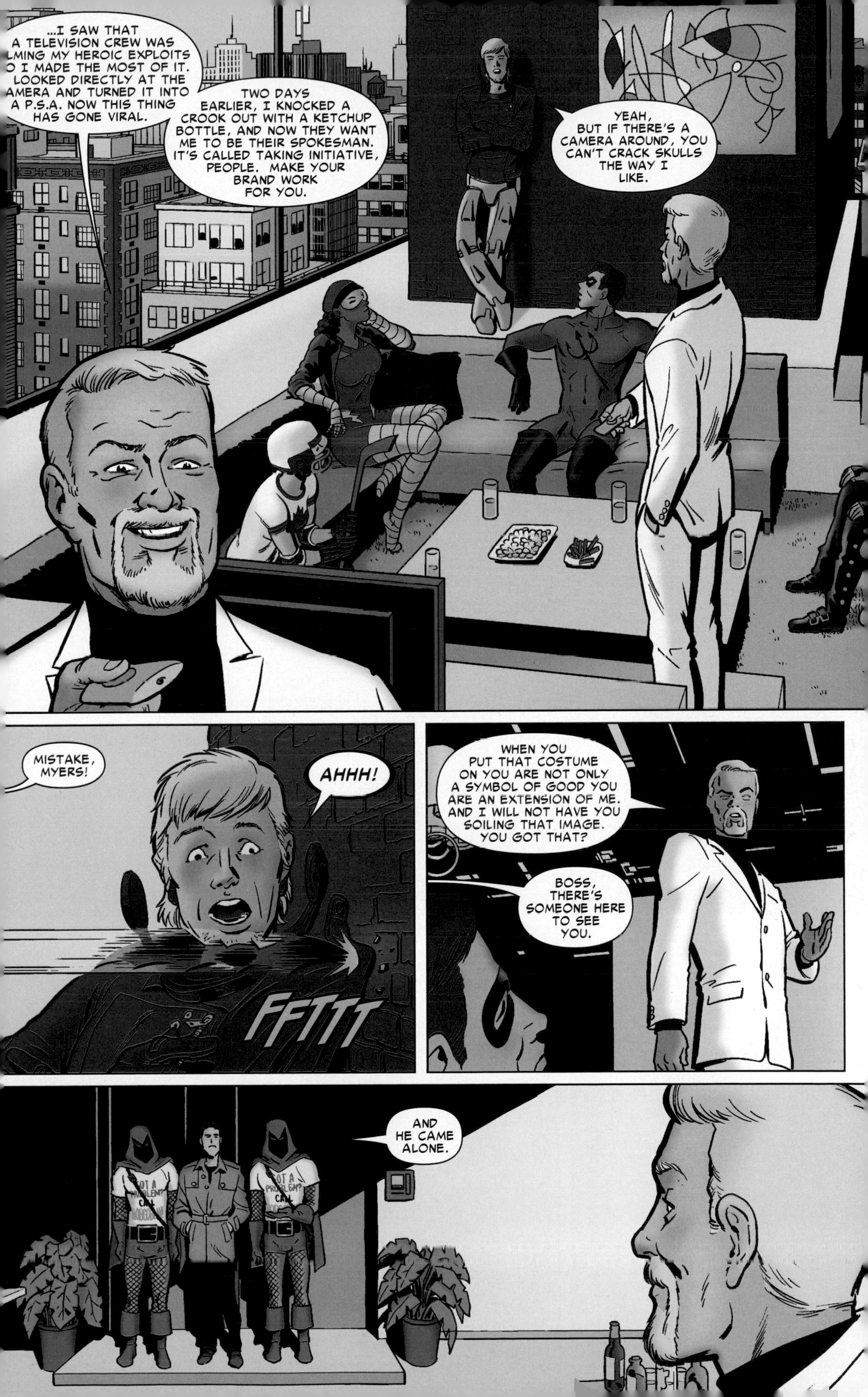

...I SAW THAT A TELEVISION CREW WAS LMING MY HEROIC EXPLOITS O I MADE THE MOST OF IT. LOOKED DIRECTLY AT THE AMERA AND TURNED IT INTO A P.S.A. NOW THIS THING HAS GONE VIRAL.
TWO DAYS EARLIER, I KNOCKED A CROOK OUT WITH A KETCHUP BOTTLE, AND NOW THEY WANT ME TO BE THEIR SPOKESMAN. IT'S CALLED TAKING INITIATIVE, PEOPLE. MAKE YOUR BRAND WORK FOR YOU.
YEAH, BUT IF THERE'S A CAMERA AROUND, YOU CAN'T CRACK SKULLS THE WAY I LIKE.
MISTAKE, MYERS!
AHHH!
FFTTT
WHEN YOU PUT THAT COSTUME ON YOU ARE NOT ONLY A SYMBOL OF GOOD YOU ARE AN EXTENSION OF ME. AND I WILL NOT HAVE YOU SOILING THAT IMAGE. YOU GOT THAT?
BOSS, THERE'S SOMEONE HERE TO SEE YOU.
AND HE CAME ALONE.

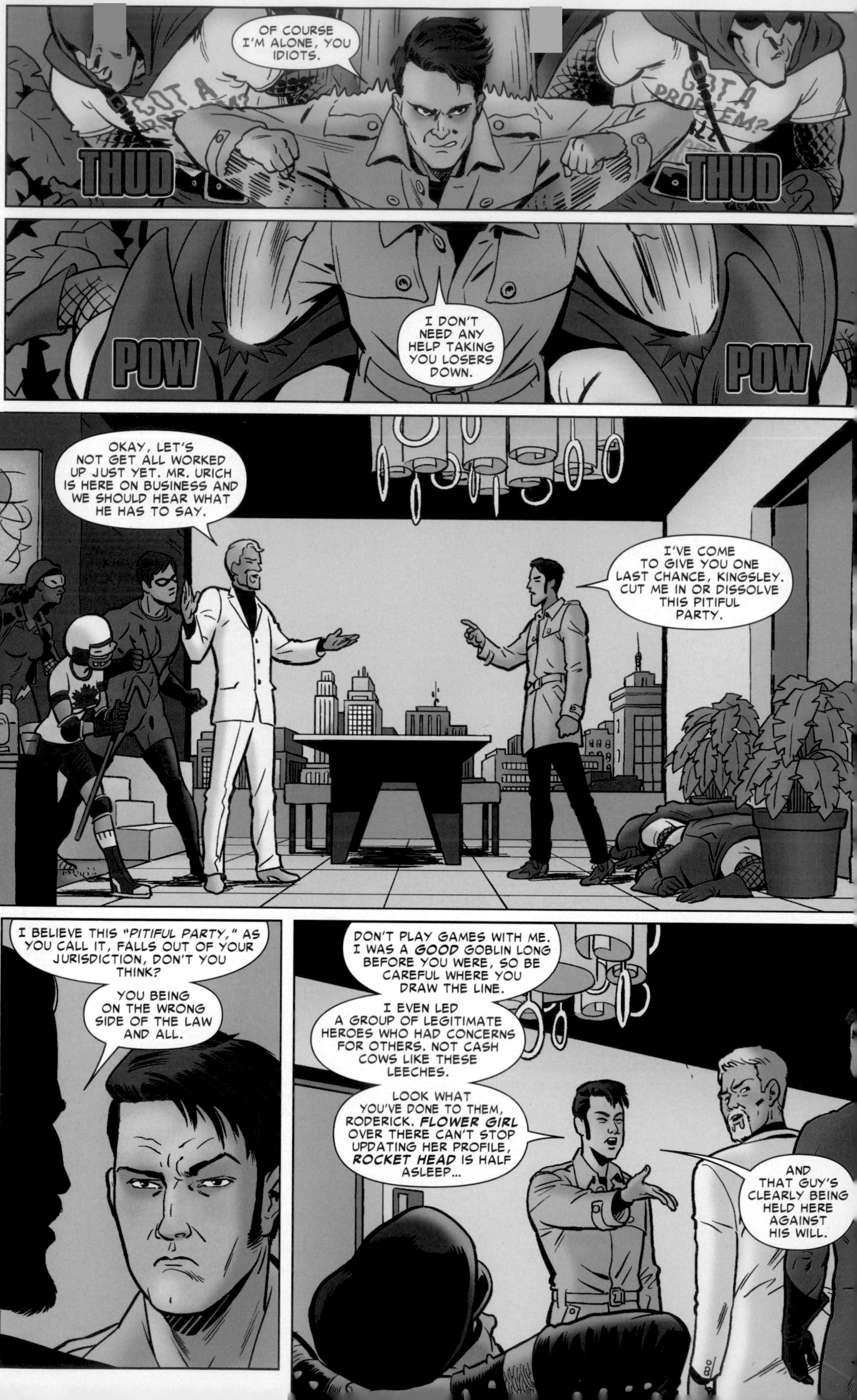
OF COURSE I'M ALONE, YOU IDIOTS.
THUD
THUD
I DON'T NEED ANY HELP TAKING YOU LOSERS DOWN.
POW
POW
OKAY, LET'S NOT GET ALL WORKED UP JUST YET. MR. URICH IS HERE ON BUSINESS AND WE SHOULD HEAR WHAT HE HAS TO SAY.
I'VE COME TO GIVE YOU ONE LAST CHANCE, KINGSLEY. CUT ME IN OR DISSOLVE THIS PITIFUL PARTY.
I BELIEVE THIS "*PITIFUL PARTY,*" AS YOU CALL IT, FALLS OUT OF YOUR JURISDICTION, DON'T YOU THINK?
YOU BEING ON THE WRONG SIDE OF THE LAW AND ALL.
DON'T PLAY GAMES WITH ME. I WAS A ***GOOD*** GOBLIN LONG BEFORE YOU WERE, SO BE CAREFUL WHERE YOU DRAW THE LINE.
I EVEN LED A GROUP OF LEGITIMATE HEROES WHO HAD CONCERNS FOR OTHERS. NOT CASH COWS LIKE THESE LEECHES.
LOOK WHAT YOU'VE DONE TO THEM, RODERICK. ***FLOWER GIRL*** OVER THERE CAN'T STOP UPDATING HER PROFILE, ***ROCKET HEAD*** IS HALF ASLEEP...
AND THAT GUY'S CLEARLY BEING HELD HERE AGAINST HIS WILL.

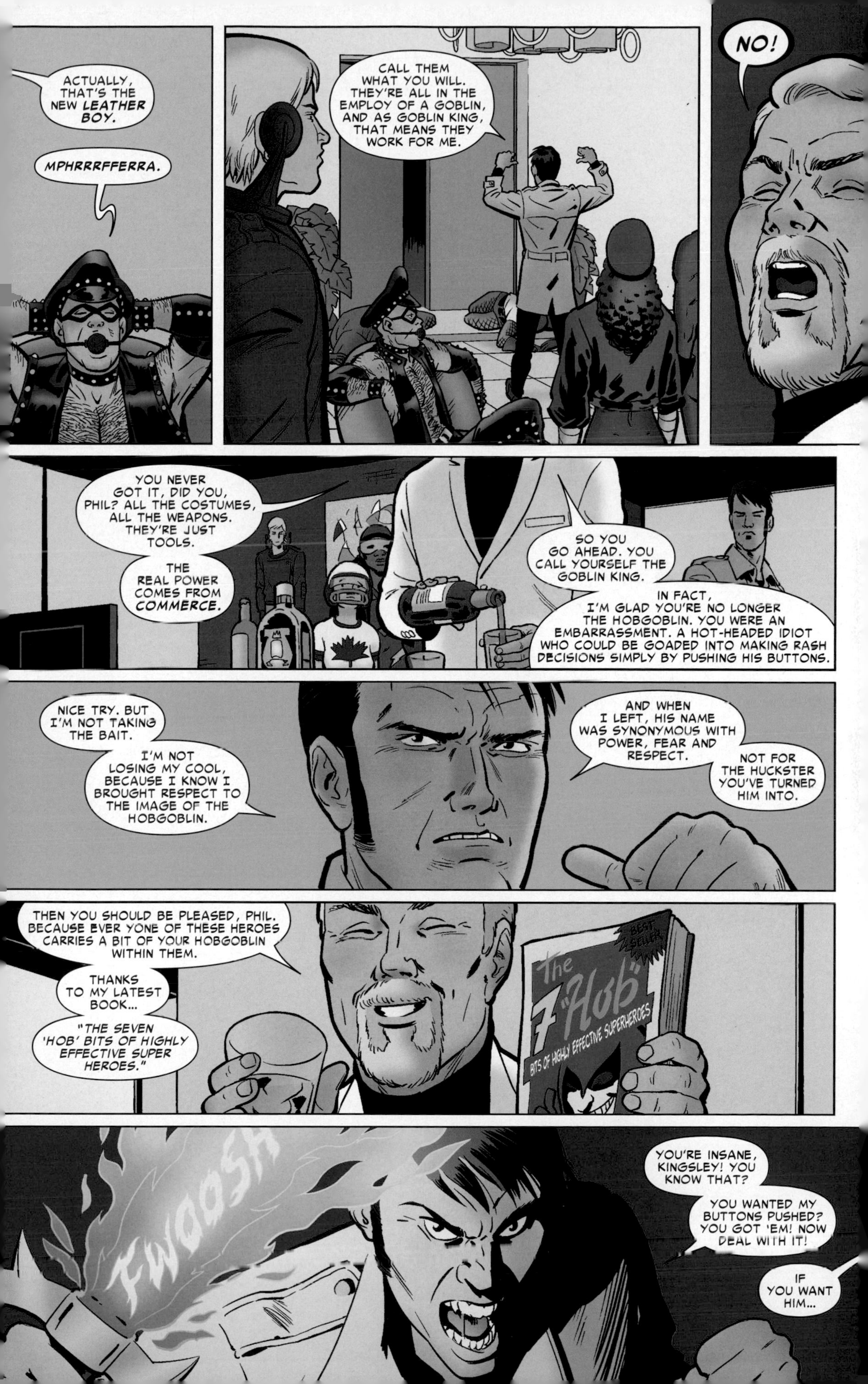
ACTUALLY, THAT'S THE NEW LEATHER BOY.
MPHRRRFFERRA.
CALL THEM WHAT YOU WILL. THEY'RE ALL IN THE EMPLOY OF A GOBLIN, AND AS GOBLIN KING, THAT MEANS THEY WORK FOR ME.
NO!
YOU NEVER GOT IT, DID YOU, PHIL? ALL THE COSTUMES, ALL THE WEAPONS. THEY'RE JUST TOOLS.
THE REAL POWER COMES FROM COMMERCE.
SO YOU GO AHEAD. YOU CALL YOURSELF THE GOBLIN KING.
IN FACT, I'M GLAD YOU'RE NO LONGER THE HOBGOBLIN. YOU WERE AN EMBARRASSMENT. A HOT-HEADED IDIOT WHO COULD BE GOADED INTO MAKING RASH DECISIONS SIMPLY BY PUSHING HIS BUTTONS.
NICE TRY. BUT I'M NOT TAKING THE BAIT.
I'M NOT LOSING MY COOL, BECAUSE I KNOW I BROUGHT RESPECT TO THE IMAGE OF THE HOBGOBLIN.
AND WHEN I LEFT, HIS NAME WAS SYNONYMOUS WITH POWER, FEAR AND RESPECT.
NOT FOR THE HUCKSTER YOU'VE TURNED HIM INTO.
THEN YOU SHOULD BE PLEASED, PHIL. BECAUSE EVER YONE OF THESE HEROES CARRIES A BIT OF YOUR HOBGOBLIN WITHIN THEM.
THANKS TO MY LATEST BOOK...
"THE SEVEN 'HOB' BITS OF HIGHLY EFFECTIVE SUPER HEROES."
BEST SELLER
The 7 "Hob" BITS OF HIGHLY EFFECTIVE SUPERHEROES
FWOOSH
YOU'RE INSANE, KINGSLEY! YOU KNOW THAT?
YOU WANTED MY BUTTONS PUSHED? YOU GOT 'EM! NOW DEAL WITH IT!
IF YOU WANT HIM...

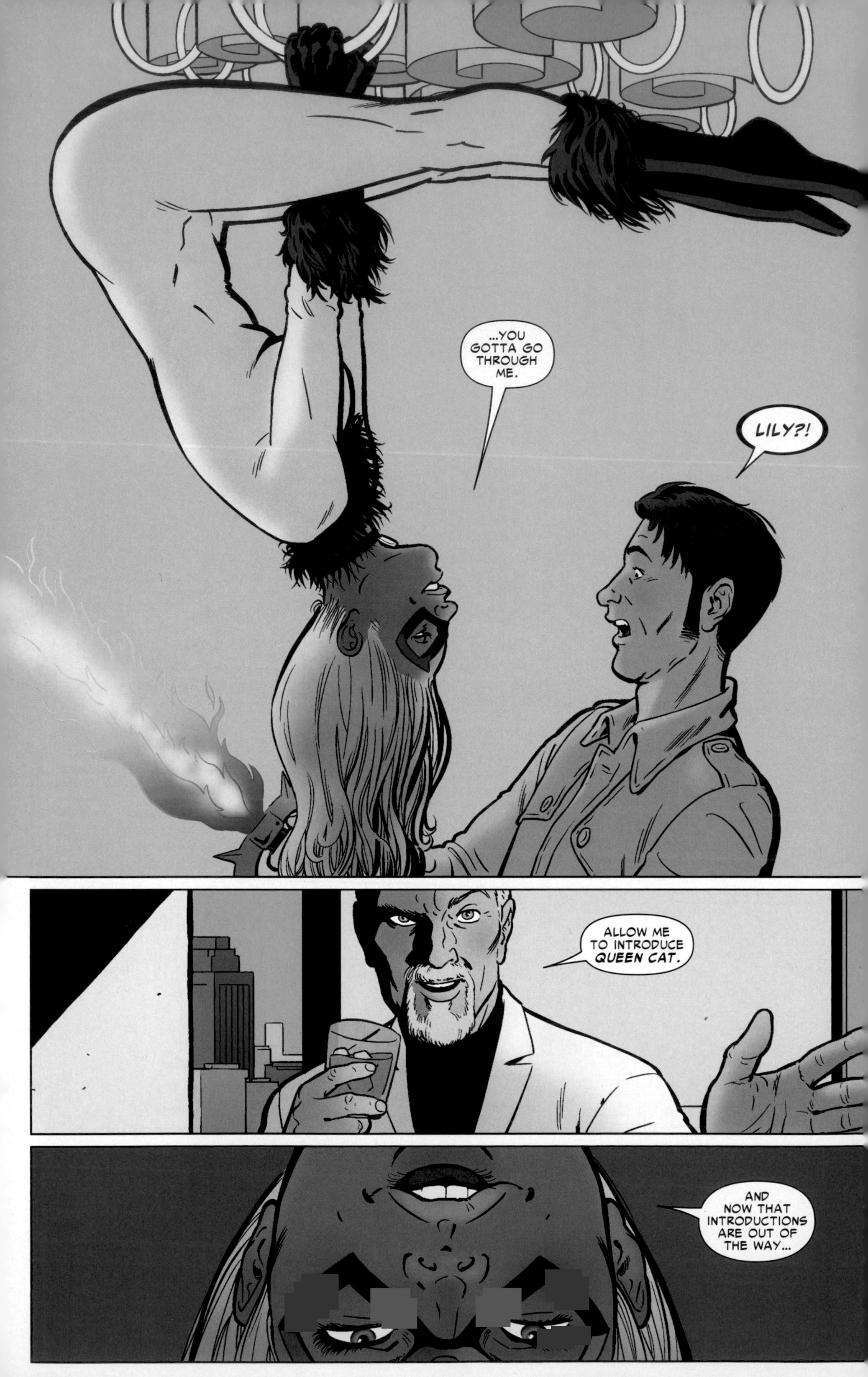

...YOU GOTTA GO THROUGH ME.
LILY?!
ALLOW ME TO INTRODUCE QUEEN CAT.
AND NOW THAT INTRODUCTIONS ARE OUT OF THE WAY...

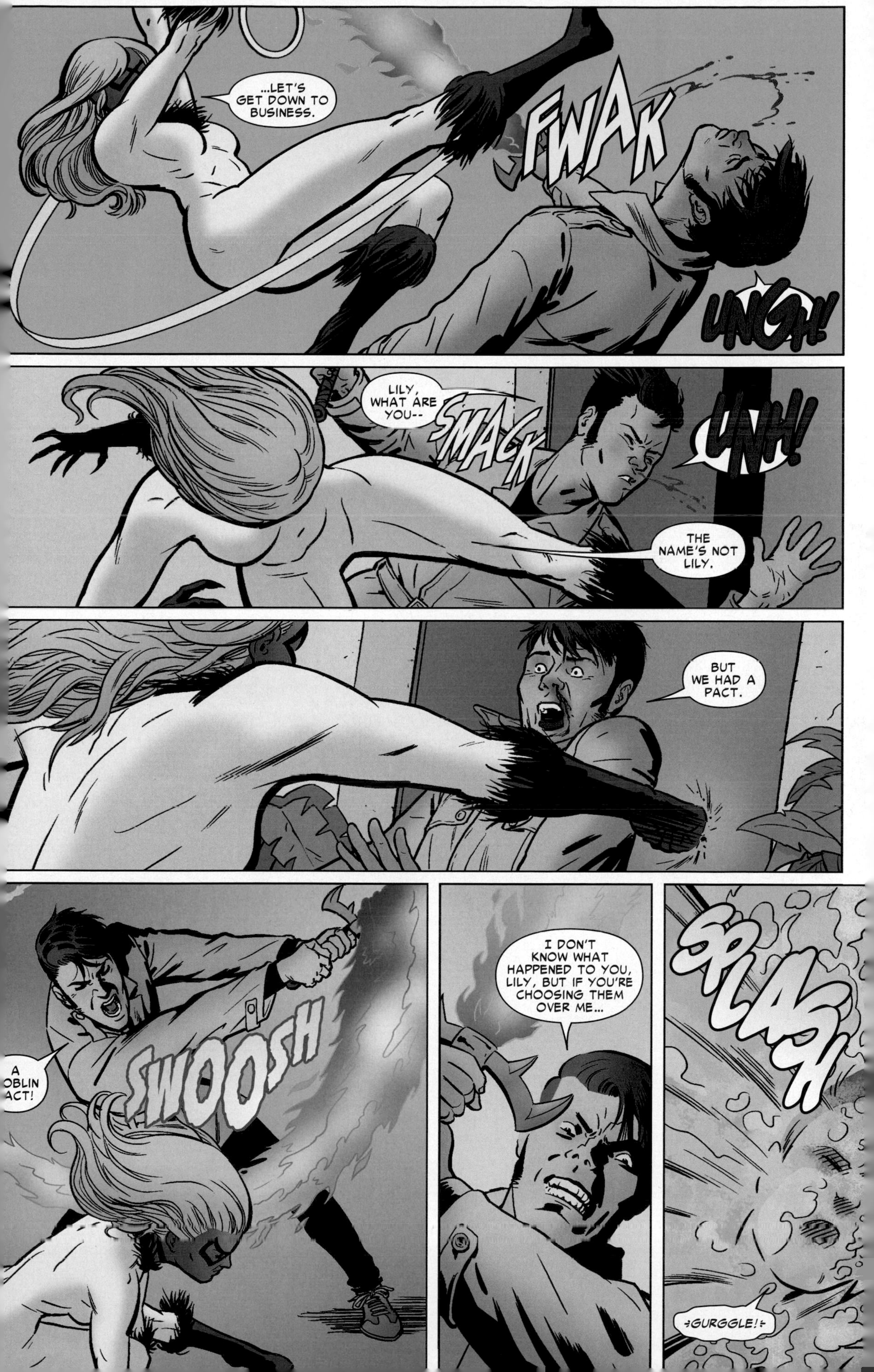
...LET'S GET DOWN TO BUSINESS.
FWAK
UNGH!
LILY, WHAT ARE YOU--
SMACK
UNH!
THE NAME'S NOT LILY.
BUT WE HAD A PACT.
A
OBLIN
ACT!
SWOOSH
I DON'T KNOW WHAT HAPPENED TO YOU, LILY, BUT IF YOU'RE CHOOSING THEM OVER ME...
SPLASH
GURGGLE!

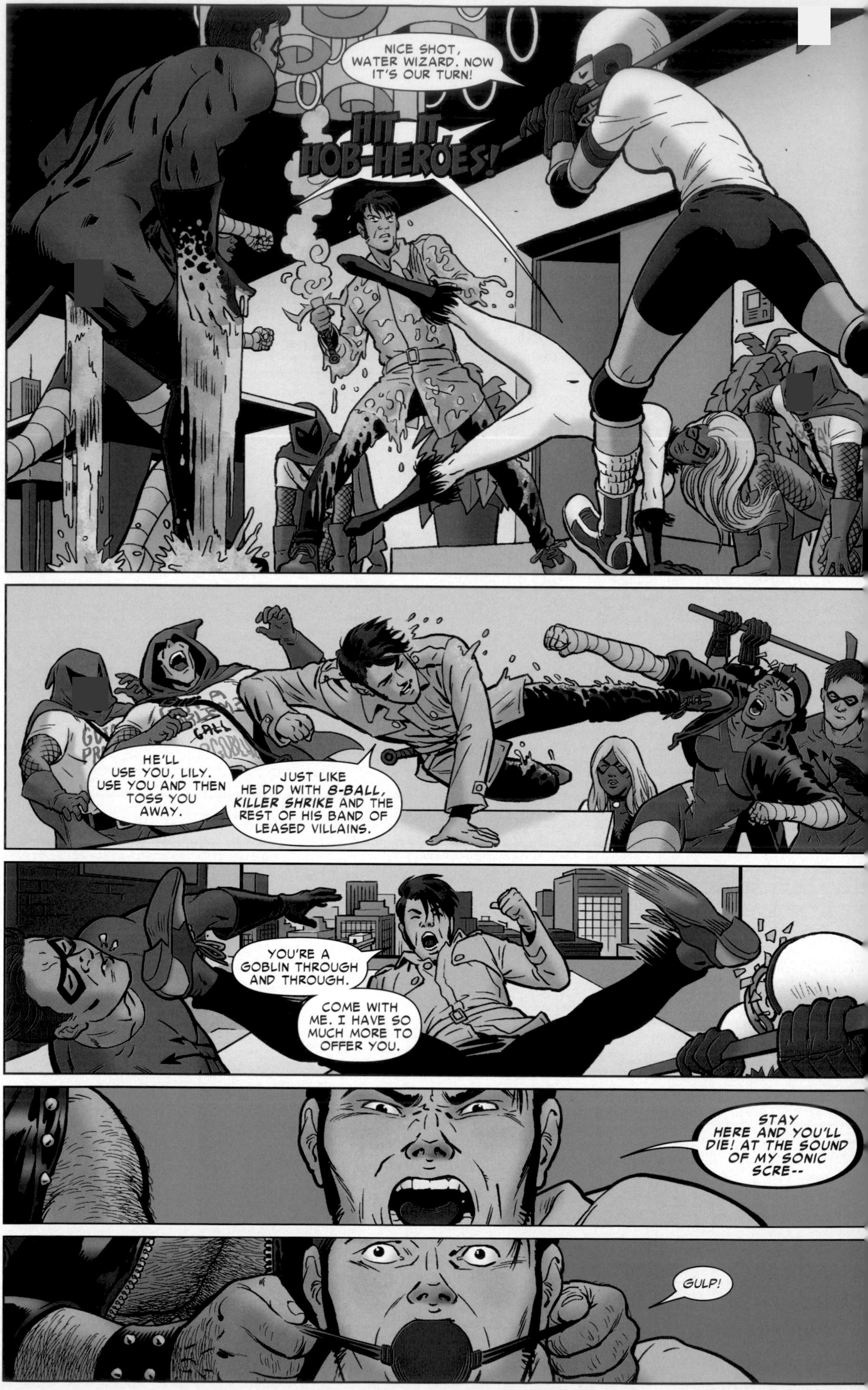
NICE SHOT, WATER WIZARD. NOW IT'S OUR TURN!
HIT IT, HOB-HEROES!
HE'LL USE YOU, LILY. USE YOU AND THEN TOSS YOU AWAY.
JUST LIKE HE DID WITH *8-BALL*, *KILLER SHRIKE* AND THE REST OF HIS BAND OF LEASED VILLAINS.
YOU'RE A GOBLIN THROUGH AND THROUGH.
COME WITH ME. I HAVE SO MUCH MORE TO OFFER YOU.
STAY HERE AND YOU'LL DIE! AT THE SOUND OF MY SONIC SCRE--
GULP!

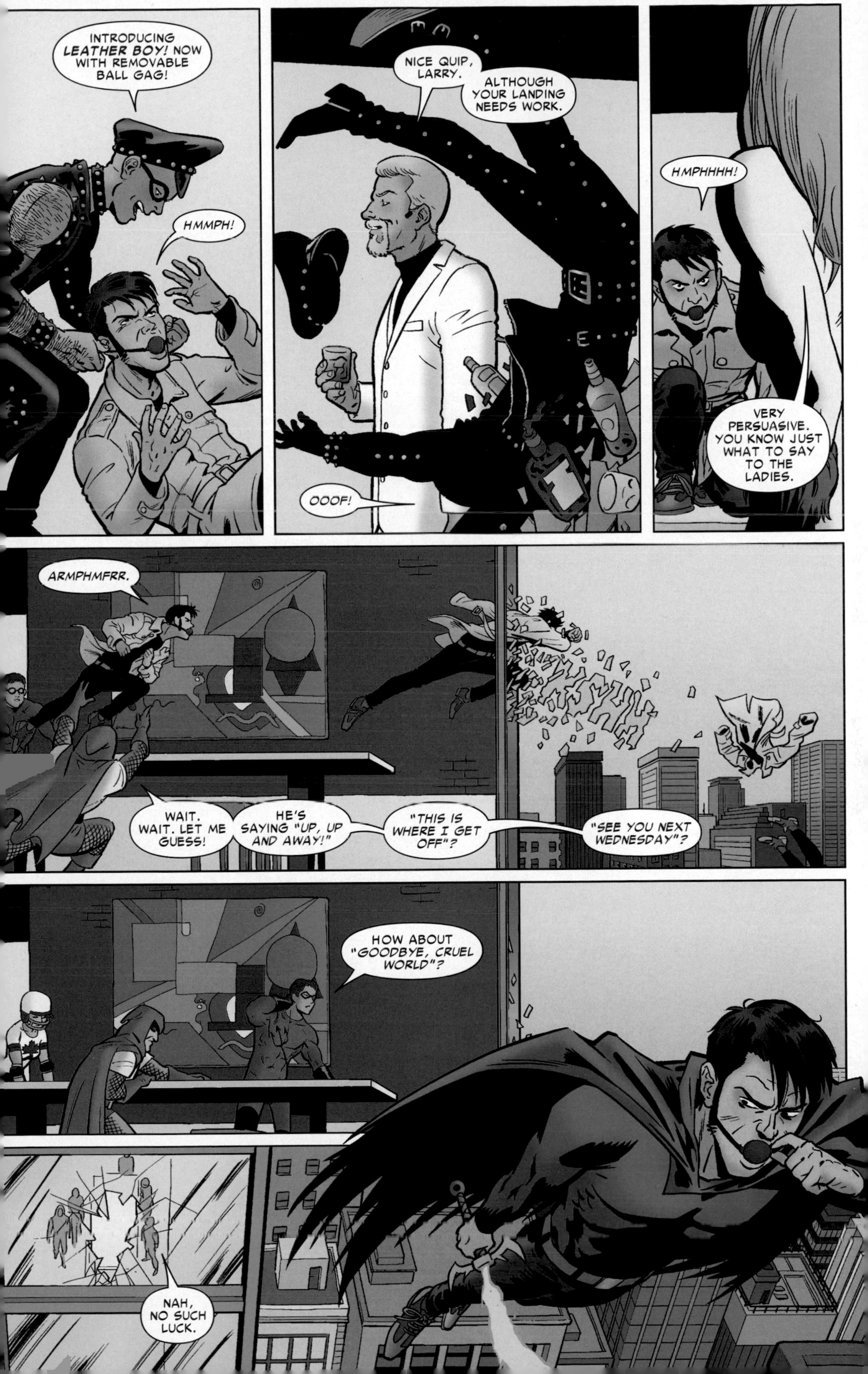
INTRODUCING LEATHER BOY! NOW WITH REMOVABLE BALL GAG!
HMMPH!
NICE QUIP, LARRY.
ALTHOUGH YOUR LANDING NEEDS WORK.
OOOF!
HMPHHHH!
VERY PERSUASIVE. YOU KNOW JUST WHAT TO SAY TO THE LADIES.
ARMPHMFRR.
WAIT. WAIT. LET ME GUESS!
HE'S SAYING "UP, UP AND AWAY!"
"THIS IS WHERE I GET OFF"?
"SEE YOU NEXT WEDNESDAY"?
HOW ABOUT "GOODBYE, CRUEL WORLD"?
NAH, NO SUCH LUCK.

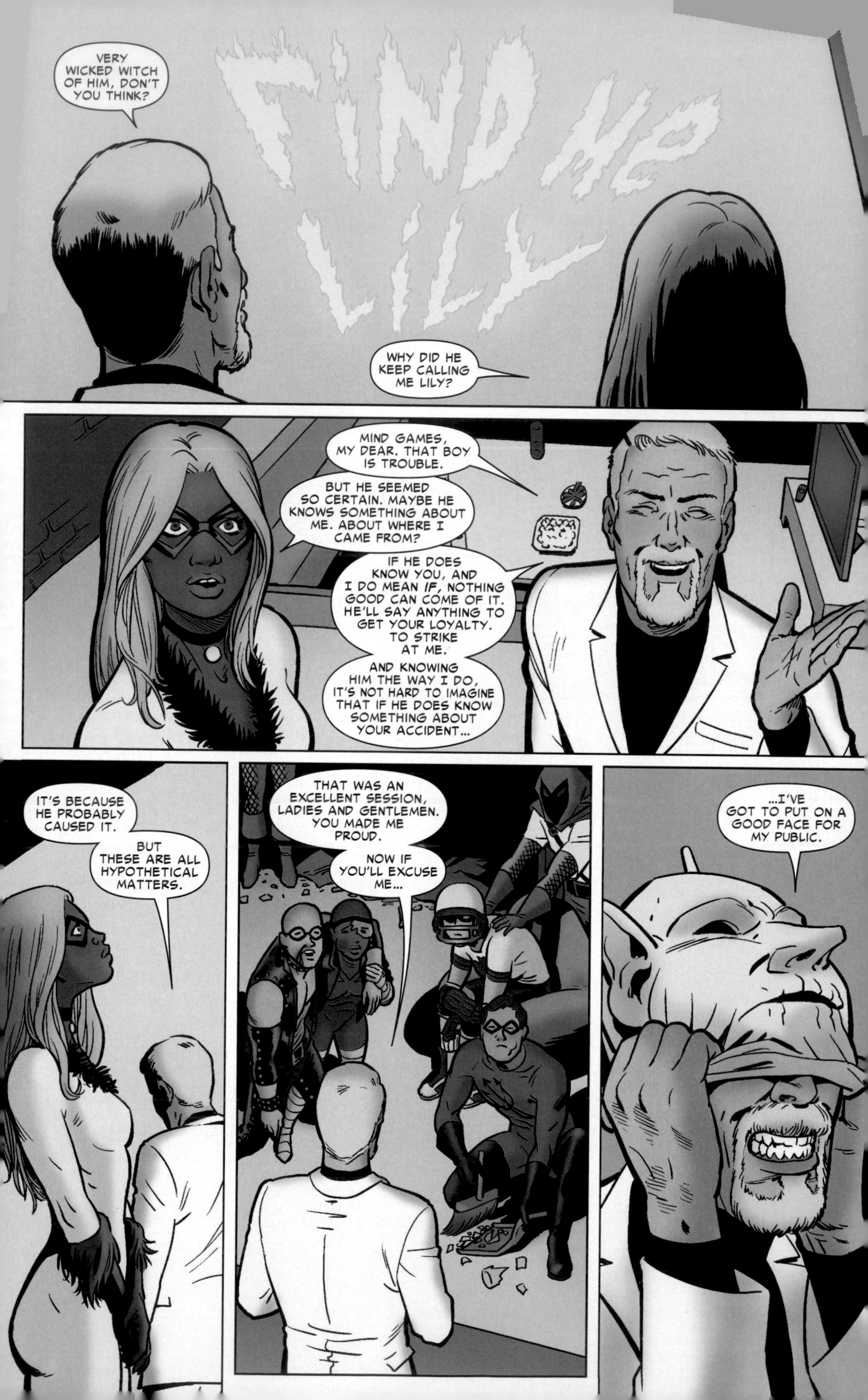
VERY WICKED WITCH OF HIM, DON'T YOU THINK?
FIND ME LILY
WHY DID HE KEEP CALLING ME LILY?
MIND GAMES, MY DEAR. THAT BOY IS TROUBLE.
BUT HE SEEMED SO CERTAIN. MAYBE HE KNOWS SOMETHING ABOUT ME. ABOUT WHERE I CAME FROM?
IF HE DOES KNOW YOU, AND I DO MEAN *IF*, NOTHING GOOD CAN COME OF IT. HE'LL SAY ANYTHING TO GET YOUR LOYALTY. TO STRIKE AT ME.
AND KNOWING HIM THE WAY I DO, IT'S NOT HARD TO IMAGINE THAT IF HE DOES KNOW SOMETHING ABOUT YOUR ACCIDENT...
IT'S BECAUSE HE PROBABLY CAUSED IT.
BUT THESE ARE ALL HYPOTHETICAL MATTERS.
THAT WAS AN EXCELLENT SESSION, LADIES AND GENTLEMEN. YOU MADE ME PROUD.
NOW IF YOU'LL EXCUSE ME...
...I'VE GOT TO PUT ON A GOOD FACE FOR MY PUBLIC.

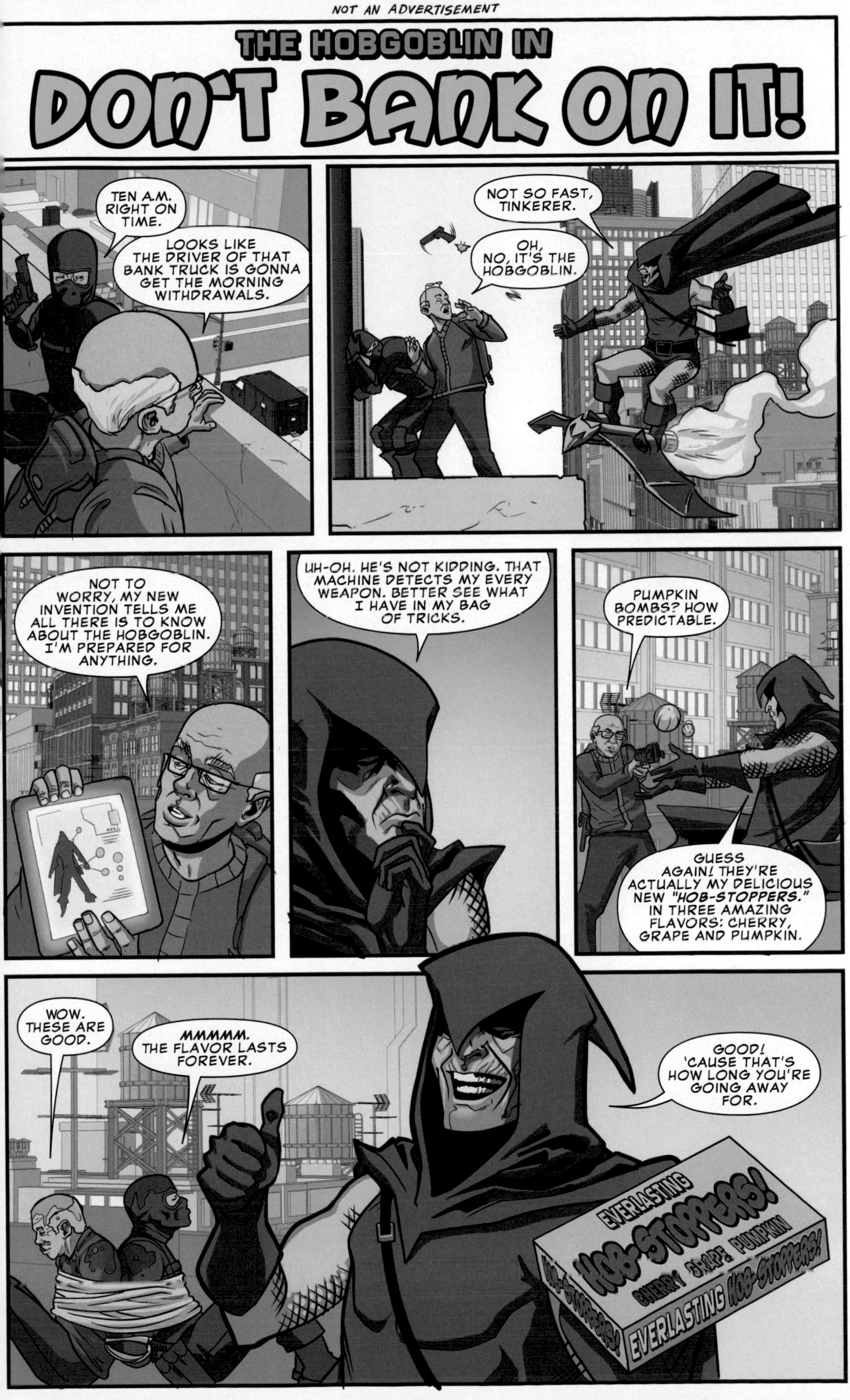
THE HOBGOBLIN IN
DON'T BANK ON IT!
TEN A.M. RIGHT ON TIME.
LOOKS LIKE THE DRIVER OF THAT BANK TRUCK IS GONNA GET THE MORNING WITHDRAWALS.
NOT SO FAST, TINKERER.
OH, NO, IT'S THE HOBGOBLIN.
NOT TO WORRY, MY NEW INVENTION TELLS ME ALL THERE IS TO KNOW ABOUT THE HOBGOBLIN. I'M PREPARED FOR ANYTHING.
UH-OH. HE'S NOT KIDDING. THAT MACHINE DETECTS MY EVERY WEAPON. BETTER SEE WHAT I HAVE IN MY BAG OF TRICKS.
PUMPKIN BOMBS? HOW PREDICTABLE.
GUESS AGAIN! THEY'RE ACTUALLY MY DELICIOUS NEW "HOB-STOPPERS." IN THREE AMAZING FLAVORS: CHERRY, GRAPE AND PUMPKIN.
WOW. THESE ARE GOOD.
MMMMM. THE FLAVOR LASTS FOREVER.
GOOD! 'CAUSE THAT'S HOW LONG YOU'RE GOING AWAY FOR.
EVERLASTING HOB-STOPPERS! CHERRY GRAPE PUMPKIN
EVERLASTING HOB-STOPPERS!

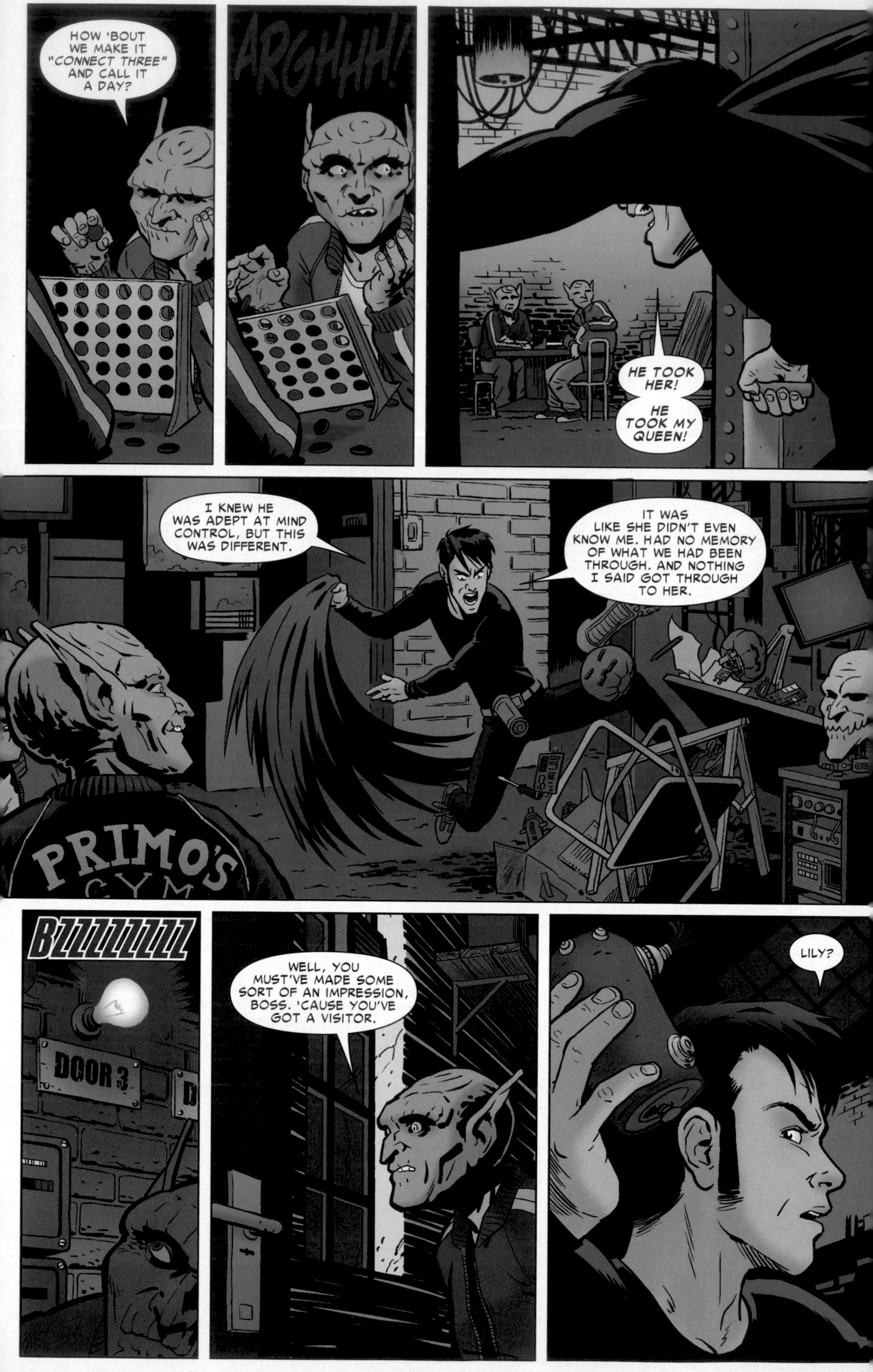
HOW 'BOUT WE MAKE IT "CONNECT THREE" AND CALL IT A DAY?
ARGHHH!
HE TOOK HER!
HE TOOK MY QUEEN!
I KNEW HE WAS ADEPT AT MIND CONTROL, BUT THIS WAS DIFFERENT.
IT WAS LIKE SHE DIDN'T EVEN KNOW ME. HAD NO MEMORY OF WHAT WE HAD BEEN THROUGH. AND NOTHING I SAID GOT THROUGH TO HER.
PRIMO'S GYM
BZZZZZZZZZ
DOOR 3
WELL, YOU MUST'VE MADE SOME SORT OF AN IMPRESSION, BOSS. 'CAUSE YOU'VE GOT A VISITOR.
LILY?

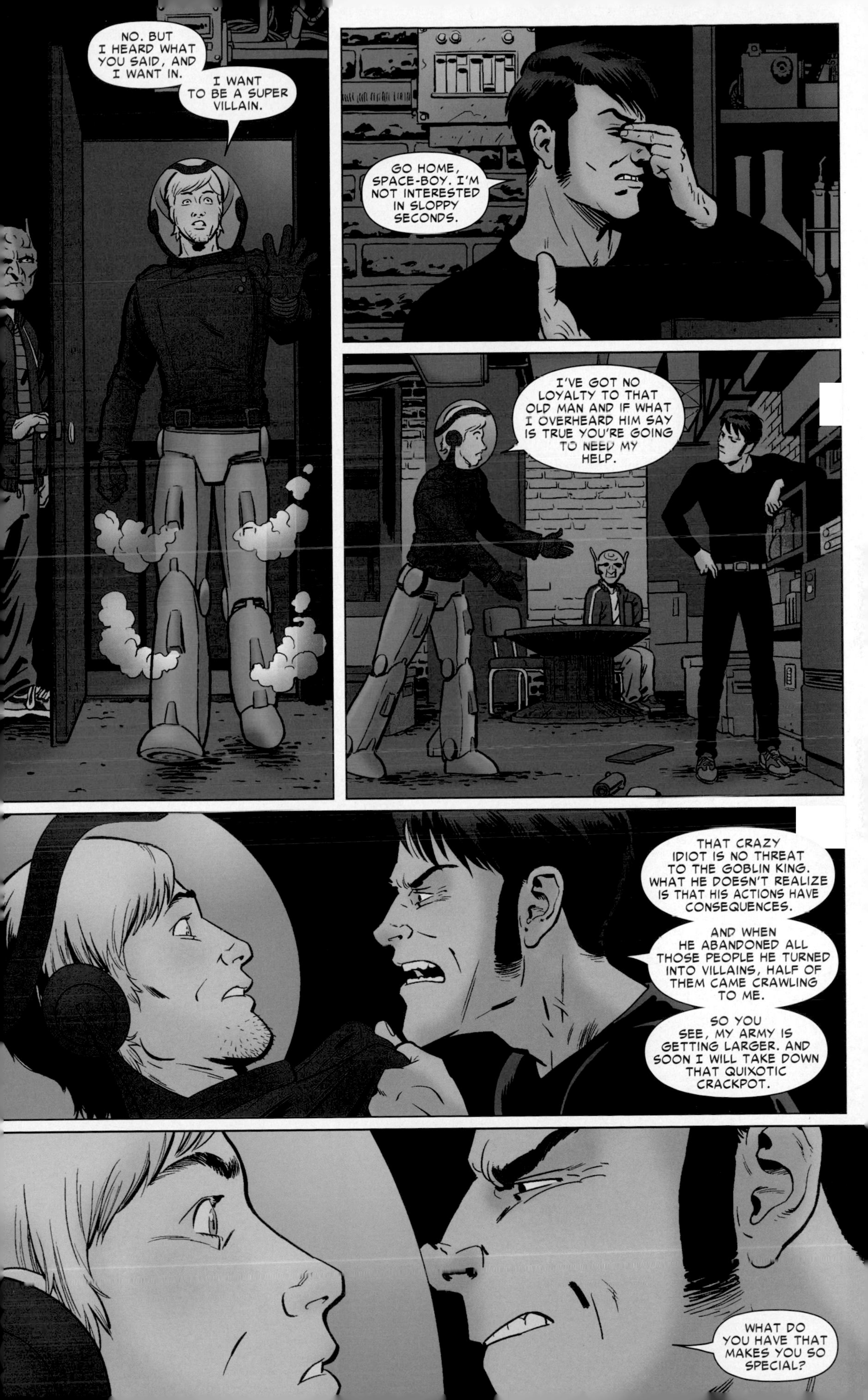
NO. BUT I HEARD WHAT YOU SAID, AND I WANT IN.
I WANT TO BE A SUPER VILLAIN.
GO HOME, SPACE-BOY. I'M NOT INTERESTED IN SLOPPY SECONDS.
I'VE GOT NO LOYALTY TO THAT OLD MAN AND IF WHAT I OVERHEARD HIM SAY IS TRUE YOU'RE GOING TO NEED MY HELP.
THAT CRAZY IDIOT IS NO THREAT TO THE GOBLIN KING. WHAT HE DOESN'T REALIZE IS THAT HIS ACTIONS HAVE CONSEQUENCES.
AND WHEN HE ABANDONED ALL THOSE PEOPLE HE TURNED INTO VILLAINS, HALF OF THEM CAME CRAWLING TO ME.
SO YOU SEE, MY ARMY IS GETTING LARGER. AND SOON I WILL TAKE DOWN THAT QUIXOTIC CRACKPOT.
WHAT DO YOU HAVE THAT MAKES YOU SO SPECIAL?

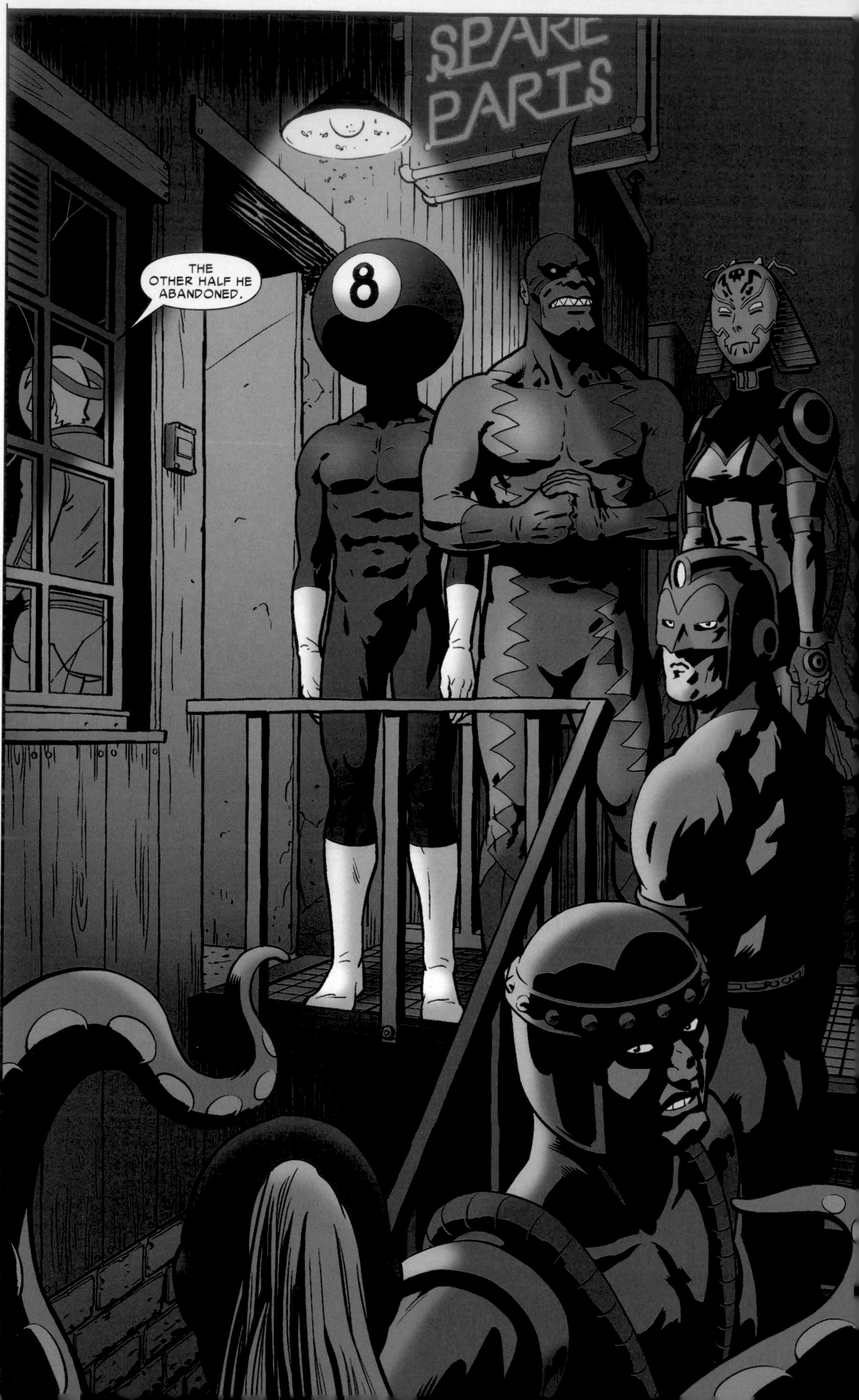
SPARE PARTS
THE OTHER HALF HE ABANDONED.

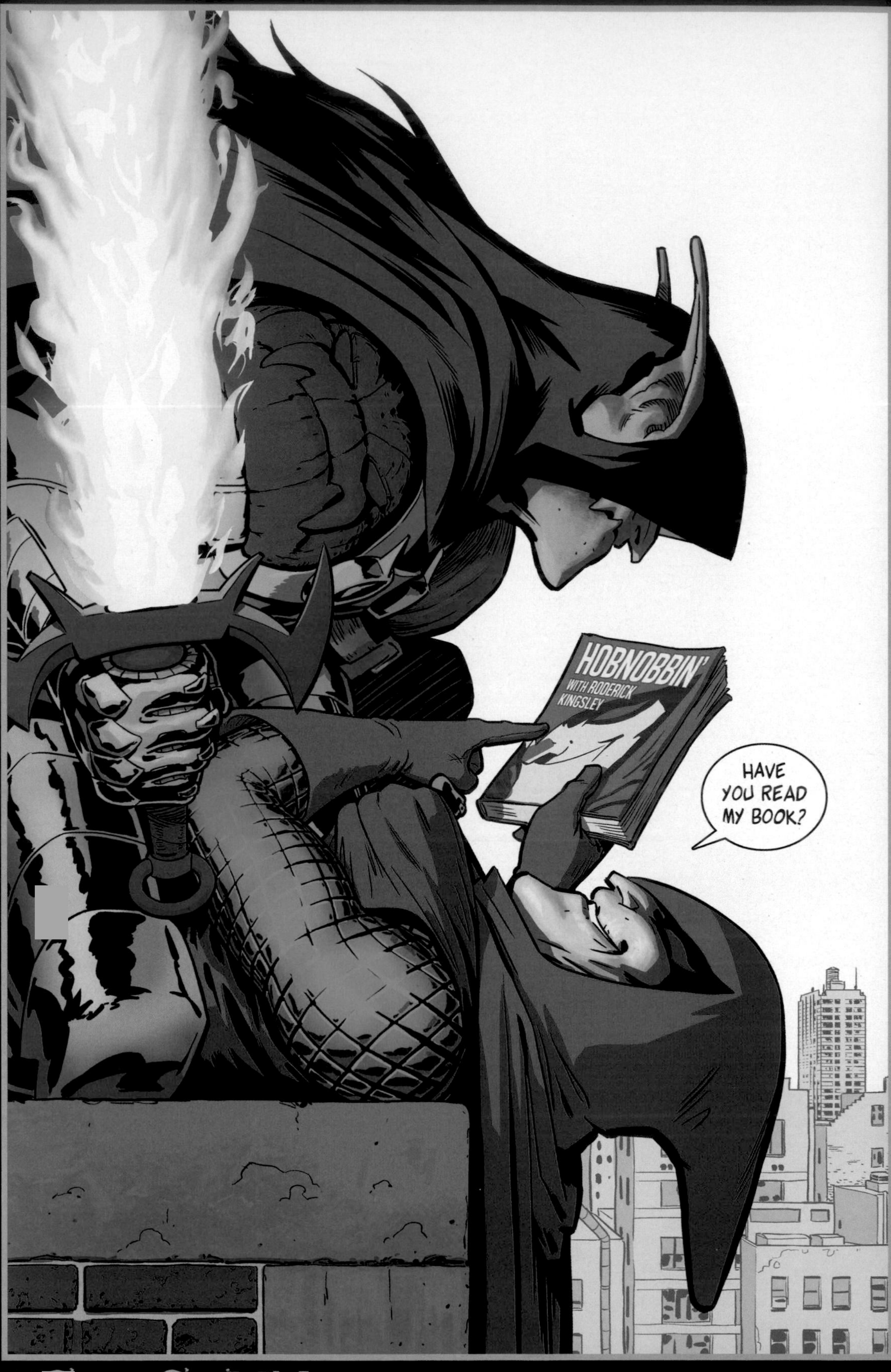
HOBNOBBIN'
WITH RODERICK KINGSLEY
HAVE YOU READ MY BOOK?

HOBGOBLIN #3

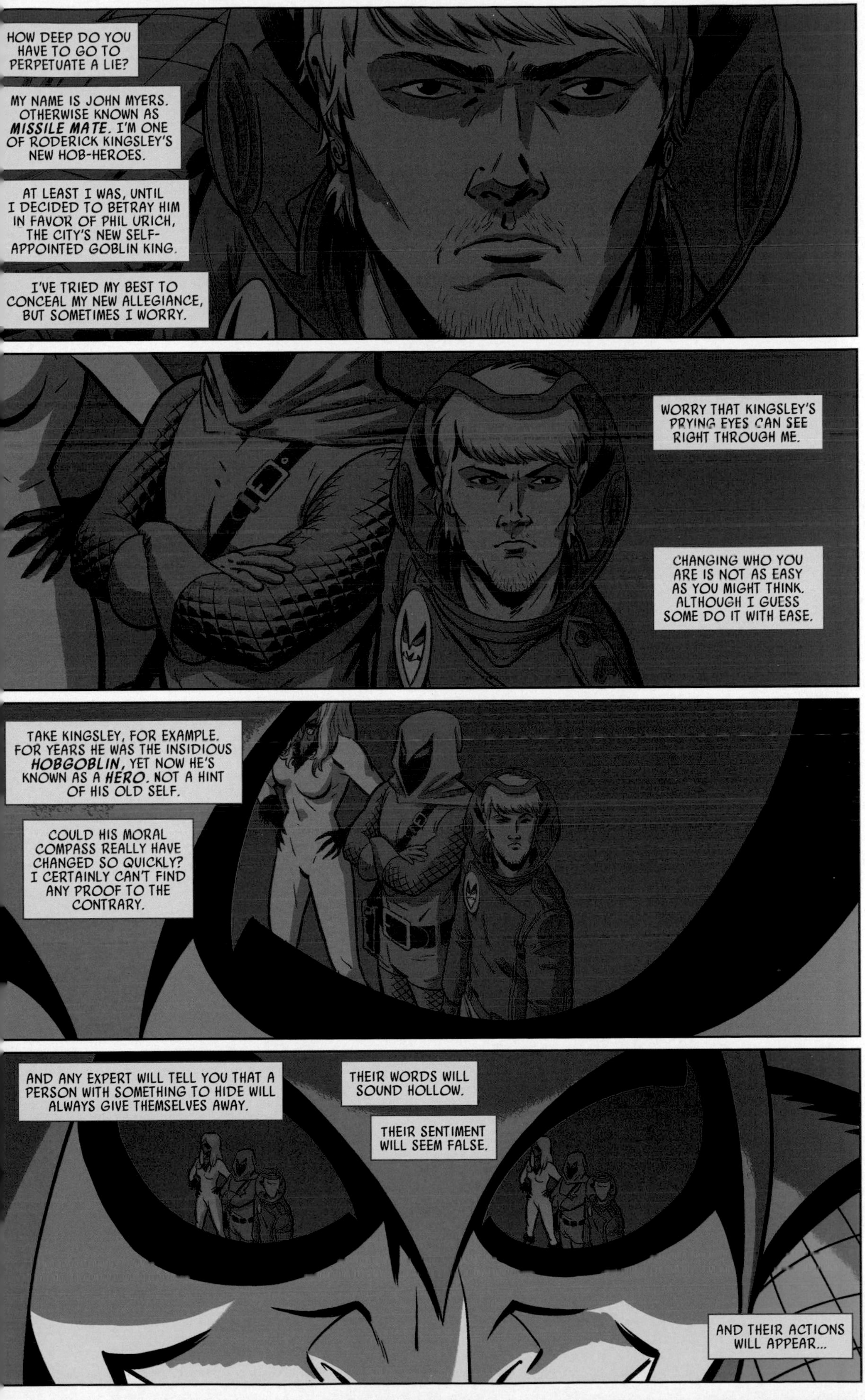
HOW DEEP DO YOU HAVE TO GO TO PERPETUATE A LIE?
MY NAME IS JOHN MYERS. OTHERWISE KNOWN AS MISSILE MATE. I'M ONE OF RODERICK KINGSLEY'S NEW HOB-HEROES.
AT LEAST I WAS, UNTIL I DECIDED TO BETRAY HIM IN FAVOR OF PHIL URICH, THE CITY'S NEW SELF-APPOINTED GOBLIN KING.
I'VE TRIED MY BEST TO CONCEAL MY NEW ALLEGIANCE, BUT SOMETIMES I WORRY.
WORRY THAT KINGSLEY'S PRYING EYES CAN SEE RIGHT THROUGH ME.
CHANGING WHO YOU ARE IS NOT AS EASY AS YOU MIGHT THINK. ALTHOUGH I GUESS SOME DO IT WITH EASE.
TAKE KINGSLEY, FOR EXAMPLE. FOR YEARS HE WAS THE INSIDIOUS HOBGOBLIN, YET NOW HE'S KNOWN AS A HERO. NOT A HINT OF HIS OLD SELF.
COULD HIS MORAL COMPASS REALLY HAVE CHANGED SO QUICKLY? I CERTAINLY CAN'T FIND ANY PROOF TO THE CONTRARY.
AND ANY EXPERT WILL TELL YOU THAT A PERSON WITH SOMETHING TO HIDE WILL ALWAYS GIVE THEMSELVES AWAY.
THEIR WORDS WILL SOUND HOLLOW.
THEIR SENTIMENT WILL SEEM FALSE.
AND THEIR ACTIONS WILL APPEAR...

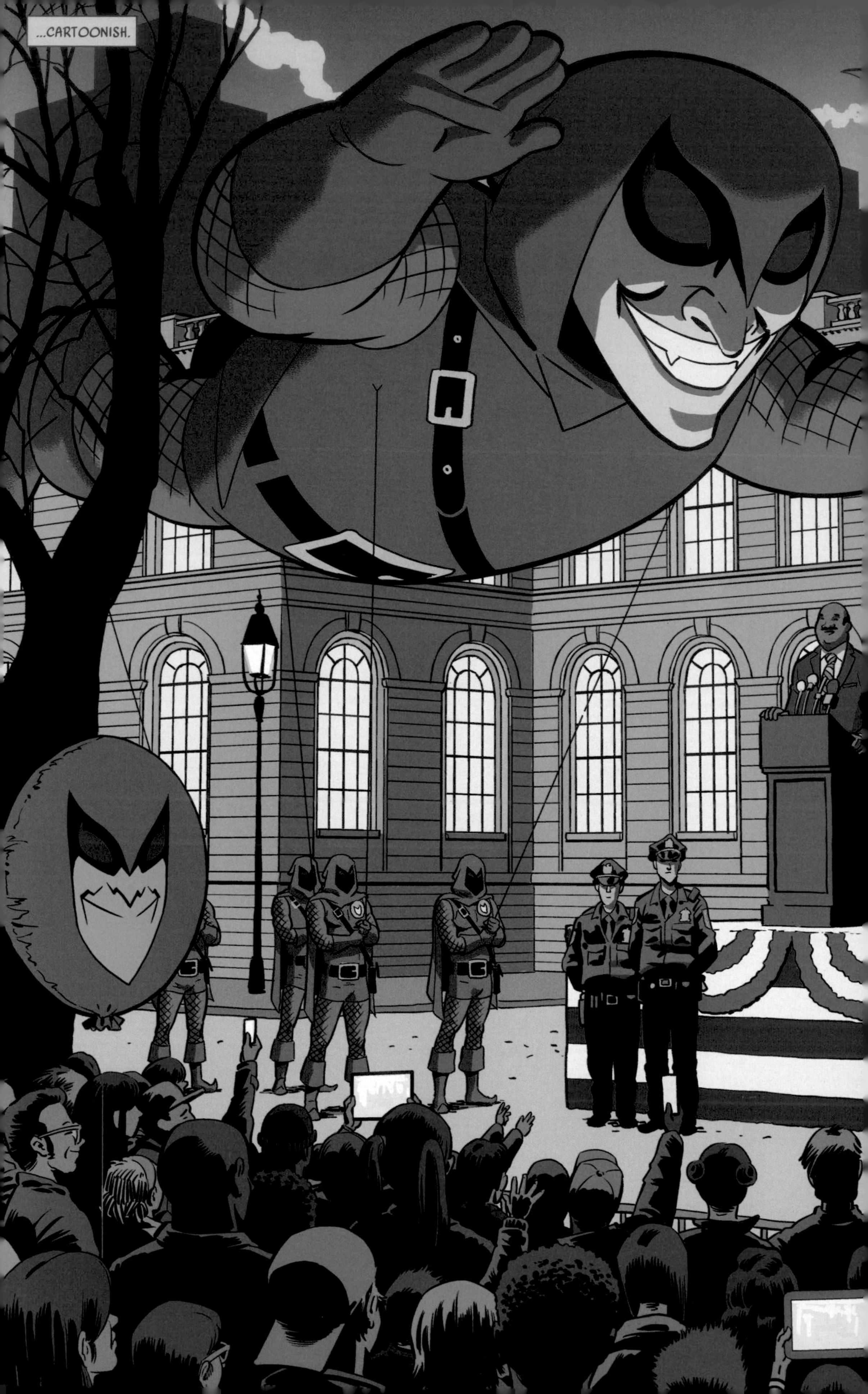
...CARTOONISH.

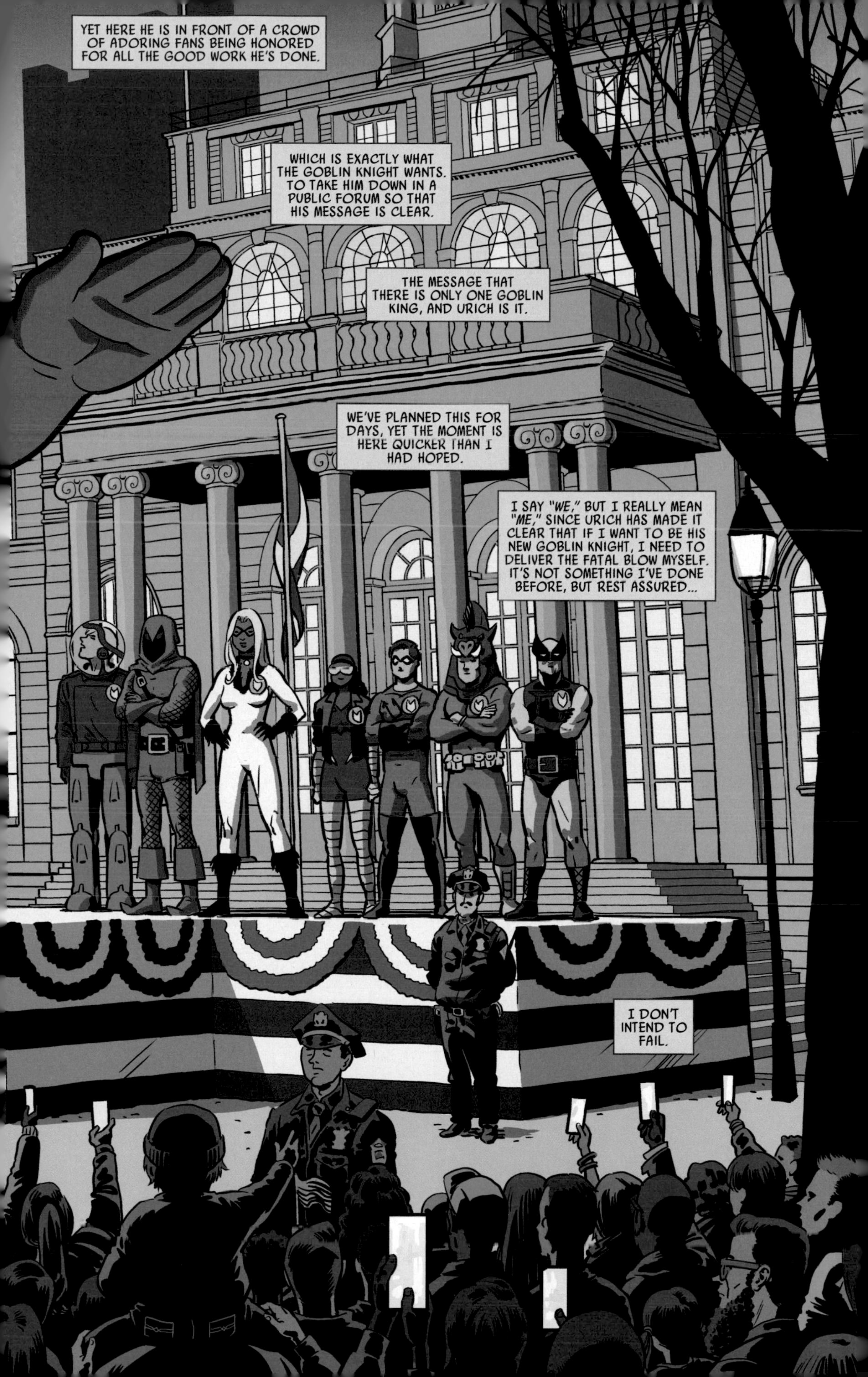
YET HERE HE IS IN FRONT OF A CROWD OF ADORING FANS BEING HONORED FOR ALL THE GOOD WORK HE'S DONE.
WHICH IS EXACTLY WHAT THE GOBLIN KNIGHT WANTS. TO TAKE HIM DOWN IN A PUBLIC FORUM SO THAT HIS MESSAGE IS CLEAR.
THE MESSAGE THAT THERE IS ONLY ONE GOBLIN KING, AND URICH IS IT.
WE'VE PLANNED THIS FOR DAYS, YET THE MOMENT IS HERE QUICKER THAN I HAD HOPED.
I SAY "WE," BUT I REALLY MEAN "ME," SINCE URICH HAS MADE IT CLEAR THAT IF I WANT TO BE HIS NEW GOBLIN KNIGHT, I NEED TO DELIVER THE FATAL BLOW MYSELF. IT'S NOT SOMETHING I'VE DONE BEFORE, BUT REST ASSURED...
I DON'T INTEND TO FAIL.

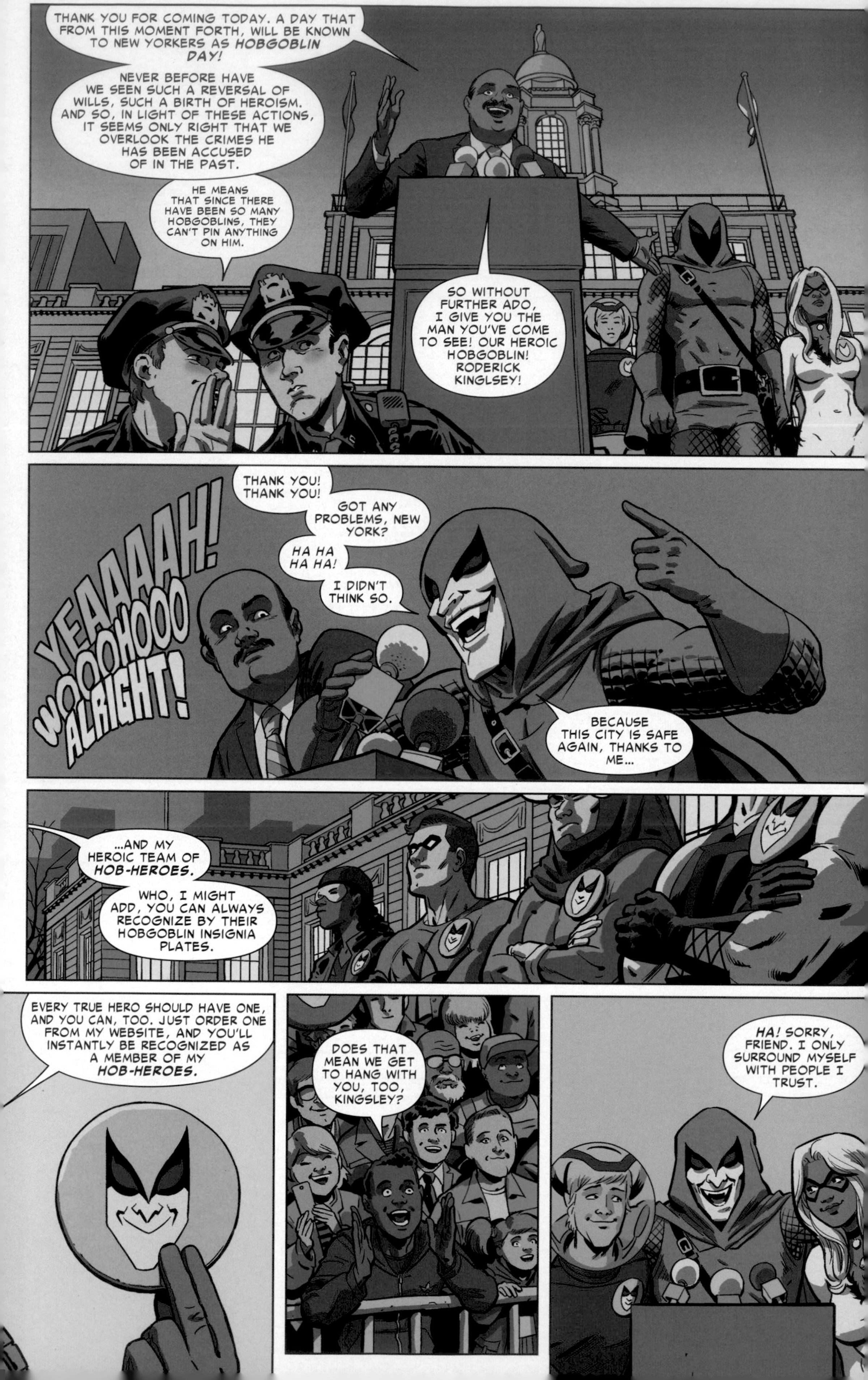
THANK YOU FOR COMING TODAY. A DAY THAT FROM THIS MOMENT FORTH, WILL BE KNOWN TO NEW YORKERS AS *HOBGOBLIN DAY!*
NEVER BEFORE HAVE WE SEEN SUCH A REVERSAL OF WILLS, SUCH A BIRTH OF HEROISM. AND SO, IN LIGHT OF THESE ACTIONS, IT SEEMS ONLY RIGHT THAT WE OVERLOOK THE CRIMES HE HAS BEEN ACCUSED OF IN THE PAST.
HE MEANS THAT SINCE THERE HAVE BEEN SO MANY HOBGOBLINS, THEY CAN'T PIN ANYTHING ON HIM.
SO WITHOUT FURTHER ADO, I GIVE YOU THE MAN YOU'VE COME TO SEE! OUR HEROIC HOBGOBLIN! RODERICK KINGLSEY!
YEAAAAH!
WOOOHOOO
ALRIGHT!
THANK YOU! THANK YOU!
GOT ANY PROBLEMS, NEW YORK?
HA HA HA HA!
I DIDN'T THINK SO.
BECAUSE THIS CITY IS SAFE AGAIN, THANKS TO ME...
...AND MY HEROIC TEAM OF *HOB-HEROES.*
WHO, I MIGHT ADD, YOU CAN ALWAYS RECOGNIZE BY THEIR HOBGOBLIN INSIGNIA PLATES.
EVERY TRUE HERO SHOULD HAVE ONE, AND YOU CAN, TOO. JUST ORDER ONE FROM MY WEBSITE, AND YOU'LL INSTANTLY BE RECOGNIZED AS A MEMBER OF MY *HOB-HEROES.*
DOES THAT MEAN WE GET TO HANG WITH YOU, TOO, KINGSLEY?
HA! SORRY, FRIEND. I ONLY SURROUND MYSELF WITH PEOPLE I TRUST.

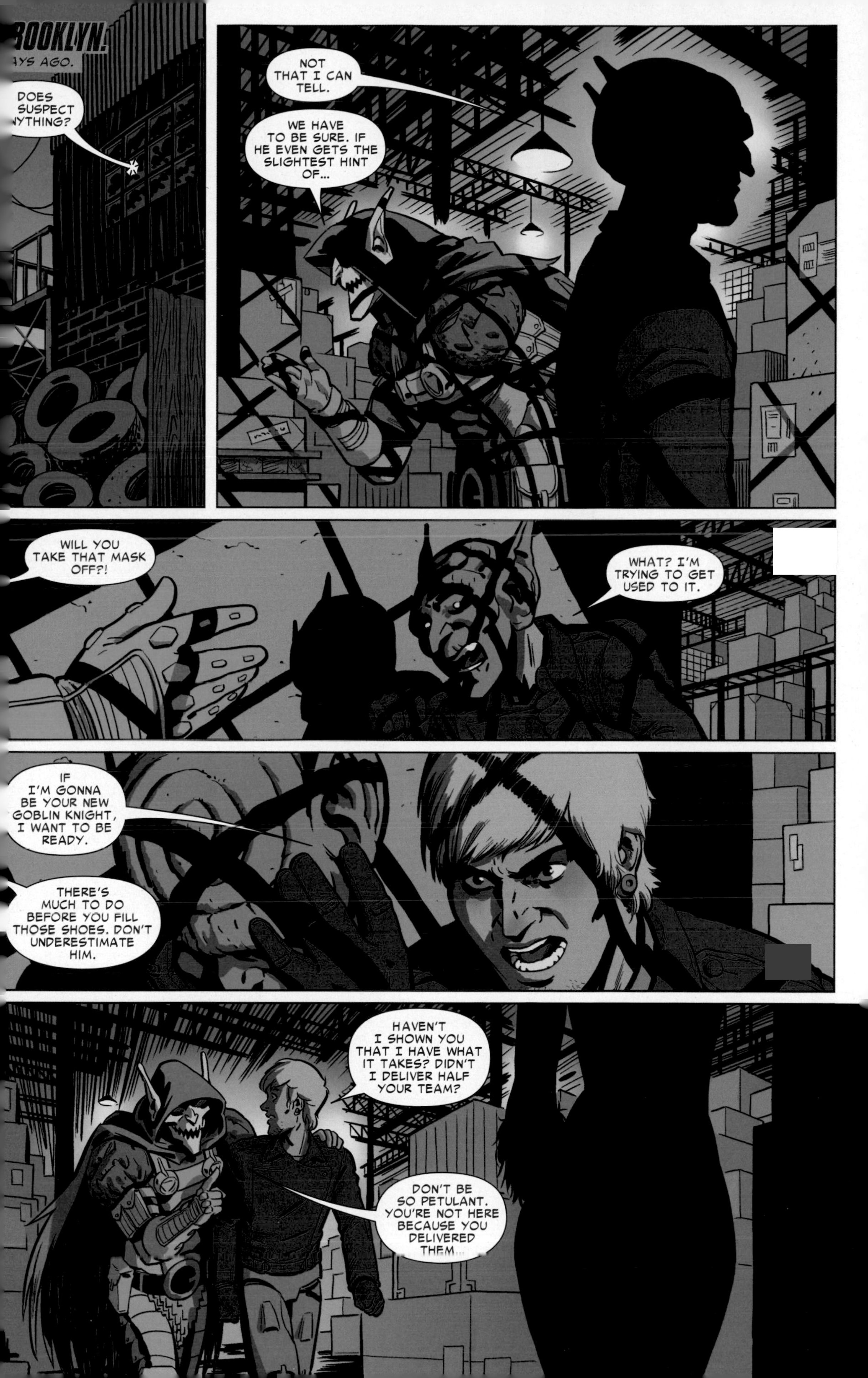
ROOKLYN.
AYS AGO.
DOES
SUSPECT
NYTHING?
NOT THAT I CAN TELL.
WE HAVE TO BE SURE. IF HE EVEN GETS THE SLIGHTEST HINT OF...
WILL YOU TAKE THAT MASK OFF?!
WHAT? I'M TRYING TO GET USED TO IT.
IF I'M GONNA BE YOUR NEW GOBLIN KNIGHT, I WANT TO BE READY.
THERE'S MUCH TO DO BEFORE YOU FILL THOSE SHOES. DON'T UNDERESTIMATE HIM.
HAVEN'T I SHOWN YOU THAT I HAVE WHAT IT TAKES? DIDN'T I DELIVER HALF YOUR TEAM?
DON'T BE SO PETULANT. YOU'RE NOT HERE BECAUSE YOU DELIVERED THEM...

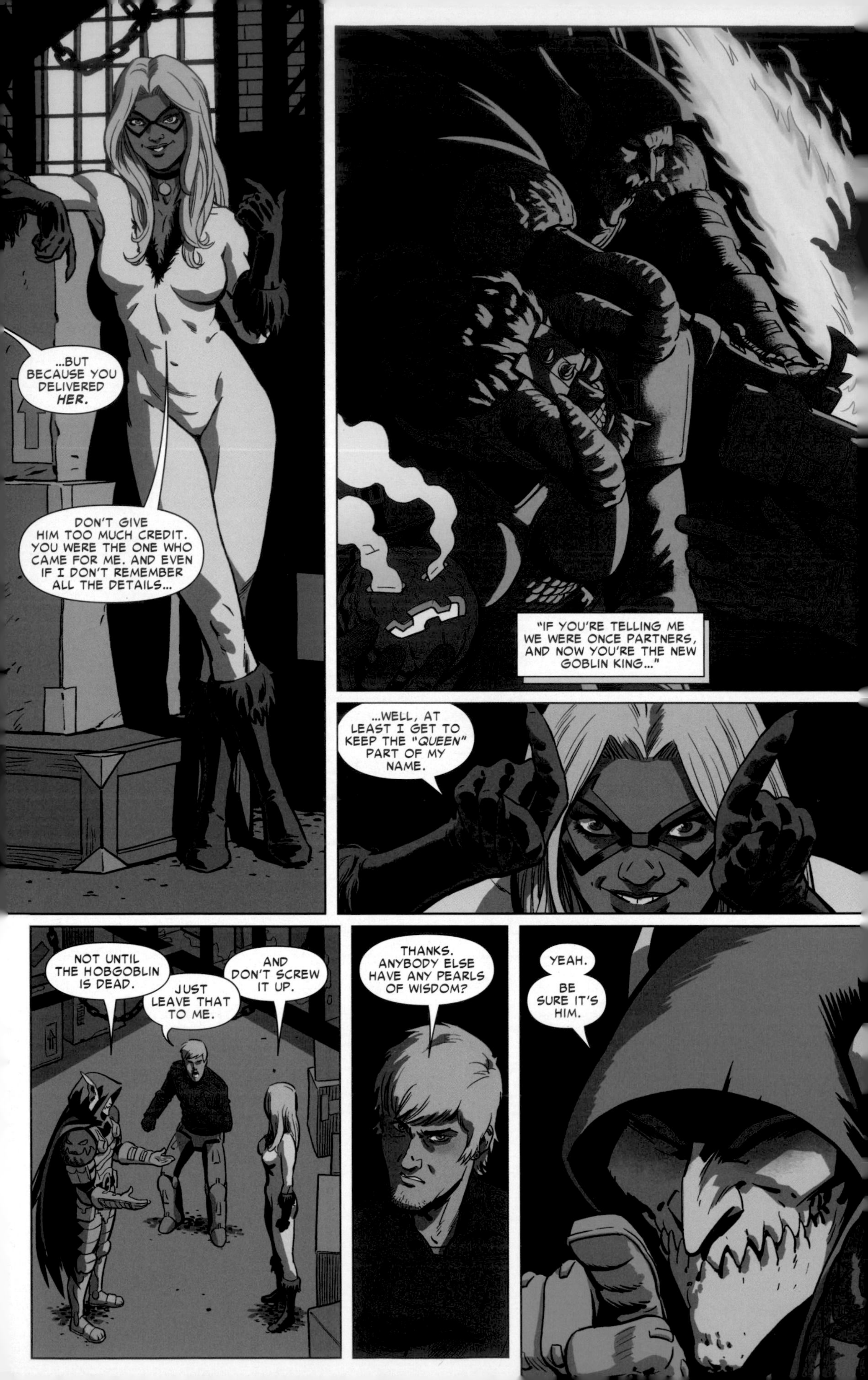

...BUT BECAUSE YOU DELIVERED *HER.*
DON'T GIVE HIM TOO MUCH CREDIT. YOU WERE THE ONE WHO CAME FOR ME. AND EVEN IF I DON'T REMEMBER ALL THE DETAILS...
"IF YOU'RE TELLING ME WE WERE ONCE PARTNERS, AND NOW YOU'RE THE NEW GOBLIN KING..."
...WELL, AT LEAST I GET TO KEEP THE "*QUEEN*" PART OF MY NAME.
NOT UNTIL THE HOBGOBLIN IS DEAD.
JUST LEAVE THAT TO ME.
AND DON'T SCREW IT UP.
THANKS. ANYBODY ELSE HAVE ANY PEARLS OF WISDOM?
YEAH.
BE SURE IT'S HIM.

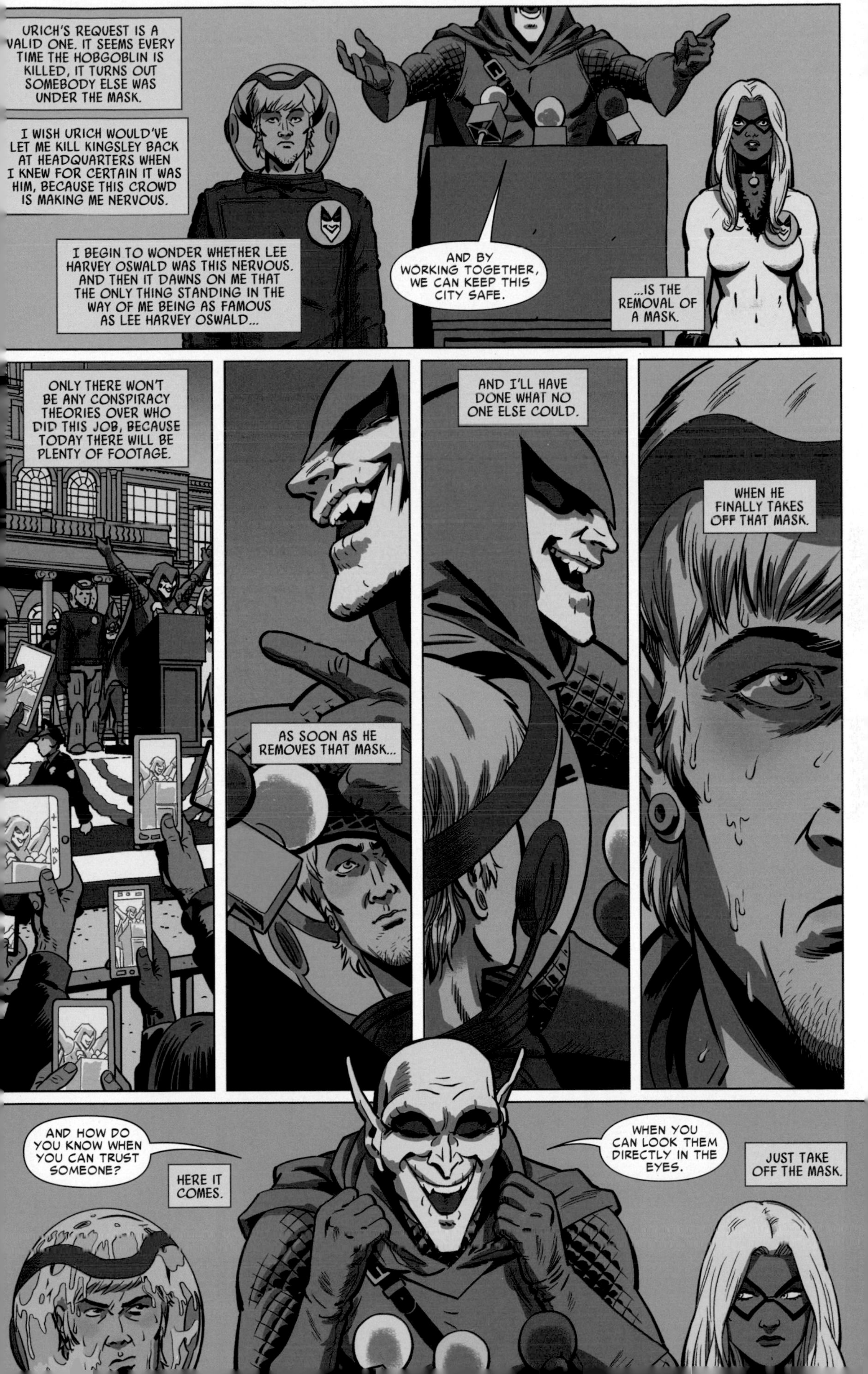
URICH'S REQUEST IS A VALID ONE. IT SEEMS EVERY TIME THE HOBGOBLIN IS KILLED, IT TURNS OUT SOMEBODY ELSE WAS UNDER THE MASK.
I WISH URICH WOULD'VE LET ME KILL KINGSLEY BACK AT HEADQUARTERS WHEN I KNEW FOR CERTAIN IT WAS HIM, BECAUSE THIS CROWD IS MAKING ME NERVOUS.
I BEGIN TO WONDER WHETHER LEE HARVEY OSWALD WAS THIS NERVOUS. AND THEN IT DAWNS ON ME THAT THE ONLY THING STANDING IN THE WAY OF ME BEING AS FAMOUS AS LEE HARVEY OSWALD...
AND BY WORKING TOGETHER, WE CAN KEEP THIS CITY SAFE.
...IS THE REMOVAL OF A MASK.
ONLY THERE WON'T BE ANY CONSPIRACY THEORIES OVER WHO DID THIS JOB, BECAUSE TODAY THERE WILL BE PLENTY OF FOOTAGE.
AS SOON AS HE REMOVES THAT MASK...
AND I'LL HAVE DONE WHAT NO ONE ELSE COULD.
WHEN HE FINALLY TAKES OFF THAT MASK.
AND HOW DO YOU KNOW WHEN YOU CAN TRUST SOMEONE?
HERE IT COMES.
WHEN YOU CAN LOOK THEM DIRECTLY IN THE EYES.
JUST TAKE OFF THE MASK.

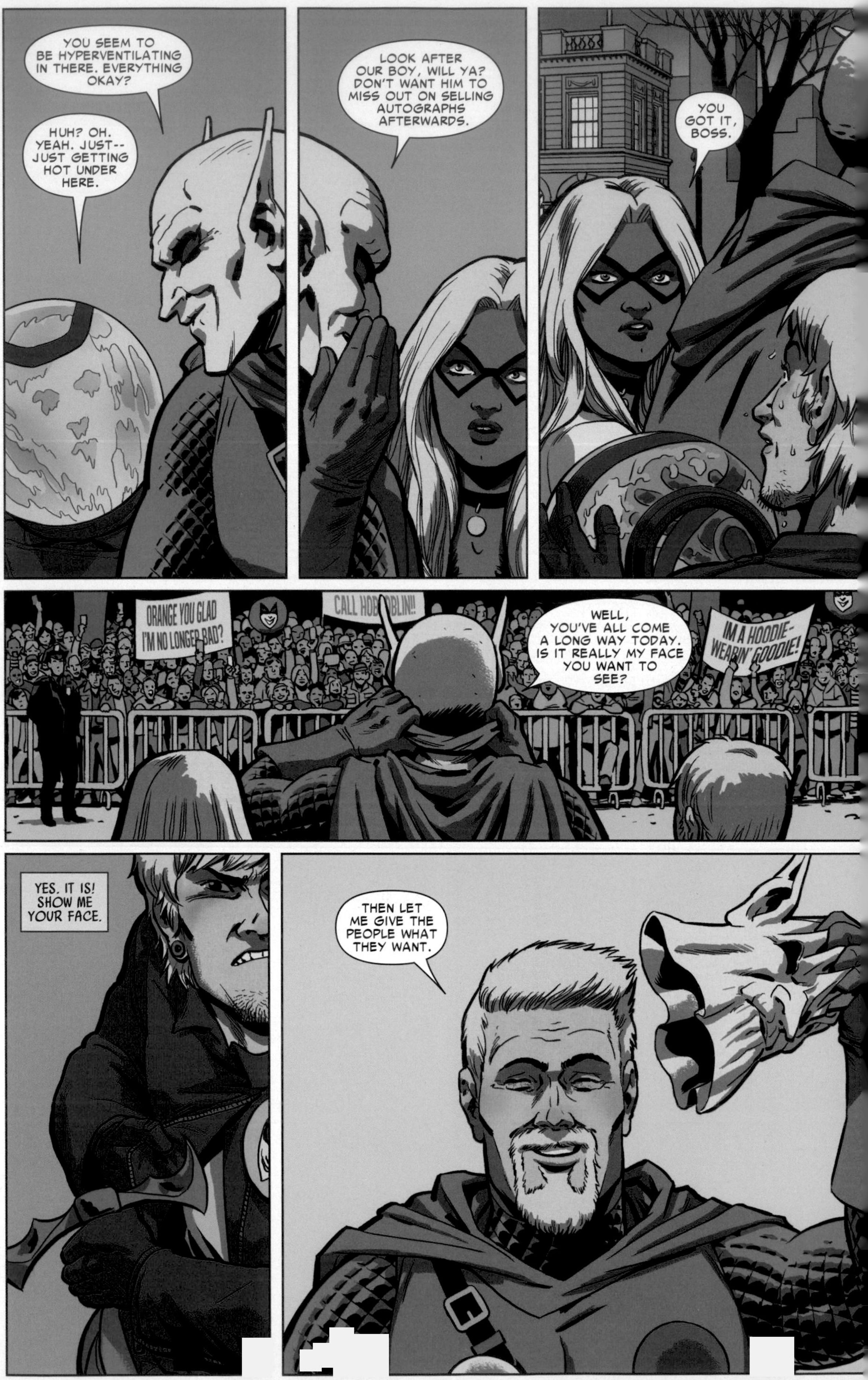
YOU SEEM TO BE HYPERVENTILATING IN THERE. EVERYTHING OKAY?
HUH? OH. YEAH. JUST-- JUST GETTING HOT UNDER HERE.
LOOK AFTER OUR BOY, WILL YA? DON'T WANT HIM TO MISS OUT ON SELLING AUTOGRAPHS AFTERWARDS.
YOU GOT IT, BOSS.
ORANGE YOU GLAD I'M NO LONGER BAD?
CALL HOBGOBLIN!!
WELL, YOU'VE ALL COME A LONG WAY TODAY. IS IT REALLY MY FACE YOU WANT TO SEE?
IM A HOODIE-WEARIN' GOODIE!
YES. IT IS! SHOW ME YOUR FACE.
THEN LET ME GIVE THE PEOPLE WHAT THEY WANT.

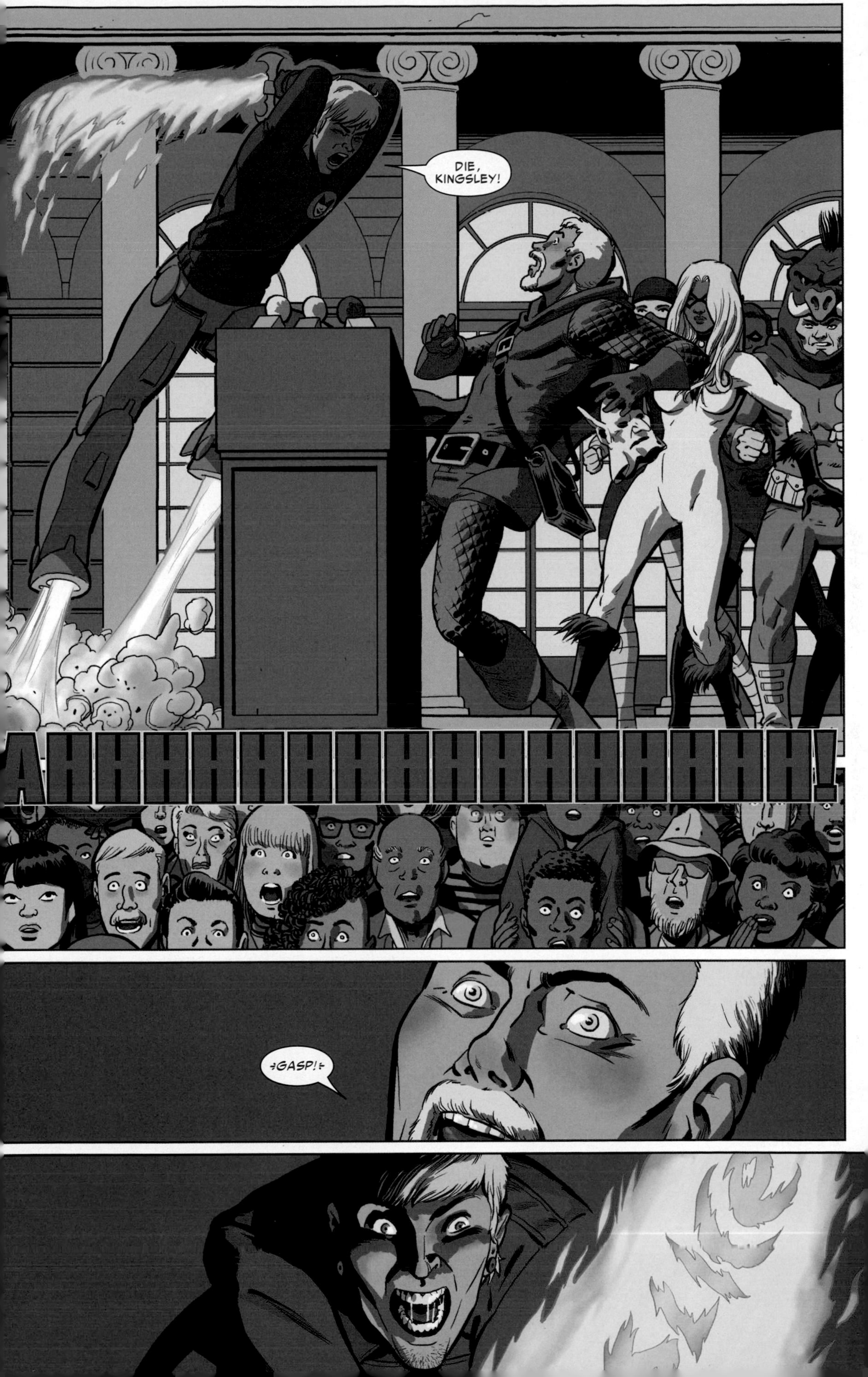
DIE, KINGSLEY!
AHHHHHHHHHHHHHHHHHHHHHH!
+GASP!+

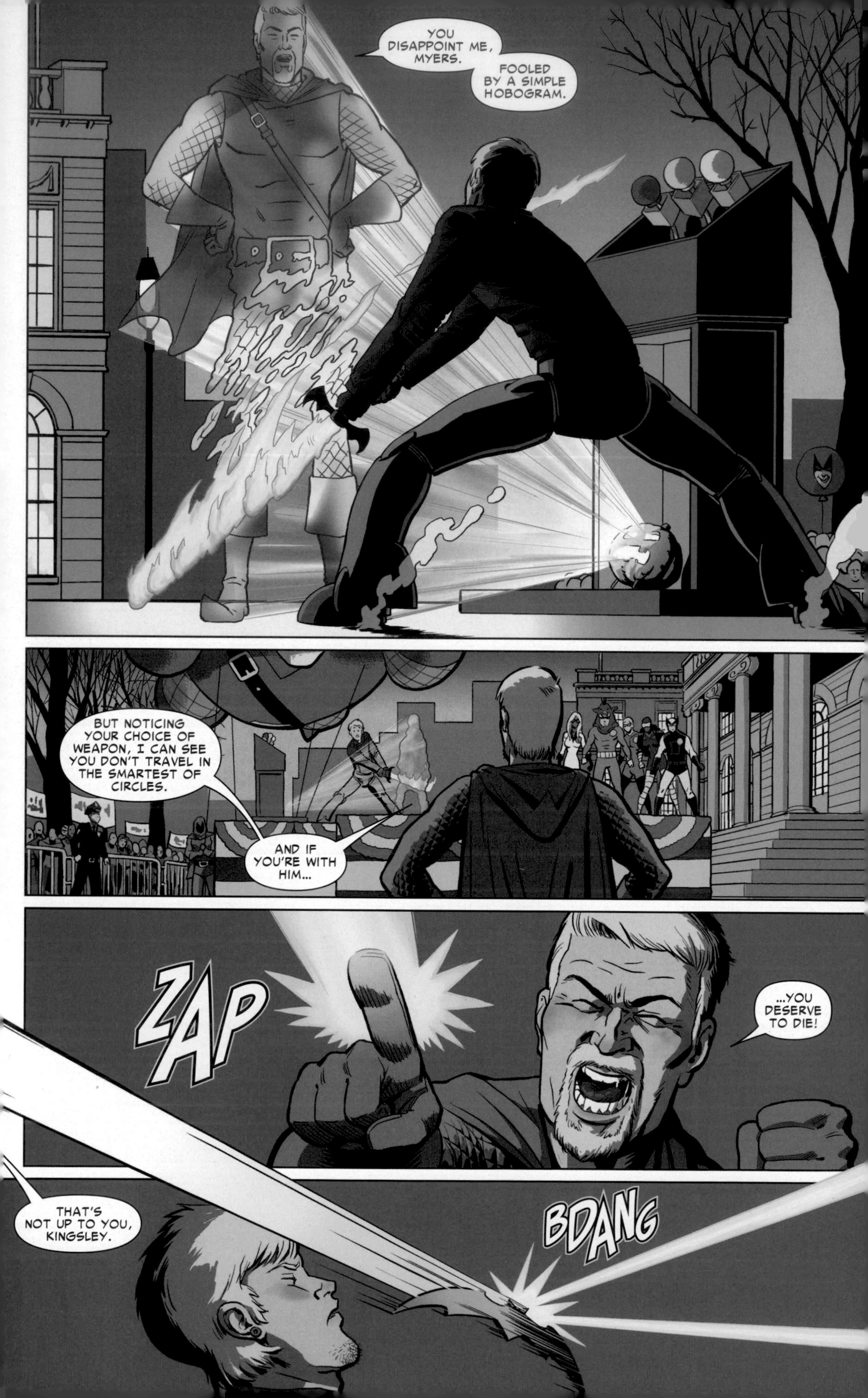
YOU DISAPPOINT ME, MYERS.
FOOLED BY A SIMPLE HOBOGRAM.
BUT NOTICING YOUR CHOICE OF WEAPON, I CAN SEE YOU DON'T TRAVEL IN THE SMARTEST OF CIRCLES.
AND IF YOU'RE WITH HIM...
ZAP
...YOU DESERVE TO DIE!
THAT'S NOT UP TO YOU, KINGSLEY.
BDANG

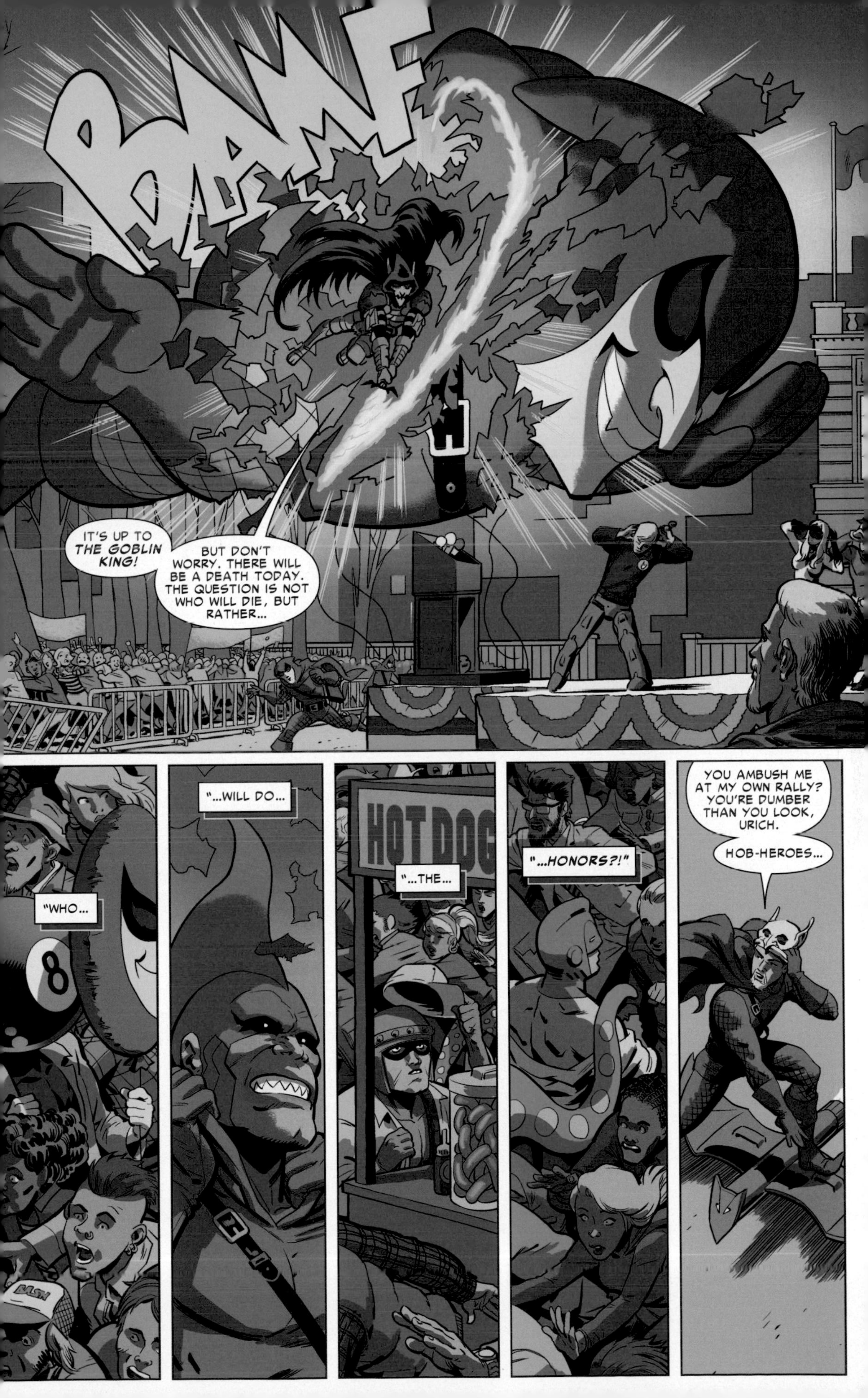

BAMF
IT'S UP TO THE GOBLIN KING!
BUT DON'T WORRY. THERE WILL BE A DEATH TODAY. THE QUESTION IS NOT WHO WILL DIE, BUT RATHER...
"WHO...
"...WILL DO...
HOT DOG
"...THE...
"...HONORS?!"
YOU AMBUSH ME AT MY OWN RALLY? YOU'RE DUMBER THAN YOU LOOK, URICH.
HOB-HEROES...

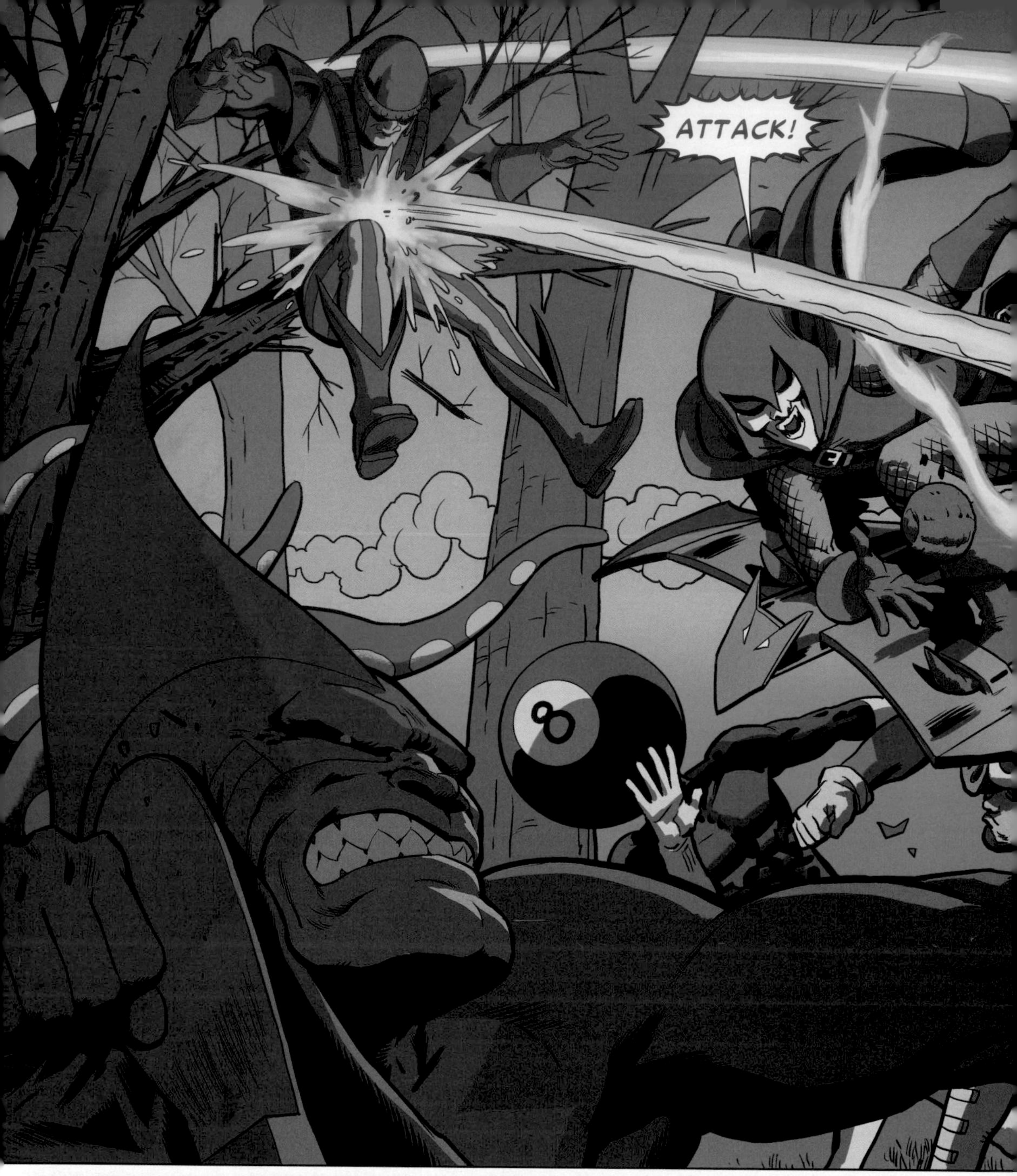
ATTACK!

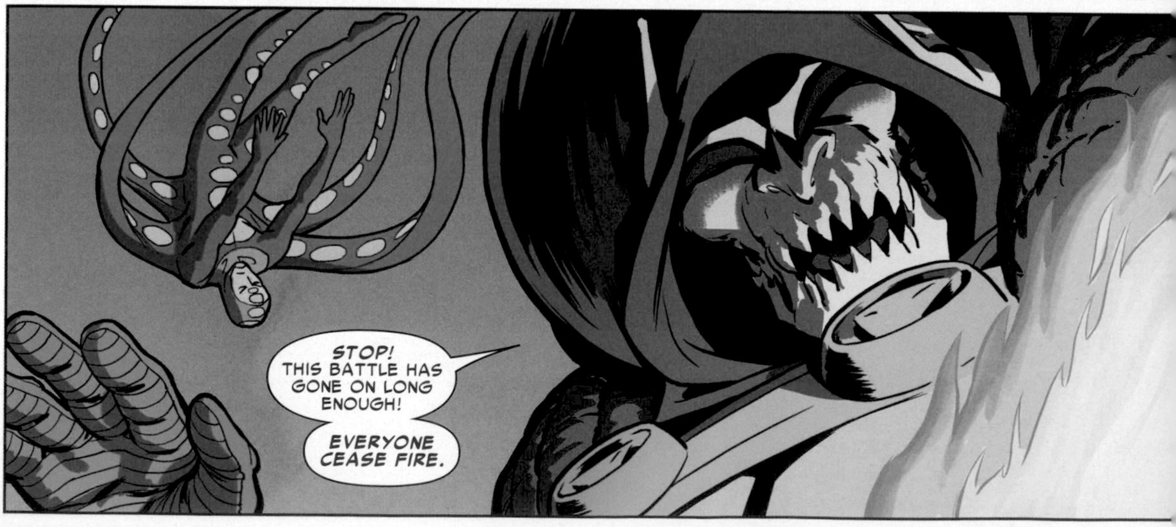
STOP! THIS BATTLE HAS GONE ON LONG ENOUGH!
EVERYONE CEASE FIRE.

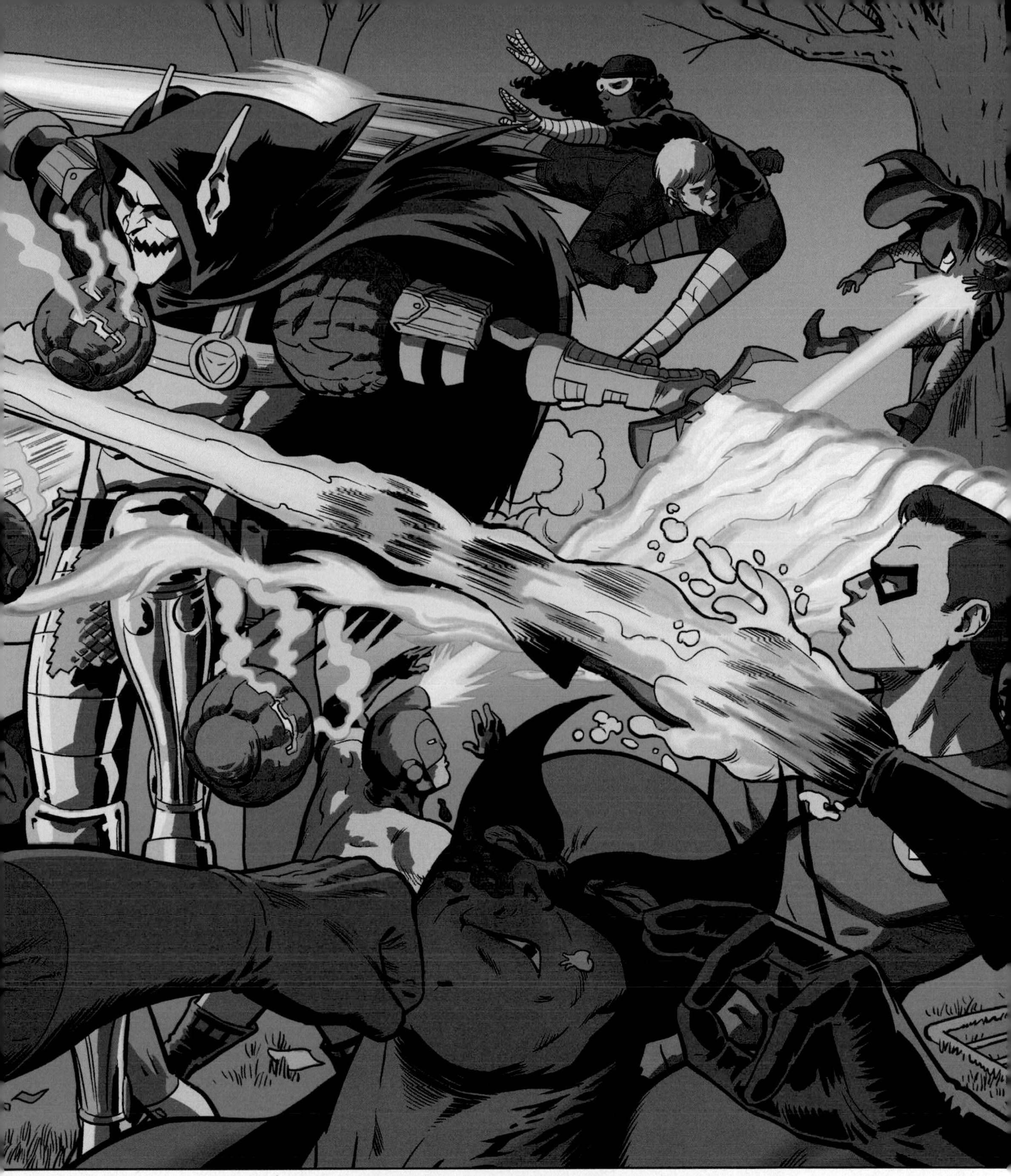

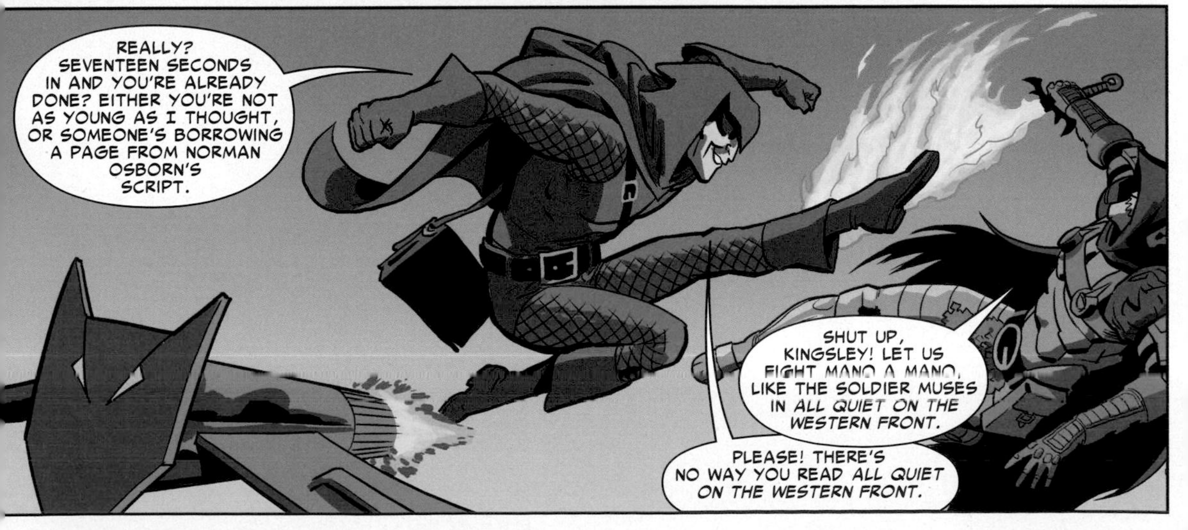
REALLY? SEVENTEEN SECONDS IN AND YOU'RE ALREADY DONE? EITHER YOU'RE NOT AS YOUNG AS I THOUGHT, OR SOMEONE'S BORROWING A PAGE FROM NORMAN OSBORN'S SCRIPT.
SHUT UP, KINGSLEY! LET US FIGHT MANO A MANO, LIKE THE SOLDIER MUSES IN ALL QUIET ON THE WESTERN FRONT.
PLEASE! THERE'S NO WAY YOU READ ALL QUIET ON THE WESTERN FRONT.

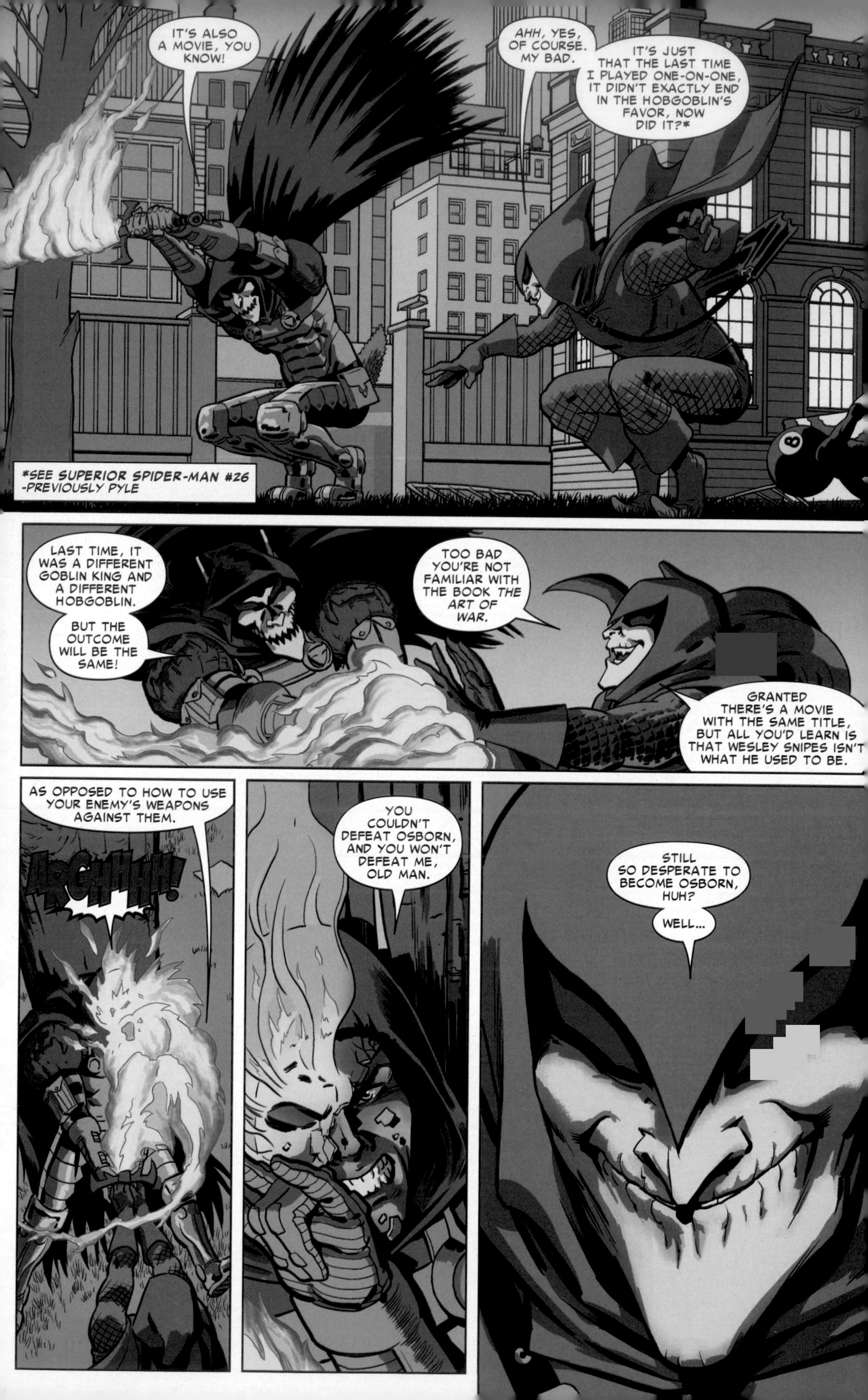
IT'S ALSO A MOVIE, YOU KNOW!
AHH, YES, OF COURSE. MY BAD.
IT'S JUST THAT THE LAST TIME I PLAYED ONE-ON-ONE, IT DIDN'T EXACTLY END IN THE HOBGOBLIN'S FAVOR, NOW DID IT?*
*SEE SUPERIOR SPIDER-MAN #26 -PREVIOUSLY PYLE
LAST TIME, IT WAS A DIFFERENT GOBLIN KING AND A DIFFERENT HOBGOBLIN.
BUT THE OUTCOME WILL BE THE SAME!
TOO BAD YOU'RE NOT FAMILIAR WITH THE BOOK THE ART OF WAR.
GRANTED THERE'S A MOVIE WITH THE SAME TITLE, BUT ALL YOU'D LEARN IS THAT WESLEY SNIPES ISN'T WHAT HE USED TO BE.
AS OPPOSED TO HOW TO USE YOUR ENEMY'S WEAPONS AGAINST THEM.
YOU COULDN'T DEFEAT OSBORN, AND YOU WON'T DEFEAT ME, OLD MAN.
STILL SO DESPERATE TO BECOME OSBORN, HUH?
WELL...

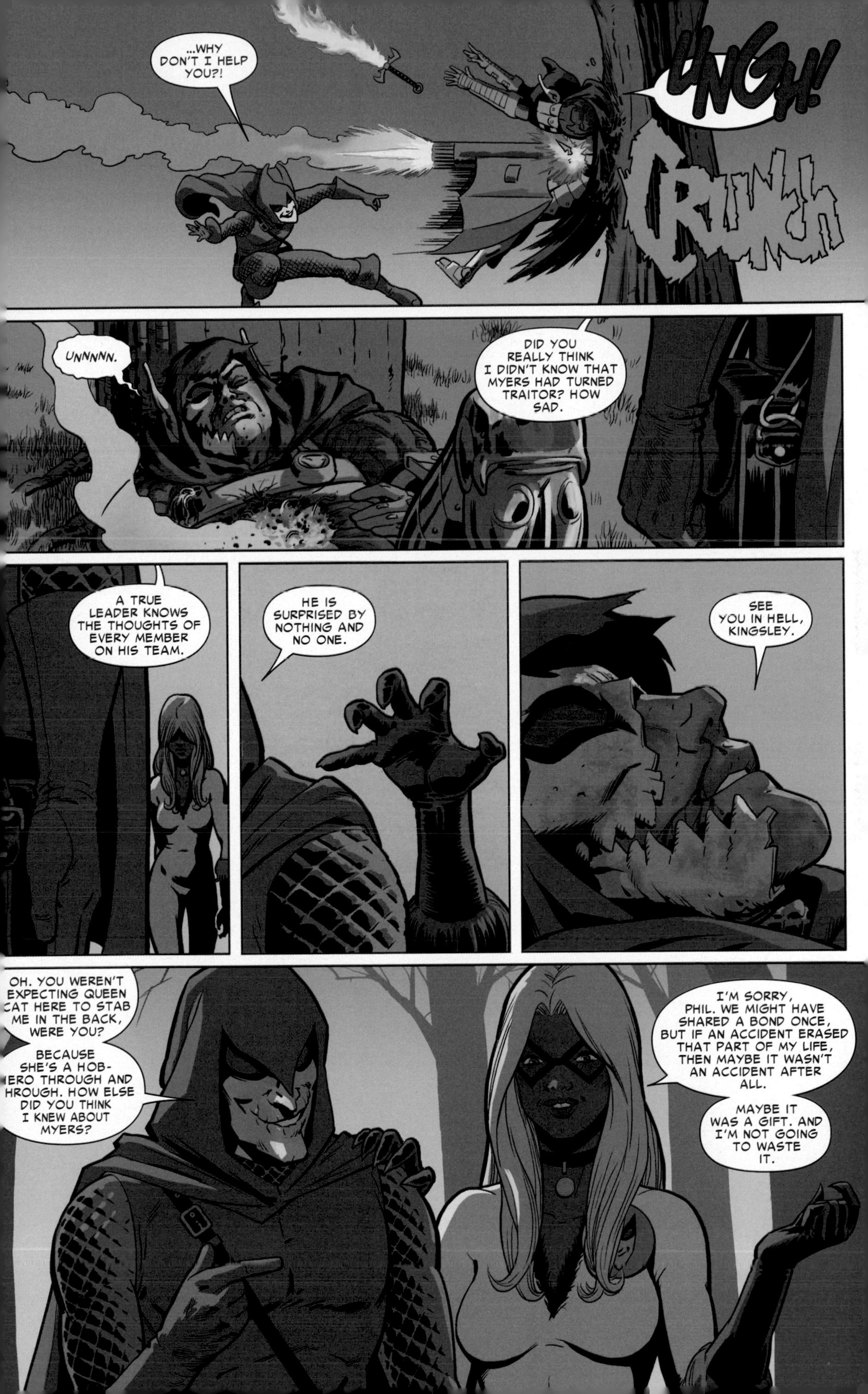
...WHY DON'T I HELP YOU?!
UNGH!
CRUNCH
UNNNNN.
DID YOU REALLY THINK I DIDN'T KNOW THAT MYERS HAD TURNED TRAITOR? HOW SAD.
A TRUE LEADER KNOWS THE THOUGHTS OF EVERY MEMBER ON HIS TEAM.
HE IS SURPRISED BY NOTHING AND NO ONE.
SEE YOU IN HELL, KINGSLEY.
OH. YOU WEREN'T EXPECTING QUEEN CAT HERE TO STAB ME IN THE BACK, WERE YOU?
BECAUSE SHE'S A HOB-HERO THROUGH AND THROUGH. HOW ELSE DID YOU THINK I KNEW ABOUT MYERS?
I'M SORRY, PHIL. WE MIGHT HAVE SHARED A BOND ONCE, BUT IF AN ACCIDENT ERASED THAT PART OF MY LIFE, THEN MAYBE IT WASN'T AN ACCIDENT AFTER ALL.
MAYBE IT WAS A GIFT. AND I'M NOT GOING TO WASTE IT.

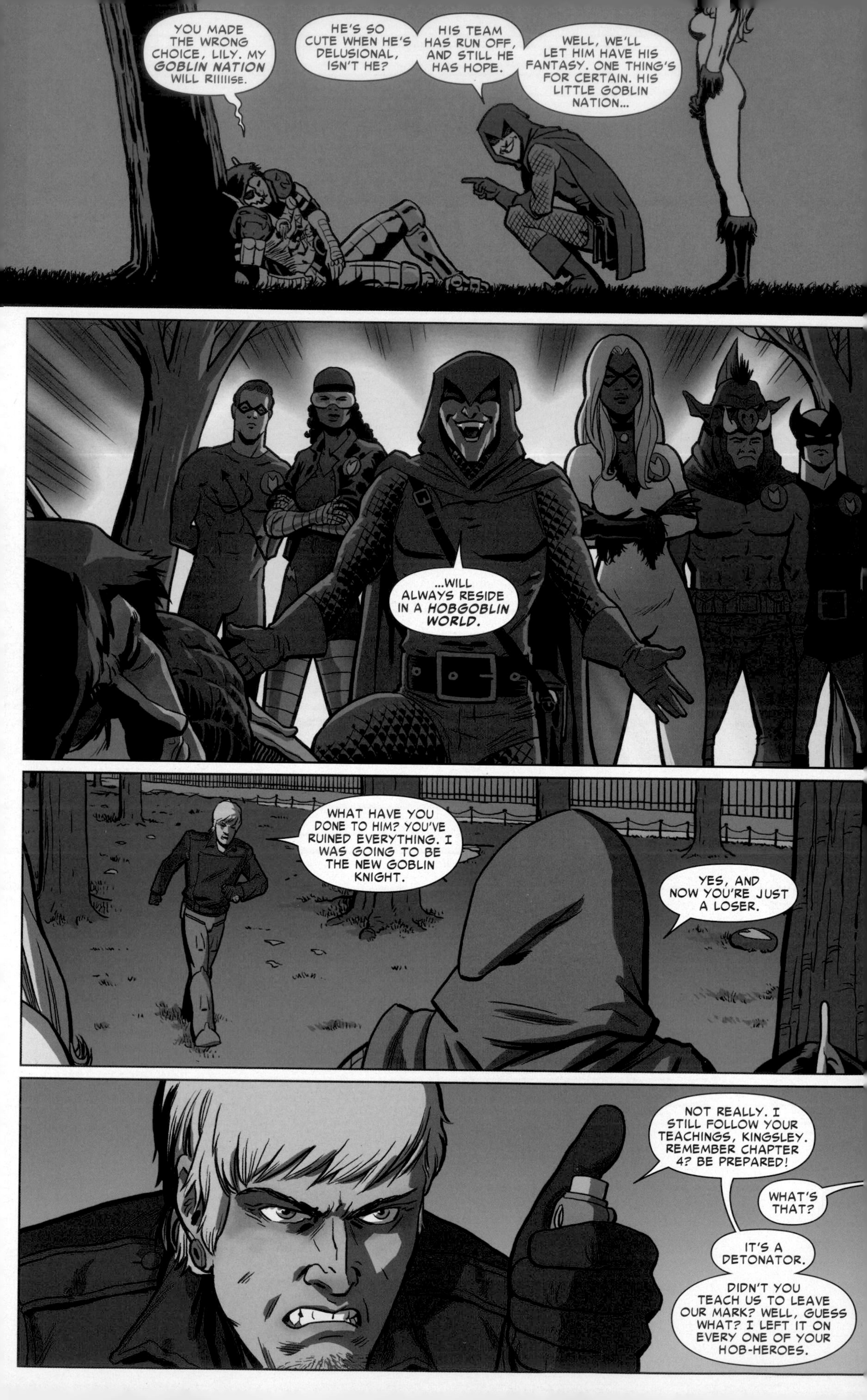

YOU MADE THE WRONG CHOICE, LILY. MY GOBLIN NATION WILL RIIIIISE.
HE'S SO CUTE WHEN HE'S DELUSIONAL, ISN'T HE?
HIS TEAM HAS RUN OFF, AND STILL HE HAS HOPE.
WELL, WE'LL LET HIM HAVE HIS FANTASY. ONE THING'S FOR CERTAIN. HIS LITTLE GOBLIN NATION...
...WILL ALWAYS RESIDE IN A HOBGOBLIN WORLD.
WHAT HAVE YOU DONE TO HIM? YOU'VE RUINED EVERYTHING. I WAS GOING TO BE THE NEW GOBLIN KNIGHT.
YES, AND NOW YOU'RE JUST A LOSER.
NOT REALLY. I STILL FOLLOW YOUR TEACHINGS, KINGSLEY. REMEMBER CHAPTER 4? BE PREPARED!
WHAT'S THAT?
IT'S A DETONATOR.
DIDN'T YOU TEACH US TO LEAVE OUR MARK? WELL, GUESS WHAT? I LEFT IT ON EVERY ONE OF YOUR HOB-HEROES.

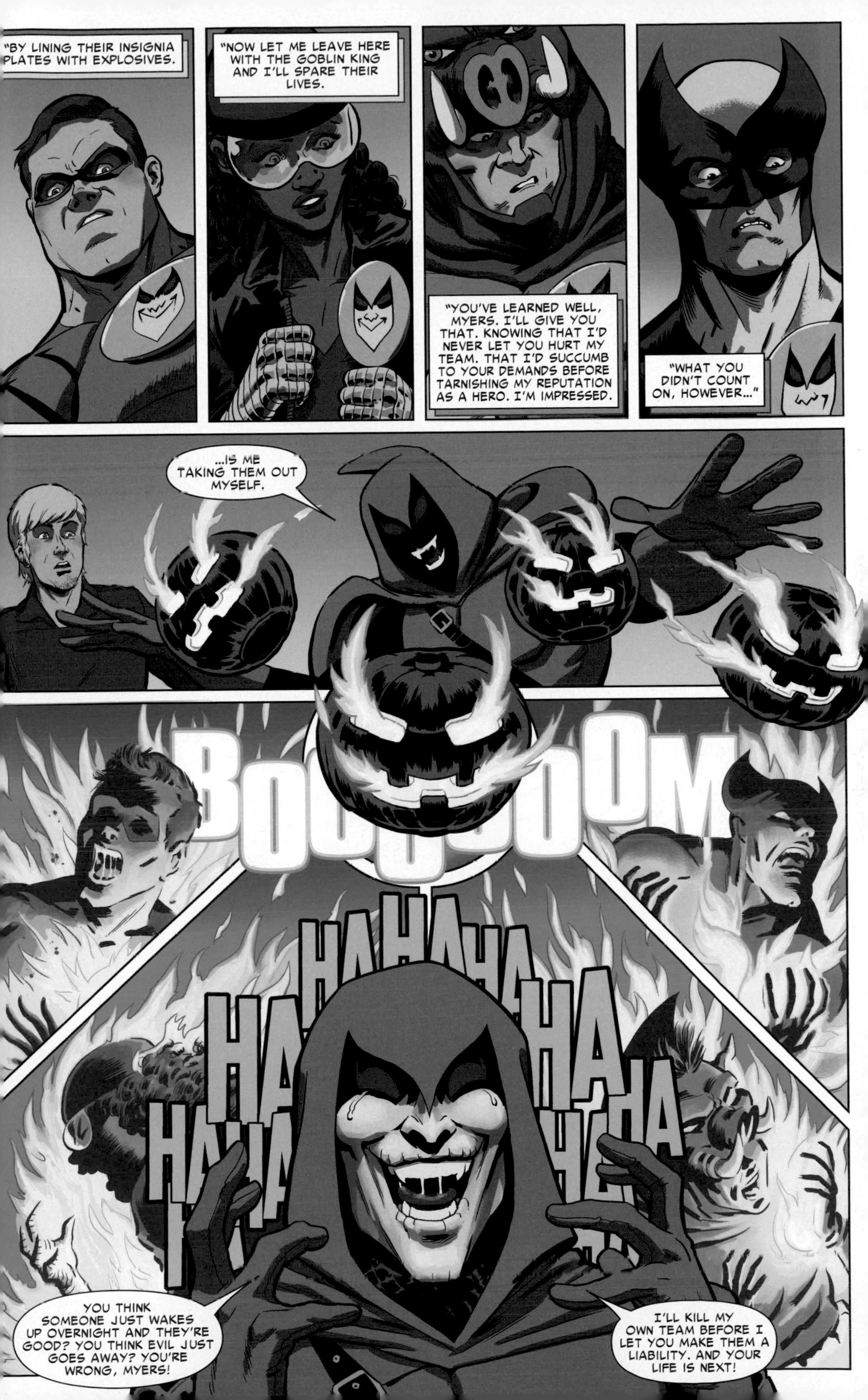
"BY LINING THEIR INSIGNIA PLATES WITH EXPLOSIVES.
"NOW LET ME LEAVE HERE WITH THE GOBLIN KING AND I'LL SPARE THEIR LIVES.
"YOU'VE LEARNED WELL, MYERS. I'LL GIVE YOU THAT. KNOWING THAT I'D NEVER LET YOU HURT MY TEAM. THAT I'D SUCCUMB TO YOUR DEMANDS BEFORE TARNISHING MY REPUTATION AS A HERO. I'M IMPRESSED.
"WHAT YOU DIDN'T COUNT ON, HOWEVER..."
...IS ME TAKING THEM OUT MYSELF.
BOOOOOOOM
HAHAHA
HAHAHAHA
YOU THINK SOMEONE JUST WAKES UP OVERNIGHT AND THEY'RE GOOD? YOU THINK EVIL JUST GOES AWAY? YOU'RE WRONG, MYERS!
I'LL KILL MY OWN TEAM BEFORE I LET YOU MAKE THEM A LIABILITY. AND YOUR LIFE IS NEXT!

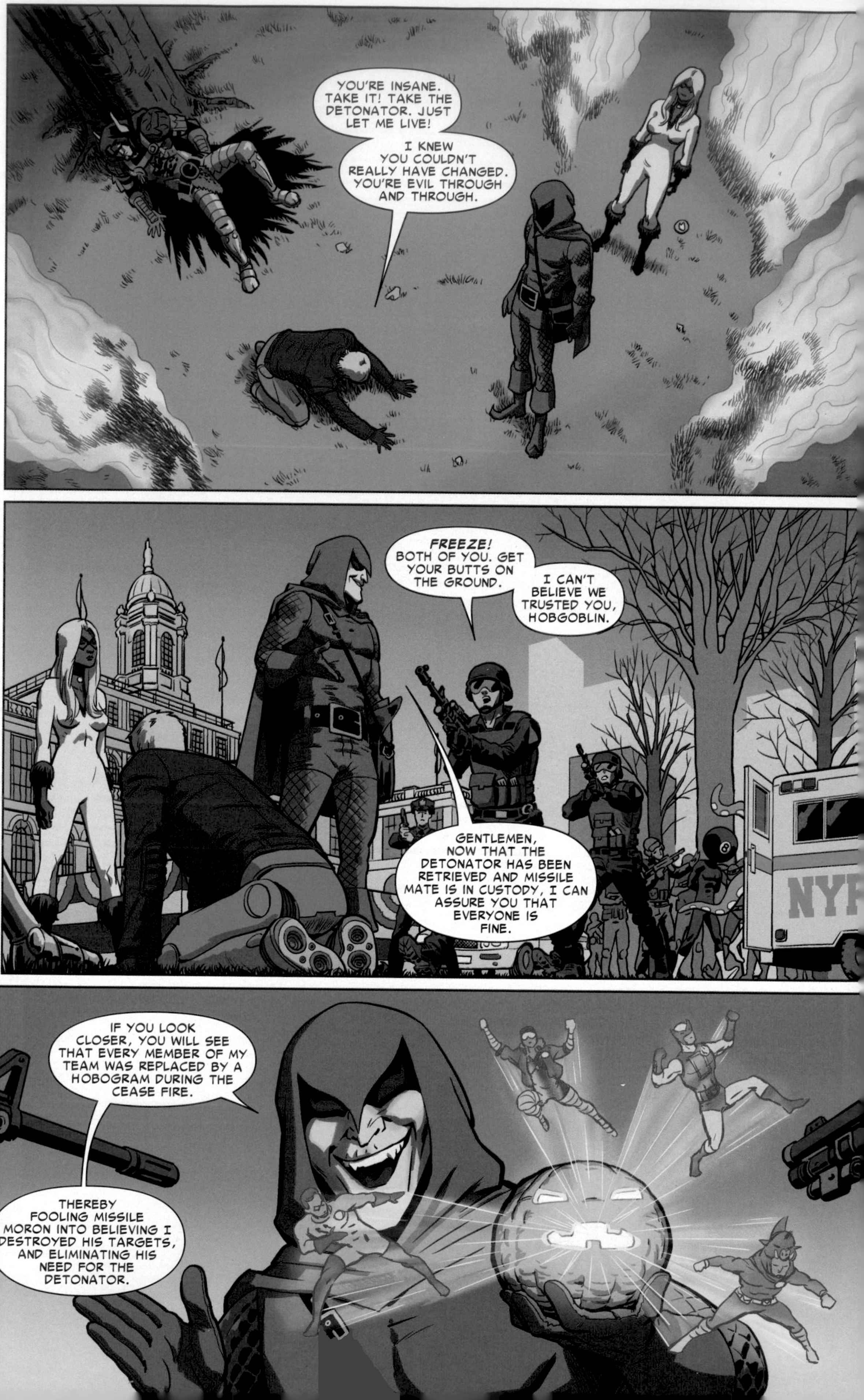
YOU'RE INSANE. TAKE IT! TAKE THE DETONATOR. JUST LET ME LIVE!
I KNEW YOU COULDN'T REALLY HAVE CHANGED. YOU'RE EVIL THROUGH AND THROUGH.
FREEZE! BOTH OF YOU. GET YOUR BUTTS ON THE GROUND.
I CAN'T BELIEVE WE TRUSTED YOU, HOBGOBLIN.
GENTLEMEN, NOW THAT THE DETONATOR HAS BEEN RETRIEVED AND MISSILE MATE IS IN CUSTODY, I CAN ASSURE YOU THAT EVERYONE IS FINE.
IF YOU LOOK CLOSER, YOU WILL SEE THAT EVERY MEMBER OF MY TEAM WAS REPLACED BY A HOBOGRAM DURING THE CEASE FIRE.
THEREBY FOOLING MISSILE MORON INTO BELIEVING I DESTROYED HIS TARGETS, AND ELIMINATING HIS NEED FOR THE DETONATOR.

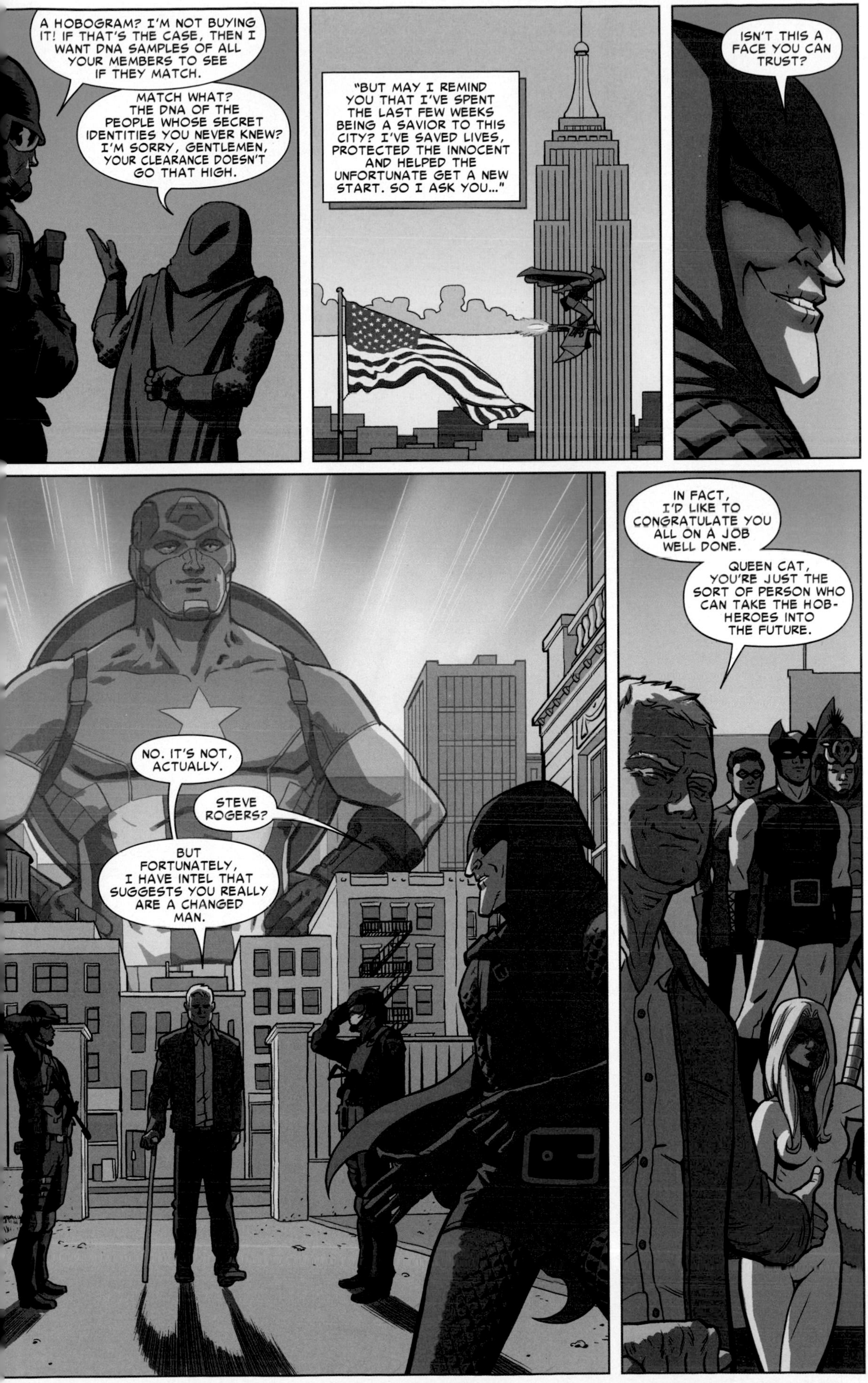
A HOBOGRAM? I'M NOT BUYING IT! IF THAT'S THE CASE, THEN I WANT DNA SAMPLES OF ALL YOUR MEMBERS TO SEE IF THEY MATCH.
MATCH WHAT? THE DNA OF THE PEOPLE WHOSE SECRET IDENTITIES YOU NEVER KNEW? I'M SORRY, GENTLEMEN, YOUR CLEARANCE DOESN'T GO THAT HIGH.
"BUT MAY I REMIND YOU THAT I'VE SPENT THE LAST FEW WEEKS BEING A SAVIOR TO THIS CITY? I'VE SAVED LIVES, PROTECTED THE INNOCENT AND HELPED THE UNFORTUNATE GET A NEW START. SO I ASK YOU..."
ISN'T THIS A FACE YOU CAN TRUST?
NO. IT'S NOT, ACTUALLY.
STEVE ROGERS?
BUT FORTUNATELY, I HAVE INTEL THAT SUGGESTS YOU REALLY ARE A CHANGED MAN.
IN FACT, I'D LIKE TO CONGRATULATE YOU ALL ON A JOB WELL DONE.
QUEEN CAT, YOU'RE JUST THE SORT OF PERSON WHO CAN TAKE THE HOB-HEROES INTO THE FUTURE.

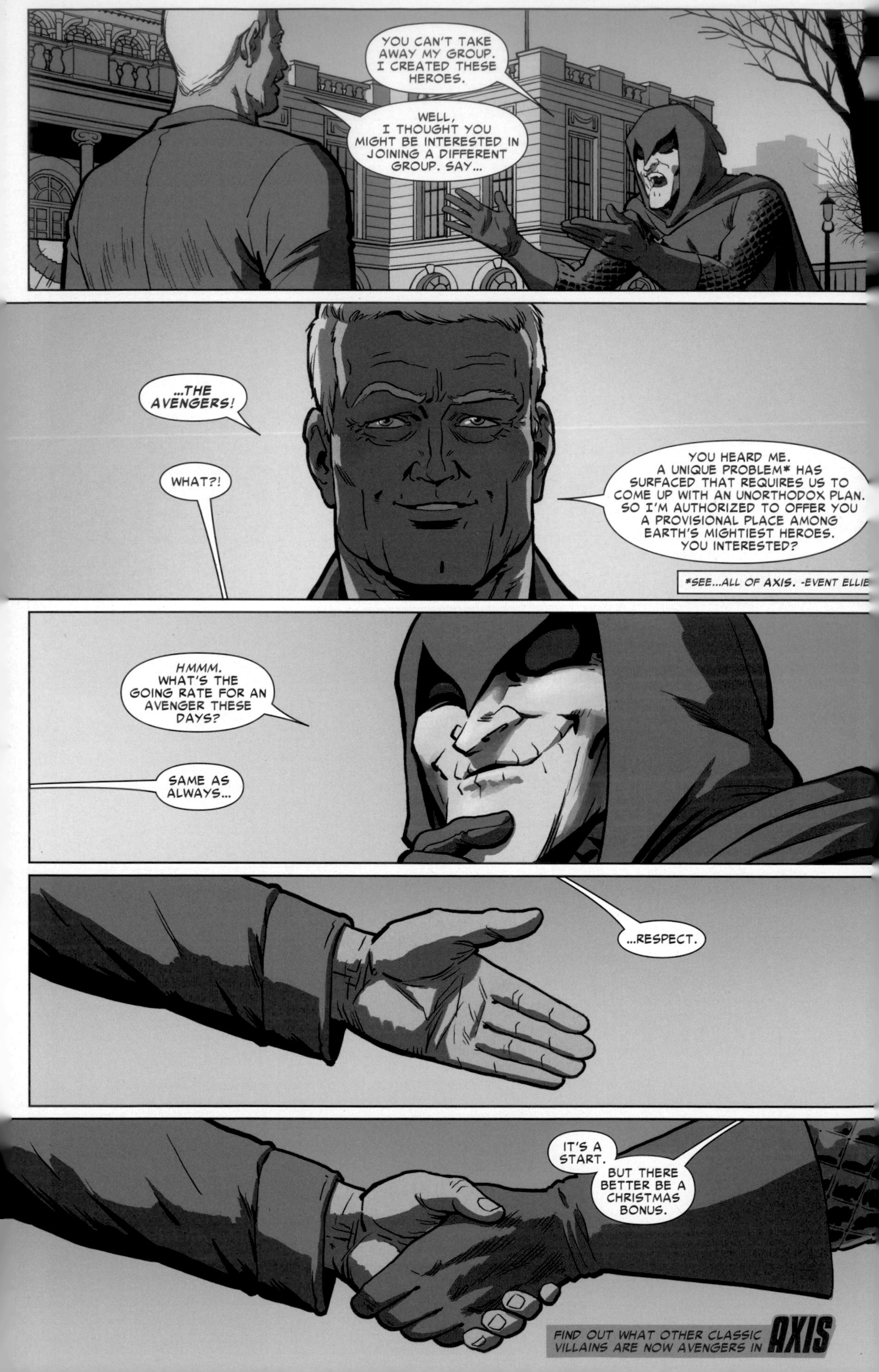
YOU CAN'T TAKE AWAY MY GROUP. I CREATED THESE HEROES.
WELL, I THOUGHT YOU MIGHT BE INTERESTED IN JOINING A DIFFERENT GROUP. SAY...
...THE AVENGERS!
WHAT?!
YOU HEARD ME. A UNIQUE PROBLEM* HAS SURFACED THAT REQUIRES US TO COME UP WITH AN UNORTHODOX PLAN. SO I'M AUTHORIZED TO OFFER YOU A PROVISIONAL PLACE AMONG EARTH'S MIGHTIEST HEROES. YOU INTERESTED?
*SEE...ALL OF AXIS. -EVENT ELLIE
HMMM. WHAT'S THE GOING RATE FOR AN AVENGER THESE DAYS?
SAME AS ALWAYS...
...RESPECT.
IT'S A START.
BUT THERE BETTER BE A CHRISTMAS BONUS.
FIND OUT WHAT OTHER CLASSIC VILLAINS ARE NOW AVENGERS IN AXIS

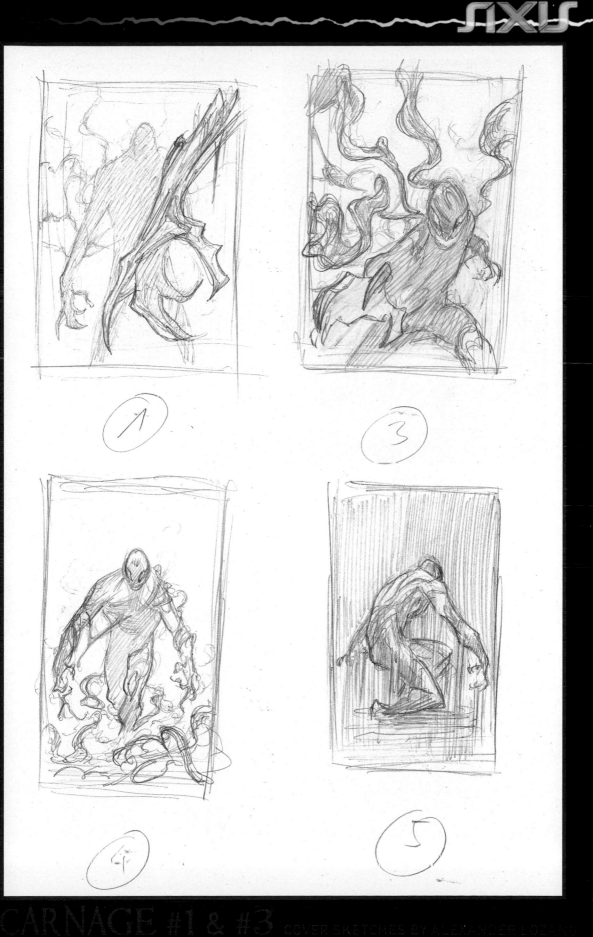

CARNAGE #1 & #3 COVER SKETCHES BY ALEXANDER LOZANO

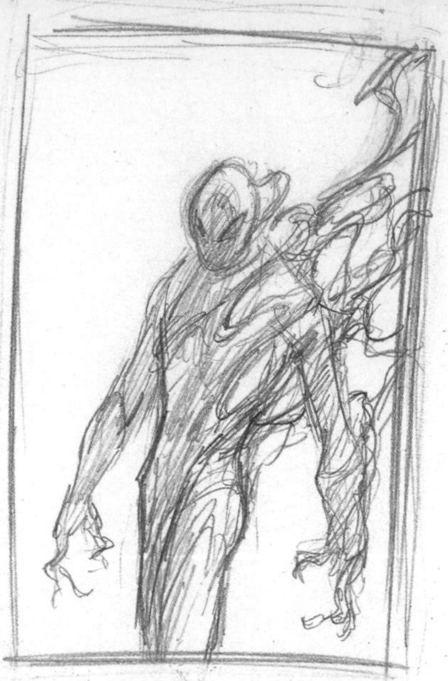

6

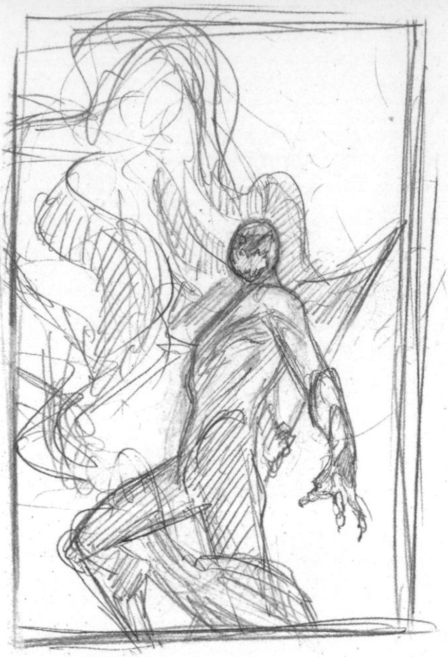

2

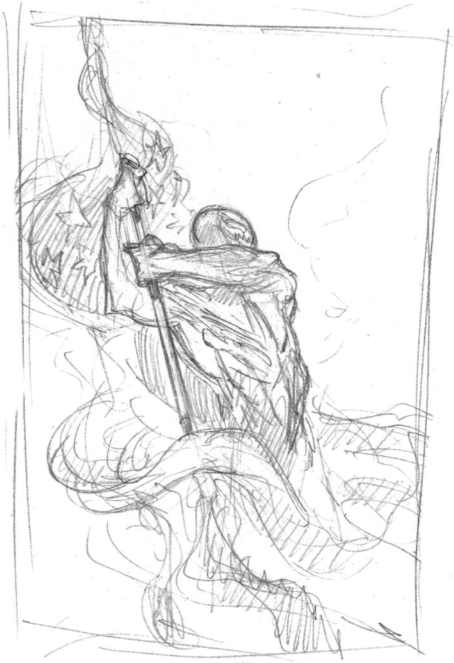

3

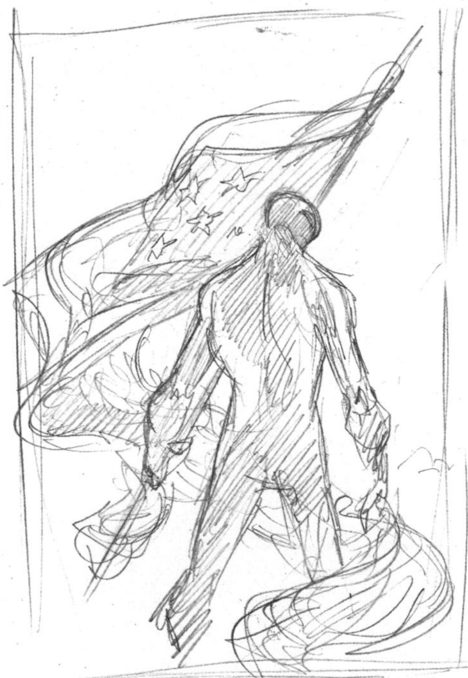

4

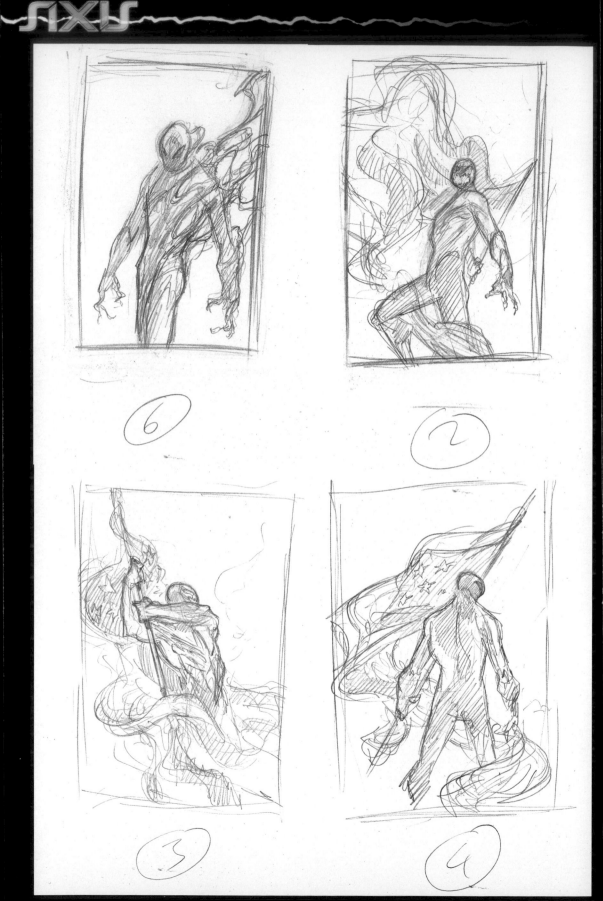

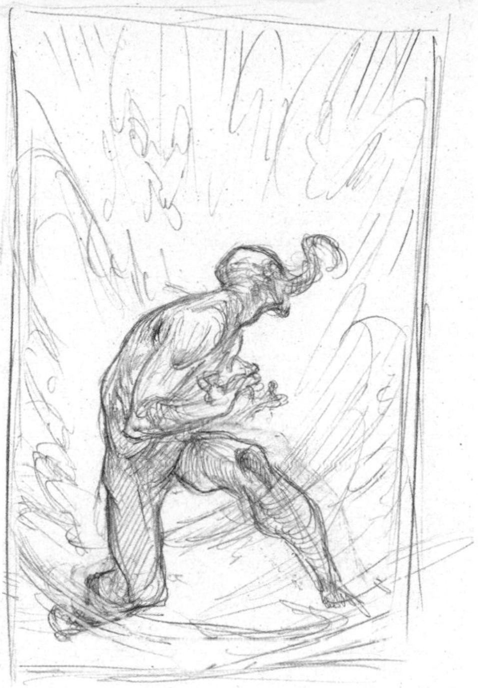

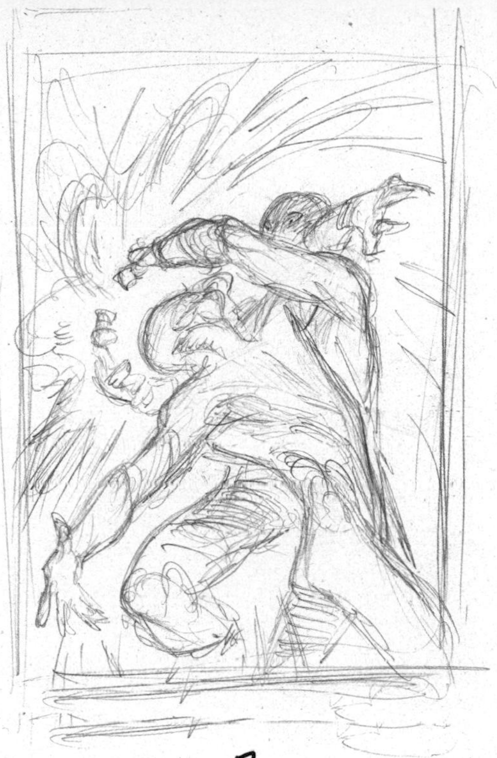

1

7

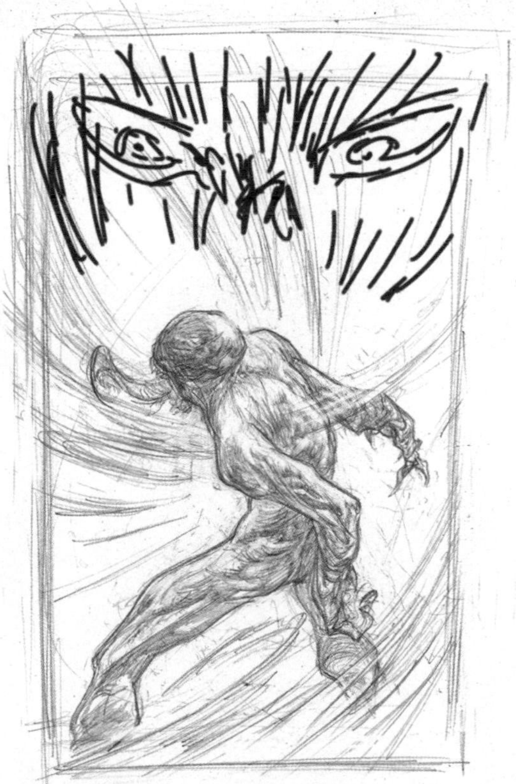

6

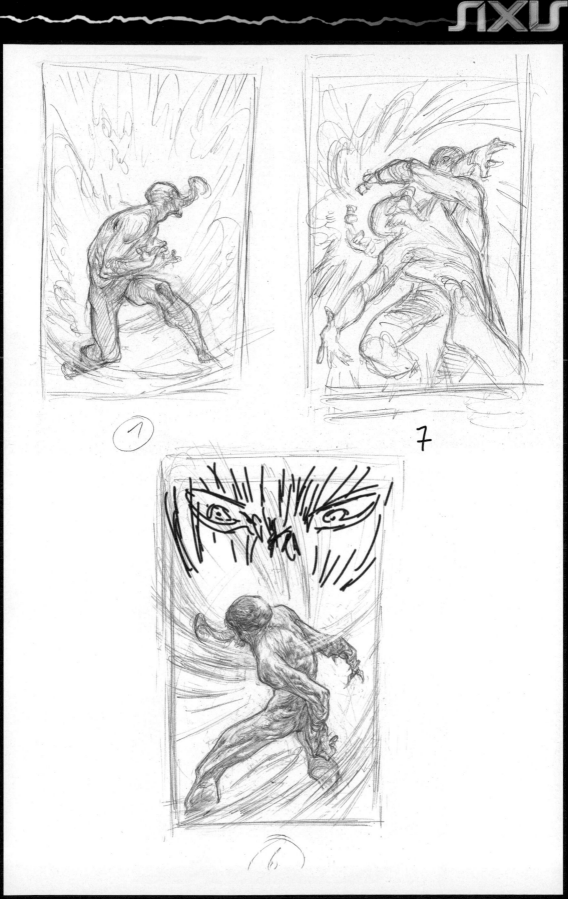

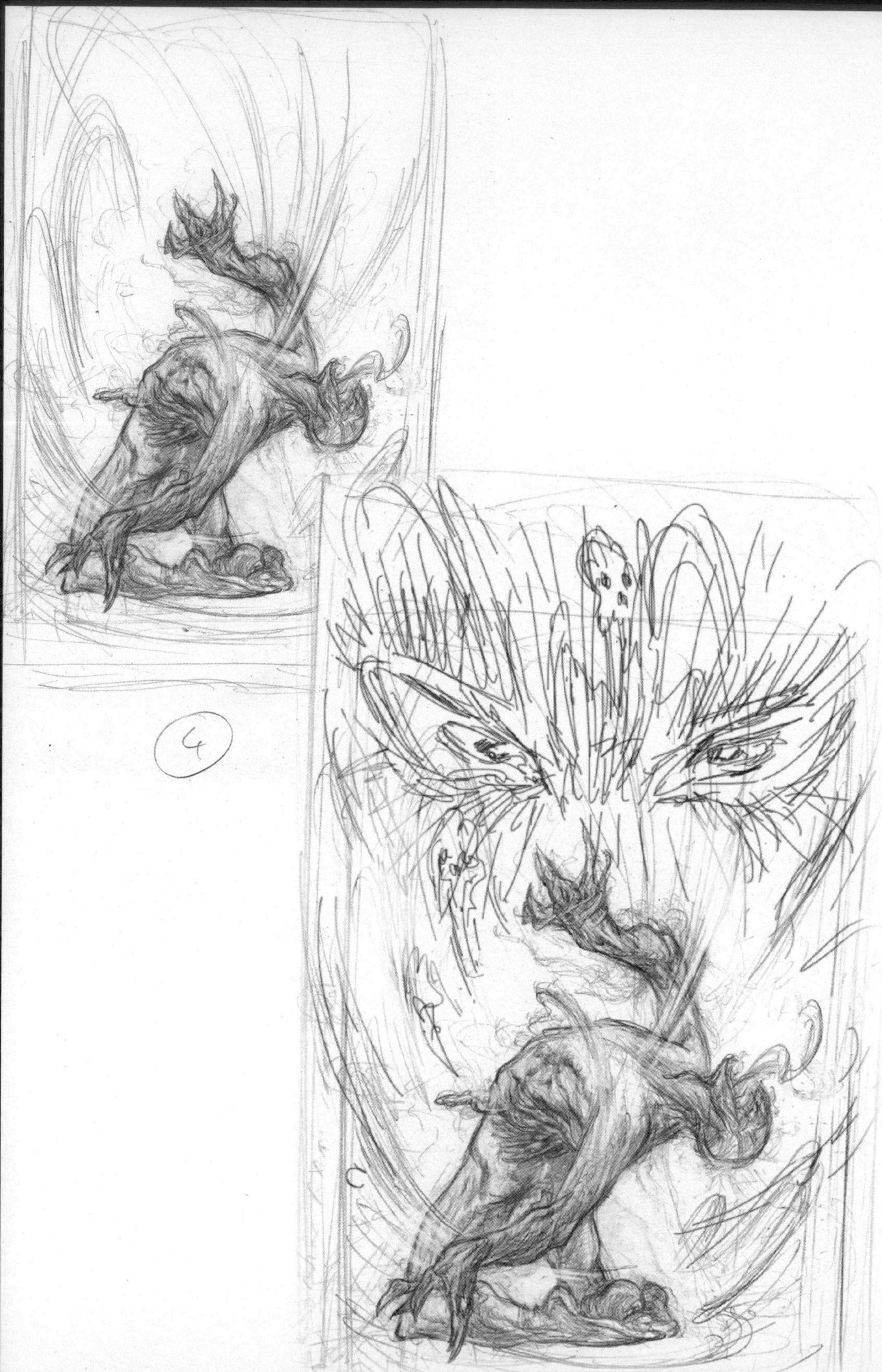
4